PRAI
BLUEWATER WALK.

M000107642

HOW WOULD YOUR LIFE CHANGE IF IT INCLUDED A WILD FAMILY ADVENTURE?

TINA DREFFIN had it all—a life living in paradise aboard a boat in the Caribbean islands with her husband and their two teen-aged sons. After twenty years of tranquil living, the family embarks upon a journey to Africa for wild adventure. Events don't always turn out well, leaving her speechless, and the journey challenges her to reach higher for mere emotional survival. She's laughing as fast as she can until the final end nearly breaks her.

KIRKUS REVIEWS: Dreffin's writing is the strongest when unpacking difficult events. A tender portrait of a clan coming into its own on the ocean.

"Tina's writing is lucid and descriptive, and she tells a story that needs to be told. Interwoven into her memoir of a brave sailing adventure is a much deeper story about the way women struggle to be mothers, partners, and individuals in a world that is still very much dominated by men. Tina doesn't shy away from things that need to be written about. This is a book you will remember long after you have finished reading it." Melanie Neale, author of *Boat Girl: A Memoir of Youth, Love & Fiberglass.*

"What an inspirational, emotional, spiritual and physical journey of a woman faced with overwhelming life challenges. Despite Tina's despair, adversity and grief, she had the determination and desire to transform negative experiences into lessons of how to achieve a better life. Her experiences produced a powerful, confident and successful, joyful mother, wife, woman, and advocate. The source of Tina's strength and survival are effectively woven through her life adventures. These are lessons we all need to learn." Diann Vanhook, QRM Director, Life Point Hospitals.

Bluewater Walkabout

---◆---

Into Africa

To Dave,

May you have many
more adventures)!

your new buddy,

Tina Dreffin
Blue Publishing, Inc

Tina

Requests for permission to make copies of any part of the work should be submitted to tinadreffin@bluewaterwalkabout.com.
Bahamas (242) 524-0156

ISBN-10: 0-9979996-1-6
ISBN-13: 978-0-9979996-1-7

Editing by Melanie Neale: Neale Editorial
Developmental Editor: Brooke Warner. Warner Coaching
Family photograph, Sue Hacking
Cover by Fiverr
Printed in the United States of America

DISCLAIMER

All the stories in this book are true, although some names and identifying details have been changed to protect the privacy of the people involved.

ACKNOWLEGEMENTS

Thanks to my editor, Melanie Neale, for her dedication in scrambling my walkabout chapters into dignified content.

Thanks to Lisa for your encouragement as I wrote this memoir over a ten-year period.

Thanks to Diann Vanhook for her unyielding support: "My prior therapists helped me to name my feelings and identify coping mechanisms, but didn't teach me how to move beyond the trauma and not only live life, but live it well, as you have."

Thanks to Brooke Warner's and Linda Meyer's the Magic of Memoir Writing Conference in Berkeley for teaching me how to dig deeper and why it's important—to save lives.

To Peter, Adam, Warren…

You taught me how to laugh. Though our bizarre travel journeys left me
flabbergasted most of the time, I realized life was meant to be
a great adventure. It made me the storyteller I am today.
I'm ready to do it again.

To all women who have been there…

May this book lift you towards freedom.

CONTENTS

PREFACE

This book originated from a joint dream to begin a journey around the globe together, formulated when Peter and I swooned in love over a meal of beans and rice and jerk chicken at a waterfront Cuban café in Ft Lauderdale. In the background, a folk song singer wailed into the mic. My heart swelled with emotion. It was a moment in life, forever foot-printed on my brain, because I knew without a doubt that I was going on walkabout.

Up to this point in my life, I seemed to be immersed on an unending treadmill towards getting a better job, a better car (other than my current jalopy), and better digs. When I got to know Peter, I quickly realized I was looking at life from all the wrong angles. It was apparent that either I went on walkabout alone or we went together.

In addition, I knew deep down that I had more than a couple personal issues to work out within myself. As a young girl from a sheltered home with helicopter parents in a small town in North Carolina, I hit more than a few roadblocks when encountering predators on the college campus and in the workplace.

In common usage, walkabout refers to the aboriginal custom in Australia where a man breaks off from the daily grind and walks in solitude across desert and bush country on a spiritual quest. The distance covered on a walkabout may exceed 1000 miles, done without aid of compass or radio. The walker finds his way, it is believed, under the guidance of a spiritual power.

I had the spiritual power. I just needed the journey.

My journey healed my wounds, for I discovered that the size of my issues were nothing compared to those women who lived in developing nations, struggling with poverty, clean drinking water, and security on a daily basis. Over time, I saw that I had overestimated my problems and underestimated myself. I realized I would never grow as long as I hid from my painful past. I knew I would only grow when I faced them.

Things went horribly wrong during my journey at times along the way, and I eventually discovered the laughter deep within myself.

I hope this book is an inspiration to you to create your own journey of recovery through adventurous travel.

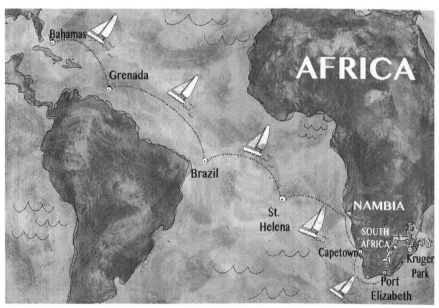

Passage from South Africa to the Bahamas

Around Africa

PROLOGUE

Young children are impressionable.

When our boys were just eight and ten years old, I created a family game for fun and dubbed it, "I Dream Of ..." We were living aboard *Scud*, a forty-five foot steel sloop, in the Bahamas. Our sons Adam and Warren completed homeschooling courses in the mornings and played island games in the afternoons with boating friends. Every night at sundown, we'd curl within the depths of a large hammock, strung across the foredeck on our boat, and take turns envisioning our innermost fantasies and dreams. As a tropical sun fell into the sea, we whispered of secret adventures, our clothes softly reflecting the brilliant pinks and purples of the sunset. On the breeze rode the sound of singing casuarinas, the pine needles playing a sweet lullaby as their tips swished together.

"Daddy, what's past the horizon?" Adam asked. My heart swelled for him.

"Great lands and people," Peter said wistfully. "Ports-of-call that few people have ever seen."

"What's it like?" Adam asked.

"Wild. Exotic. Exciting," Peter answered with a twinkle in his eye.

"Can we go there?" Warren pleaded.

In their eyes, I saw my dreams reflected. As a child, I was most comfortable alone with my daydreams. Hidden within tall blades of grass, I gazed up at white shapes galloping across a limitless sky and imagined traveling to someplace distant and strange. I curled up on the top bunk in my bedroom that I shared with my two sisters and got lost in a stack of National Geographic magazines. Inside the glossy pages, bronzed women stared back at me. They sprang out of flowing waterfalls, crowned with flowering garlands. They danced around night fires adorned in bright ankle beads and carried jugs of water atop their heads. The exotic images fueled my desire for wanderlust. I knew I would go one day.

My husband shared my dreams. As a student, he backpacked across Europe, collecting a treasure trove of outrageous adventures before I knew him. Whenever he pulled out a distant memory from a faraway journey, I begged for more details. I constantly asked for more reflections and descriptions.

"Show me on the map," I begged.

We dreamed of sailing to the South Pacific, knowing one day we would go there, but never knowing when.

And then came 9/11. It took our country off its axis, and our outlook forever changed. In just four short years, our sons would be gone, and the window of opportunity would be lost.

Follow your dreams now, came the ghost whispers. Our dreams fast-forwarded. Instead of a wistful dream, it became our new reality. We called it South Pacific Expedition. It would be our last hurrah as a family before our sons began lives of their own.

I listed and sold our island-hopping boat while Peter hunted for a strong ocean-going catamaran as a replacement to *Scud*. Whatever we couldn't fit in a suitcase was either sold or stored for the next boat. I turned off emotional attachment and got the job done. Within a matter of time, Peter found a catamaran, and together we signed the papers. In just six months, our new boat would be ready for delivery from South Africa.

1.
INTO AFRICA

On Safari: Kruger National Park

Twenty years from now you will be more disappointed by the things that you didn't do than by the ones you did do. Explore. Dream. Discover.

—Mark Twain

Within a month of signing a sales contract for a new catamaran in South Africa, I was well on my way to paradise ... and slight madness. With my husband, Peter, and our two teenage sons, we were en-route to *J'borg* (Johannesburg). From there, we would take delivery of our new boat in Port Elisabeth. We would then sail from South Africa to the Caribbean, catching big waves to surf along the way. Adam and Warren were marvelous adventurers. Their outdoorsy, curious natures were an asset on all journeys. Adam was tall with summer blond hair and carried a mature demeanor that belied his youthful looks. At sixteen years of age, he could easily single-hand *Scud*. Everything he learned was either directly from a book or gained through osmosis.

Warren, aged fourteen years, was the movie star in the family and had the handsome looks to go along with it. He could out-charm, outwit and outdo any raconteur. When the two brothers came to near blows, he was the gifted peacemaker. Together, the two were close enough in age to relish the same sports and the same ideas.

Right from the start, the expedition was my idea. I was an adventure addict. It fed my soul and stuck to me like two sides of Velcro.

My craving for the outlandish budded when my parents frequently moved during my childhood years. When first arriving in a new state, my two sisters and I went in search of our daily adventure fix. Over the years, we lived in South Carolina, Kentucky, Mississippi, Alabama, Florida, and North Carolina. I attended six different middle and high schools. It didn't matter which state we resided in as they were all the same after the second move: new kids, new street, new school.

On weekends, my sisters and I piled into the battered Volkswagen Beetle, our sole family vehicle, and roared off-road through fallow cornfields. We were happiest when lost on distant country roads in search of somewhere and going nowhere.

As we rumbled through the wide-open territory, streamers of our long hair spewed from open windows and rock tunes thundered from a squeaky radio. I spun the radio dial, looking for distant AM stations—Chicago, New York, Lexington. The signal crackled from heat lightning over Cumberland Falls. We rode the summer breeze down skinny roads, coursing along a maze of roads as if navigating a magical flying carpet. Lilly slid across the slippery back seat when Carol powered around curves. Society life in the small town of Corbin, Kentucky consisted of a big white church and three cars in the General Store's small parking lot. A sign hanging over the door, lit by an otherworldly glow, announced: "Best notions! Anywhere!"

I craned my neck to see out the VW Bug window. Fallow fields, forests, and ponds flashed past. People had turned toward the noise of our car before they saw us. Stalks of wild corn studded fields. Leaves were frayed and bitten to the cane. The Indian tobacco was brown and wilted from the earth. All of it was brittle and rattled as if folded from sheets of cigarette paper.

We explored the fields, looking for abandoned buildings to rummage. Through big barn doors, we came upon tobacco leaves suspended from giant rafters. When we clambered back into the Bug, the August sun beat against the roof, squeezing beads of sweat from our skin.

We laughed maniacally like a bunch of loony bins bent on speed, belting out Sarah McLachlan's lyrics "Thelma and Louise" style as we roared by telephone poles. When we careened around corners, pedestrians rushed roadsides to escape our path of impending fury. At stoplights, we skidded to a stop, practically doing wheelies in front of the town boys. Once, we ended up in a ditch.

• ━━ ◦ ● ◦ ━━ •

Later in life, when I discovered such an addiction to adventure was not normal behavior, I sometimes wondered what was wrong with me. But then I met Peter. And as luck would have it, he adored my wild side. Life was never boring after that. He had no idea–nor had I–how far our adventures would take us. And now, I wondered if I might be over my head this time around.

What about this South Pacific Expedition idea of mine? How did that come about? I wondered. I don't even surf! I hate exposing my body to roiling waters. As soon as my twinkle toes hit surf waters, I was instantly thrown back on top of the beach with a mouthful of sand and half my bikini missing. Besides, I was terrified of sharks. When a predator approached us on our family free-dives, I scampered up Peter's back faster than a squirrel up a tree, sinking us both. But I could tell he was laughing when bubbles rushed from his snorkel to the surface, looking like the spin-off froth from a turbo prop. If I could not see what was eating me for dinner, I was not going swimming.

I wanted our sons to engage in life from outside themselves by experiencing the world. I wanted them to learn the ways of those whom we visited, so they brought those impressions home, further enhancing cultural understandings. Call me naive, but wars would not be initiated if more of our countrymen traveled to foreign lands and stayed awhile.

Peter wanted to be foreign, where blue sky and turquoise-blue waters greeted him every morning. Philosophical considerations just got in the way and wasted time, according to Peter.

"You think too hard," he said one day. "Let's just go. Forget why."

South Pacific Expedition was an experience dedicated to the boys—I was along for the ride. But it held great promise of guaranteed adventure. The best part, we were en-route for a rendezvous with lions and elephants before taking delivery of our boat in South Africa.

Despite the buzz of excitement, events were unfolding a little too fast for me. I felt short of breath. I talked big, but I carried a wimpy stick at times. And right now, my nerves were on overdrive.

It was Martha's fault. She was from Capetown and now lived in the Caribbean. Over coffee one morning she got me rattled.

"Keep your windows and doors locked at stop lights. Never, *ever* go outside at night. Do not answer your hotel door at night unless you know the person. Never pick up hitchhikers. Never take the train alone. Never even travel alone!" she said.

Blah, blah, blah. True: South Africa had one of the highest crime rates in the world.

"You could die there!" Martha said.

"Thanks. Just what I needed to hear," I said, speaking facetiously. I doubted she caught my glib comment.

But I wondered how I could keep our kids safe on this South Pacific Expedition. They didn't even listen to me under normal circumstances. On top of it all, Sam and Gary, both brothers and friends of our sons, were joining us for part of the way. I wondered if they would follow my marching orders in times of chaos or danger. Teenagers had a mind of their own. They expressed their intentions—yelled out, rather—openly and without regard. I liked Sam. But he requires the personal space of a barn, which worried me.

I first became undone at the Atlanta airport terminal when queueing to collect our tickets to J'borg. Peter was ahead of me, busy with a ticket agent. Around me, surfboards were stuffed into black bags and stacked in piles resembling body bags. Warren was weary of the slow crawl in the queue at the ticket counter and began to chat up the young man next to him. Warren possessed a confident bearing and relished talk with eclectic strangers: international students, backpackers, musicians. His easy-going, self-effacing manner drew them in.

"You headed to Jeffrey's Bay?" Warren asked the traveler.

"Yeah, dude. Jeffrey's Braai was wicked!" he said in the vernacular with a thick Afrikaans cadence. I listened with new ears.

Atop the Afrikaner's head, sun-bleached hair protruded in all degrees of the compass, and tattered flip-flops and khaki shorts announced him as a serious surfer.

"Dude, monstrous waves there! Two minutes on one ride alone—you're going to wig out!" The South African dude said.

Jeffreys Bay was on the southeast coast of South Africa and had the best waves in the entire world. Stormy seas brewed in the great Southern Ocean off Antarctica and rumbled towards Africa. When they hit J-Bay, long barrels crashed one upon the other against immense sand dunes. At J-Bay, World Championship surfers competed on waves dubbed "Supertubes." It had been our sons' dream to make the pilgrimage to the Mecca of Surfing ever since the Hollywood hit "Endless Summer" was filmed there in the 1980's. After hearing of Dude's account, Warren's body writhed with eager anticipation, and the whites of his eyes grew wide.

"What about sharks? Any great whites?" Warren asked.

"J-Bay is the backyard of great whites, Man. South Africa has some serious shark issues. A white bumped a kid off his board last summer. Kids were so freaked out, they wouldn't paddle out for the surf contest. Old dudes had to float around on the water acting as decoys before the kids agreed to get back out in the water. It's not just the surfers—whites like to eat boogie boarders too. Those urchins wear black wetsuits and fins. Atop a black boogie board, they look like frigging seals to the whites from underwater. Sharks hit a couple of boogers last year: two fingers, a couple of toes … they didn't recover from the hospital for months. It's going to be frigging cold there too, Dude," he said.

"Yeah?" Warren asked.

His right leg jerked back and forth, as fingers tap-danced against thighs in a frenzy of nerves. He and Dude gesticulated in a secret code only surfers knew. Dude described the event in terrifying detail. The kid bumped high from off the surf board, thrown into the sky and bitten by two great whites simultaneously.

"I got the video footage to prove it if you want to see," Dude said, eyes bulging.

"Nah, that's okay," Warren said.

I was glad Warren turned down the offer. The morning became more serious than a fun day at an airport. *Just give me a tennis ball so that I can nail this guy*, I thought. My eyes scanned the perimeter of the airport in search of Peter. But he was nowhere to be found.

Dude kicked at his surfboard, shuffling it along in the queue. The surfboard swathed with the ubiquitous black bag. I wondered if any of us would be coming home in one. The news headline of "Kid Mauled in Shark Frenzy" accompanied by a family photo flashed across the inner screen of my mind.

I turned around with probing eyes to study Adam's reaction—he's the boogie-boarder in our family. He was eighteen months older than Warren, and the more sagacious one of the two brothers. Where Adam had assumed mannerisms and gestures from his Dad, Warren had assumed mine. Poor kid. He'd have Velcro dilemma the rest of his life.

Adam relished a big wave like any other sportsman, but Dude's account had shaken him. His face was frozen, and his eyes glazed over.

Warren moved to jab his brother in the tines of his ribs.

"Bro, you hear that? Monstrous waves!" Warren said.

I watched the two of them intently, growing mildly hysterical. I couldn't decide how to react.

Warren glanced at my arched eyebrows and curled lips.

"Mom, only six people died worldwide from shark attacks last year, compared to 150 from coconut clunking fatalities. So, just chill," he said with a huff.

Then he rolled his eyes toward me like a lame horse rolls its eyes back in its sockets moments before being shot out of misery.

"I'll try to avoid sitting beneath a coconut tree," I said.

Once onboard our flight to J'borg, I tried to decompress from Dude's disconcerting stories. Twenty-two hours to J'borg—way too much time to think. My nerves roared like a Ferrari out of control and wide open on a desert highway. In my cabin window, I saw my reflection. Beneath my eyes, deep circles were etched. Looking into the pane glass, I gazed back into the glazed eyes of a sleep-deprived insomniac.

Back at home, once we had implemented the South Pacific Expedition, we shared our intentions with those around us. To our friends we shouted: the adventure of a lifetime! The opportunity to see the world! They were delighted, but our parents were concerned.

"What do you mean you won't stop at night at sea? Where will you stay, exactly?" they asked.

"We'll sail all night long and take night watches. We can't stop. The waters are too deep and the boat too far from shore," I said.

Our plan sounded exotic. The feeling of high anticipation rode with me for months … until now. Thanks to the Dude, nibbles of doubt began to plague my spirit. To my list of grave dangers, I now added: great white attack. I had already dealt with other less serious concerns. For example, one could fall overboard. The kids were required to don lifelines and life jackets, but they would probably refuse. I couldn't get our kids to wear life jackets on our regular passages between the USA and the Bahamas. Even Peter refused to use a life tether, except in gale conditions , when it was like pulling teeth from a dog to get him to use a life line.

Violent crime pervaded in South Africa. No one was allowed to leave the boat at night. The kids snuck out, regardless. There was also a high rate of HIV and AIDS, so I spent sleepless nights hoping I'd raised my boys to respect the physical dangers of the night life. Among our less serious concerns were dysentery, typhoid, staph infection, and injury.

I gazed out my flight cabin window at the expanse of the ocean below, gaping in shock at waves like white horses vaulting over a tumultuous sea. They were on a never ending racetrack that stretched to a distant horizon. *I'll be down there in a little boat with four teenagers. Four teenagers*, I thought. There would be no way to fly home—even if I had a home.

Once we landed in South Africa and boarded our new boat, our plans were to sail along the Shipwrecked Coast from Port Elizabeth to Capetown. From there, we were scheduled to sail around the Cape of Good Hope, known amongst sailors as the Cape of Storms. And from there, we were to sail up the Skeleton Coast of West Africa and on across the Atlantic Ocean. The first time I studied the nautical charts, hostile words leapt off the pages: Shipwrecked Coast, Cape of Storms, Skeleton Coast. Who in their right mind would even try such a thing from just looking at bathroom wallpaper? Why didn't I study the map first? It was right there in front of me, words that spoke of death and bones and the sinking of ships. I blamed it on my seductive husband and sunsets, and not Martha this time.

The voyage from South Africa to the Caribbean was expected to take three months. We faced months of fear, loneliness, boredom, and fatigue. Although our destination was the Caribbean, we planned to sail on towards the South Pacific—assuming all had gone well (no loss of the ship or life).

I slid closer to Peter and gazed into his Robert DiNiro look-alike face. Soft brown eyes stared back at me, eyes that were benevolent and calmed me in the midst of all gales. Where I was unpredictable, untamed and spontaneous, Peter was steady and sedate. He called me 'his firecracker'. Like a trusty compass, his insouciant style gave me direction, pointing up and due north without fail. I slipped my hand into his large one, which was rough from handling heavy sails in the tropics over the years. It swallowed my own and I decompressed, allowing his warmth to lift me up. Instantly, liquid light shot up my arm like a vaccine. Friends sought him out for sage counsel: now that time was for me.

"Relax," he said. "Everything is going to be fine. Where's your cheer-leader hat? Remember the day you saved my favorite hat?"

I laughed. His funny side always cheered me.

2.

OVERBOARD

Biscayne Bay, Miami: Barracuda

Be yourself. Everyone else is already taken.

—*Oscar Wilde*

I hadn't always been a wuss. Early in my relationship with Peter, boats dominated our life together. He taught me about the sea life. It all started in Florida many moons ago soon after our relationship had blossomed.

We were sailing aboard the *Antilles*, a forty-six foot classic wooden boat. Tim was a good friend of ours and served as crew. Conditions were favorable, and I relaxed in the rhythmic cant of the vessel.

A novice to yacht sailing, I had no idea on how to become a valuable crew member. Mostly, I stood out of the way. Confusion announced itself all around me. Great piles of ropes dangled from lifelines and rigging like a spaghetti factory of drying noodles. Bulbous fenders ballooned from corners. A giant brass bell for dense fog lay suspended from a cockpit bulkhead. A litany of electronics used for navigation flashed puzzling numbers. I felt out of place, assailed with incongruous juxtapositions. The foreign chaos enhanced my spirit immensely.

A Beechcraft plane drifted overhead, towing a sign that announced instant pleasure: Welcome to Paradise Bar and Grill. Beneath a clear blue sky, a sea breeze filled the sails. On it rode the sweet scent of the land: frangipani, date palms, and seaweed. The *Antilles* scudded along on a sapphire-blue sea against the backdrop of South Beach condominiums in Miami. Seagulls circled the mast. Fish skidded across short waves, flushed by the boat's wake. A pod of bottle-nosed dolphins gamboled across the bow, squeaking in low-pitched tones. Peter and Tim chatted animatedly, trading mechanical tips.

Tim had a knack for jerry-rigging just about anything in need of repair aboard a boat. He sailed his ketch in Florida and the Bahamas. He and Peter gesticulated wildly as sea yarns were shared. Their merry eyes sparkled. I had never experienced anything like it before. The wonder of sailing, the sea, the camaraderie—it all made my heart soar. *I belong on boats*, I thought.

"Ready about!" Peter announced, preparing to tack.

Tim handled the lines skillfully. As the large mainsail swept across the forward deck, a puff of wind caught Peter's large-brimmed canvas hat and tossed it into the sea.

"That was my favorite hat!" he shouted as a fist smacked against the helm in frustration.

Behind him, I stood high from atop the stern cabin. From my vantage point, I followed the hat as it drifted into the distance with the boat's wake. I dashed to the back of the boat and dove into the sea. Cold water filled my sundress as it billowed around me, dragging my pace as I stroked. The hat was only a short distance, and as an avid swimmer, I reached it easily. Grabbing it, I spun around to shout with joy. Panic suddenly assailed me.

The *Antilles* was gone. Peter was gone. *Gone.* My heart pounded in my ears. Did anyone see me go overboard? *Surely...*

When I turned, I found a dark shadow watching me. A torpedo of flesh. Rows of jagged teeth studded toothy jaws that gaped open and closed, open and closed, in waters clear as mountain air. When the fish finned towards me, a dozen primal alarms tripped. My breath halted.

Cuda.

In Florida and the Bahamas, you learn about the great barracuda—they can bite off fingers. A barracuda can rip a dog in half. Weighing up to 110 lbs., the great barracuda can race through waters at a top speed of 36 mph. Advice was always the same: "When approached, back away slowly and never try to outswim it."

My fingers fanned the waters, barely discernible. Casually, I slid my cubic zirconium ring around backwards to hide its twinkling lights, announcing me as prey. *Stay cool. Make no sound.* Cuda and I faced off, watching each other. When I treaded water a little bit to the right, Cuda followed me. When I finned backwards, it came for me. Jagged jaws opened and closed. I waited.

Cuda waited.

Seconds became minutes. Minutes seemed like hours. In my peripheral vision, I saw the *Antilles* turn around.

In time, Peter brought the boat up close. He spilled the wind from the sails until the boat sat motionless in the water. Casting caution aside, I left Cuda at my tail and rushed to the side of the boat. Peter's large hand reached down for me. In one swift grasp, he yanked my 5'3", 102-pound body from the sea and placed me gently on the deck. I stood mute, unsure of what to do. Peter was an experienced sailor. Would he lecture me like a school girl who'd lost her lunch? Say I was a hazard at sea?

Suddenly, guffaws of laughter resounded through the rigging. I went limp with relief.

"That was amazing, Babe! You'll be great when the anchor chain runs out-of-control and free-falls. We'll send you in to retrieve the end," Peter laughed. A merry twinkle flashed my way. When he took me in his arms, I was wild with desire.

The event lived in my head with gorgeous reality. It pulled me in like a magnet, offering a missing link. To stand where nature and the sea ran the show–not a man–was a miracle in action. It was the missing link in my life. I needed it. *Nature.*

On the flight to South Africa, I felt my mojo flood back into me. I was ready for Africa. Ready for whatever way she would reveal to me. Just take the first step. The rest will fall into place.

3.
New Love And Pain

Bahamas

There are two ways to live your life. One is as though nothing is a miracle. The other is as though everything is a miracle.
—*Albert Einstein*

My world was altered profoundly the day I first met Peter. Since then, my life journey has been a whirlwind tour of the globe. Inside the cabin of Flight 658 from Atlanta to Johannesburg, I gazed out of the cabin window at the sea far below. The Atlantic Ocean was a sparkling sapphire-blue. I thought about Peter. I thought about the boat. I thought about the incredible events that had brought us together. Dr. Wayne Dyer and Dr. Deepak Chopra talked about synchronistic moments. They talked about odd events that occurred without notice, and how you need to take notice. They talked about people who continually pop up in your life. I could almost hear them saying, "Let go. Let your intentions lead you."

Peter was that man. He appeared one day, and I thought nothing of it. But then he kept reappearing in my life, popping up all over the country. I had to wonder about it. Images came to mind of the first event that triggered our union. It had led to another event, which had led to some other event, which had led to some person. In the end, all the events were stitched together into one, very remarkable, final scene–a synchronistic happening, a blessing.

The funny thing was that it all made sense today. But back then, I was the last to see the synchronicity unraveling at the time.

"I knew you and Peter were meant to be together," Mom said one day out of the blue.

The first time we were together remained forever etched on my mind. Had I known what lay ahead, I may not have stumbled so badly on one certain day.

I charged out of the door in darkness at 5 A.M. for the two hours of driving the Conway-Houston commute on I-45 to the downtown area. I was late already. I just knew it. A closing on a commercial property sale met at 8 A.M. The buyer was my client. Rush hour traffic was a virtual feeding frenzy. An undulating wave of humanity spanned six lanes of the freeway. Every few miles I passed by a stranded motorist, glad the sorry bum was not me. Not a day went by where I did not pass an accident alongside the road. Whirling red and blue lights littered the freeway shoulders at rush hour like toy trucks slung from a child's play in a suburban driveway.

I was new to freeway shambles. I grew up in North Carolina far from freeways and high-rises. I drove wide-eyed, jerking my head back and forth like a rooster pecking dirt. My small shoulders cradled the big steering wheel, eyes barely peeking over the rim. My face pecked the driver's window to check on surrounding traffic. People passed, staring with their mouth open at the absent Chevy driver. Of course, I could make my way just fine, except I could never relax. Driving in pre-dawn darkness was even worse. I gripped the steering wheel with white knuckles, distraught from the frenetic activity. Who in their right mind would drive at this hour? It seemed like all the world was going to work in downtown Houston that day.

Despite the moving cluster of lights, my tardiness had me in a panic. If I didn't meet the round table of fat cats on time, I was out of a job. I was history to my boss. At six-five and nearly 220 lbs., my boss had hair the color of a towhead. He was skinny enough that a light breeze could topple him over headfirst. His youthful looks belied his experience. At staff meetings, he bragged on how he had walked door-to-door in Angola for two years selling the Mormon religion. Mr. Tough Guy. Guess that was supposed to pump us up for the day's record sales. The boss was intense. I imagined that he ate pencils during coffee breaks. His nails were down to the quick, and when he walked, he spun like a toy top.

My earnings were based on commission only. So far, I had not sold one bit of land, despite having pounded the pavement to pitch corpulent oilmen for an entire year. And today was my first closing on a sale. I was selling a dilapidated warehouse in the slums—loose change for some people, but it was food in the fridge to me. My bank account was void of sustainable funds. I needed this deal to close like a granddaddy needed teeth. Last night, I had opened a can of tuna for dinner–again.

Pedal to the metal, I pushed my trusty Chevy across congested traffic lanes like a mad woman bent on Benzedrine. When a red light flashed on the dashboard, I took stock of the fuel gauge, nearly half-full, and the oil gauge, full. I vowed to see a mechanic later, just in case. My Chevy was ancient, but she always carried me to where I needed to go. I ignored the red warning light since all the dials were normal.

At the first paling of dawn, a driver gesticulated wildly at me from his window. The whites of his eyes were like winking saucers amidst a fluorescent dashboard. I ignored him too–you get all kinds of weirdoes on freeways. I sped past the driver, leaving him to choke in the fatuous fart of my Chevy. Soon afterwards, yellow tendrils of smoke trickled from beneath the hood. They were slight. I ignored them too. I consoled myself that the engine temperature would cool down in the parking garage while I was at work. The red light had illuminated many times before today—not to worry. Besides, I was seeing the mechanic on my way home from work.

A glance at my watch revealed fifteen minutes before the roundtable face-off.

A sign ahead announced the Post Oak Boulevard exit. My heart raced. I pressed on. The building that housed my office–a cubicle in a maze of others–was located just around the corner. I thought I could just barely make it. But then the yellow smoke trickling from the hood darkened. It soon widened into mustard smoke, billowing from beneath the hood. In a short time, it blanketed the Chevy, looking like a rising nuclear mushroom cloud. I drove through it. The turn-off lay just a couple hundred yards ahead. My office was right there. I pressed on.

Horns blared. Vehicles roared past. They merged around me at high speeds. I felt like a smoking tree on fire in the middle of a buffalo stampede. A loud clanging from under the hood signaled impending doom. Orange tendrils ballooned in front. They spiraled into the sky, looking like devil tongues. My heart sank. I knew I was in deep trouble. Just one more mile to go. I was mere blocks from the high-rise. I could see its signature rooftop.

Beneath the cloverleaf underpass, the Chevy surged forward and then jerked backwards, forward and back. My forehead whiplashed against the top rim of the steering wheel, and I saw stars. The engine rattled and sputtered. A semi tractor-trailer behind me sounded its horn. I panicked. There was no room for the semi to maneuver around me. There were too many vehicles in the entangled web of pressing metal. I struggled to steer my Chevy out of harm's way. But it was unresponsive. The steering wheel was hot.

I navigated through the yellow smoke and turned the Chevy onto the shoulder, pulling to a complete stop. When the semi lumbered past in a blur, I gaped in horror. I took a deep breath. A moment passed. And then I pushed my thumbs into my eyes and seized my battered briefcase. I opened the hot door and tore off my high heels. I took off running, leaving the smoking hulk behind me on the side of the road.

I grabbed my skirt ends and leaped over steel girders like a gazelle. I dashed across exit ramps and dodged cars at stop lights. When I spotted a cop, I slowed to avoid attracting suspicion. Once he turned away, I took off again. I darted around pedestrians with espressos and lattes balanced atop briefcases. I sped past delivery boys on roller blades, their arms weighted down with packages. I tore past the security guard at my office building. His scowl was hot enough to melt chocolate on ice cream. I ignored him too.

Before pin-wheeling to my desk, I detoured to the loo. Inside the granite toilet room, a heavy cherry smell wafted. I smoothed my skirt, pinned my wild hair, and scoured grit and grime from sweaty limbs. Mascara streaks snaked down my cheeks. Trickles of blood ran down my legs, cut from girders. My faux leather heels were ruined, the fabric torn and one heel severed. Twisting the heel, I backed it onto an embedded screw. I adjusted my facial expression to brandish a winning attitude, feeling far less confident than I looked. I just *had* to close the deal.

I left the loo and headed for the boardroom. My eyes darted left and right for a coffee pot. I had skipped the caffeine fix in a hurry to scurry out the door. A year ago I'd started drinking instant coffee without the hot water—quicker to get ready for work that way. Then I started stopping into one of the Houston coffee bars situated on every corner in the downtown area. It took me twenty minutes to make up my mind which of the two dozen types of designer coffee beans and liquid confections I wanted. But I could no longer afford the luxury.

I rounded the corner from the loo and found Al Freeman silently watching me. He stood beside the gold door to the boardroom, blocking my entrance. He was the buyer of the dilapidated warehouse that we closed on today. He was in his late fifties. Loosely curled hair cradled a fleshy face. His fat thighs were as large as my waist. His paunch (Belly-by–Budweiser) bulged from beneath a shiny jacket. I wondered who poured him into his Newman suit, straight off the rack of Valentino's on Savile Row.

"Good morning, Mr. Freeman," I said, putting forward my hand. "All set?"

"Hi," he said, giving me a limp handshake. "Call me Al." Then he flashed a wink at me. Beady, ferret-like eyes scanned me left and right, up and down, like an x-ray machine. The eyes were rheumy and heavily tinged with the redness of booze. A spider vein ran the length of a beak of a nose. It looked as if someone had squashed it with a boot. The guy was doing one of those subtle flexes, where you're trying to look like you're not flexing. Shirt sleeves pressed against smooth silk without much impact. The big guy was a show. He might have been a wrestler in high school or a bouncer at a local bar before he struck it rich in oil futures.

Call him Al? What's up with that? I wondered. Up to now, we had been on strictly formal terms. We had met twice at his glitzy, high-rise office. His secretary had been present and had taken notes.

"Say, how 'bout some breakfast after our little soiree?" Al Freeman suggested.

"Sorry, Mr. Freeman, but I'm busy with clients," I said.

"Ah, well, just a little snack to celebrate the deal then," he said. "Look, honey, maybe we could…"

I felt my pulse race. Honey? Did he just call me that?

"Sorry, Mr. Freeman," I said. "I can't." I planned to spend the next six hours cold-calling.

"Ah. Well then. Say, what's a young girl from Carolina doing in a place like this? How old did you say you were?" Al Freeman loomed over my tiny frame. The alcohol fumes stung my eyes. I drew up my hand to my mouth and gave a polite cough. In my head, a forklift beeped a back-up warning.

"See you inside, Mr. Freeman?"

I eased away to avoid instinctively punching him in the nose. I entered the boardroom with a purposeful stride. Not the wobbly walk of a recent highway refugee. I lowered myself into smooth leather rimmed in chrome that looked straight from the set of *Starship Galactica*. Breathing deeply, I tried to quiet the hungry rumble in my stomach. I looked down into my lap, pretending to smooth down my skirt. Silently, I willed myself to enter into a calm state of being. When I looked up, I felt better, but my mind still begged for caffeine. *Where's my Brazilian Almond fix?* After my freeway dash, my body begged for a shower, and my soul: a vacation in a place with palm trees.

Al Freeman entered, filling the doorway and blocking any natural light. He chose the chair next to me. At six-eight, nearly 350 lbs., Big Al was far too bulky for the chair and far too bulky for the room. He needed the personal space of a football field.

I organized my documents, as Big Al continued to flash his sick charm. No one offered coffee. It was nowhere to be seen, just when I needed it most. Right now, I needed the Cuban espresso stuff. Forget the wishy-washy Brazilian Almond stuff. Around me, unnatural office light glared, faces were pale, eyes blinking.

I placed my notebook directly in front of me, my pen just so. I went over talking points in my head. Suddenly, a wet hand grasped my thigh from beneath the table. I nearly sprang out of my chair. My knees bumped against cherry mahogany. Instinctively, my arms flung out, sending pens and notes onto the carpet. A weak squeak bubbled from my ruby lips.

"Oh, let me help you there," Big Al implored. He bent down with fake gentleman zeal to retrieve spilled contents. I wheeled back in the rolling chair to make room for his ample girth. When he paused to collect my notes and pen, I felt my body stiffen. He wallowed by my ankles, dropping contents and then collecting them again. When he finally rose, it was in slow motion. He stopped midway, lingering for a second too long. I felt a rushing in my ears when slimy hands raced up my legs and between my thighs as he slowly straightened up.

I squeezed my knees together so tight a sesame seed would not fit between them. My heart flapped in my chest.

When Big Al came up, he gave me a purely physical smile that lacked any warmth whatsoever. He reeked of feral intention. I kept up the eye contact though nobody was home in those ferret eyes. It was like looking into the windows of a lost soul. I maintained the stare longer. His skin looked like pink plaster of Paris that might dissolve should it get wet.

I sat silent and unmoving as a statue. I tried to smile, hide my feelings of disgust, but I do not know whether my face cooperated or not. I heard a man cough as if he were trying to dislodge a lung. It was time. The air around me crackled with intensity. I took a deep breath.

Settle, girl, settle. Reel 'em in.

All eyes met mine. My closing spiel was executed with zeal, like warm honey on Sunday pancakes. I sold the sizzle. Feeling entirely confident, I eased the bill of sale over to Al Freeman for his executive signature.

The look that met my eyes made little fire ants race up and down along my skin. A tiny reptilian smile came to Big Al's lips. It was one that touched no part of him as if the lips separated from the rest of the body. I knew that look too. It meant me and more, in exchange for his signature.

No way. It struck me that he was one sick fake. My face lost color. My stomach took a nosedive. I pushed my faux reading glasses–used for impression and age enhancement–up my nose and jiggled my notes. I left the bill of sale on the table in front of him. I waited. Al Freeman placed a fat palm, as big as a ham, by the signature, fingers splayed. A gold pinky ring flashed darts from morning light like signals from a lighthouse. He stared into my eyes. There was a small and nearly imperceptible twitch in his left eye. He knew my predicament. Everybody did.

I froze. I wanted to stop and run out the door—my caffeine craving like a magnetic pull—but I pushed on. I held it together, so much so that I could feel the quake beginning in my lips. All I knew was that I could not trade in my integrity for this gritty slime of a man. The back-up warnings in my head blared. I waited, holding the gaze and offering nothing except what was physically on the table.

Hang tough, sweetie.

I exchanged a telling glance with Big Al and he withdrew his meaty hand. He left the contract unsigned and packed up his briefcase. As the members of the Fat Boys Club filed out, the ubiquitous questions assaulted me.

"Honey, can I buy you dinner tonight? Where you from in Carolina, did you say? How old did you say you were?" the fat cat said.

Twenty-two, to be exact, you big, fat bully!

Up to now, I had spent several years in college and in the field learning and practicing commercial real estate. Though the training had landed me this potentially lucrative position at a very young age, I clearly had more to learn than what books could teach me. I felt drained.

Insulted and deflated, I sought out the only available space for privacy—the loo. I sat down in the privacy of a cubicle, my knees hoisted up to support my bowed head, my arms wrapped around my shins. I closed my eyes, clenched my fists, and pressed my mouth against my knees to keep from wailing. I wanted to be numb. The quietness of the toilet stall comforted me. The day had gone horribly wrong. I was weary of the Big Boys Game. I hated Houston. I hated my job. Men refused to take me seriously. They refused to respect me. They accosted me in the parking garage. Their business practices were disturbing. The concrete forest was depressing. The commute was disastrous, if not downright deadly. Most of all, I missed the beauty of nature. Birds. Night stars. Wild animals. Natural light.

I'd given it all I had. No one deserved that much of me.

My bank account shouted out into nearly zeros. In an effort to find a better paying job, I had strolled half-heartedly into a head hunter's office last week that promised high paying jobs. After filling out an application and passing along my resume, the career agent had arranged a meeting with a man looking for a pretty girl to showcase his product on the Johnny Carson Show. I would stand on stage and act all dumb and pretty, smiling broadly, as the spokesman pitched his new product. Clearly, this turn of events was not my most shining moment, but it sounded sane to me. The cash number was impressive. Zeros speak loudly in a bank account.

I had met the man after work last week. Taking the elevator to the top floor of a high rise, I was invited into a private suite and interviewed by him. *Normal enough,* I thought, *but strange that we're in a hotel suite for a job interview.*

He looked to be in his sixties, with ordinary features, and graying hair at the temples. He wasn't portly, but wasn't particularly fit either. I remember his name as Thomas.

I passed the interview. Thomas shook my hand and brought in a bottle of champagne.

"To celebrate!" he announced.

I didn't want to ruin a good thing, so I placated him by saying, "Sure, why not?"

The pill must have already been dissolved in the glass when he retrieved the flute from the tray. I remembered nothing after the first sip.

I awakened with my dress up and my bra torn, sans panties, in a bed, alone. A Polaroid camera lay on the bedside table. The camera was familiar to me, as I used it in photographing real estate properties for appraisals. After shooting a property, an image pushes out from the bottom of the camera. A rushing sound came from the bathroom. It sounded like someone taking a shower.

Fear and dread held me in panic. I feared for my life like never before. I bolted out of bed, and ran into the adjoining suite where the interview had taken place. Where were my shoes? On my way out of the bedroom door, I saw nude photos of me on the dresser. I snatched them up faster than a cat on a cricket. As I ran, Thomas opened the bathroom door. "You can't take those!" he shouted.

I tore them into tiny pieces in the two seconds it took him to reach me.

"Those were *mine!*" he yelled. Aggression raged through every molecule of his body. Terrified, I grabbed the door handle as he leapt after me. I ran. I ran and ran and ran.

—•◦•—

I am still running from Thomas. I was so terribly ashamed that I never told anyone but the career agent who sent me. I could not let another young girl fall victim to this awful predator.

When I called the career agent, my shaky voice and flood of tears spoke the truth. She was stunned and wanted to be certain I wouldn't sue the company. I couldn't even bear to make a police report, I felt so ashamed.

This wasn't my first rape or sexual assault. A college boyfriend date raped me when I was a virgin. For a long time, I didn't understand what making love was about, since sex seemed to be equated with violence, betrayal and fear. Later, when I married Peter, I began to learn the true meaning of love. I was brought out of the darkness and back into the light.

For nearly four decades I was too broken to tell of my trauma from sexual assault and rape—until the writing of this book. I told my best friend first, simply because she was in town and my sister wasn't.

"Leave out the mickey and rapes. Keep it a secret," she said.

"Why?" I was incredulous.

"It's tragic. I only want to read happy books."

"Rape and sexual assault are an epidemic. According to the Dept. of Justice and the CDC, 1 in 6 women have been raped and sexually assaulted in the USA, not to mention the horrific genocide rapes occurring in the Middle East and Africa. A rape occurs every 107 seconds in the USA; 20% of college women are raped before graduation. What if my telling saves even one life? The more we talk about it, the more others can too. Our shared stories bring power to the victims."

"It's still too negative," she said.

I next told a loved one. She told me of similar experiences. I was aghast. How did I not know? We had shared our youth together. "Why didn't you tell me when we were kids?"

"I was too ashamed," she said. "I had no one to turn to. You know how it is. People would have said it was all my fault. I couldn't face their betrayal."

I felt terrible. I should have seen her pain. I would make it up to her by being an intimate part of her adult life. I would protect her at all times. Look after her. Support her. Be more involved in her life.

I next told Amy Ferris, a memoirist and author of *Shades of Blue*, at a writing conference. Grimacing, she shared a similar story. "Sexual assault predators are dirt bags," she said.

"Castrate them all. Like other countries do," said her friend, who was standing next to her. I laughed.

"Amen, Sister!" We high-fived. How many more victims were amongst me?

I next asked my friend, a former military officer, if I should right about it. "No. Keep out the mickey in your book," she said.

"Are you kidding? Are you telling me you've never been harassed when you were young? Think about what we're covering up. It only proliferates if we don't speak out."

"Okay, right. Yes, put it in," she said. Then she looked down at her napkin.

According to Mother Jones, an estimated 26,000 rapes and sexual assaults took place in the military in 2012. Only one in seven victims reported their attacks, and just one in 10 of those cases went to trial.

According to mental-health experts, the effects of military sexual trauma and sexual assault (MST) include depression, substance abuse, paranoia, and feelings of isolation. Victims spend years drowning in shame and fear as the psychological damage silently eats away at their lives. Many frequently end up addicted to drugs and alcohol, homeless, or take their own lives.

Bewildered with the various responses I received, I asked a successful business woman, VP of a wealth management firm, and a friend of mine. "What do you think about leaving the mickey out?"

"Leave it out. It's not your job to save the world."

Bewildered, I consulted a spiritual mentor.

"Of course. You have to leave it in! We enter this world and choose our experiences. It's our greatest sacrifice. You must then learn how to rise above it and teach others. Only then, will you have sought your greatest accomplishment in life," she said. "You, indeed, will save lives."

At least in sharing my trauma, I knew that if I told it enough times, I would no longer feel the pain and punish myself for it.

My self-discovery rang true in the end.

* * *

At one time in college, I recall wandering a railroad track at night, going somewhere, and nowhere. I was depressed over my boyfriend's sexual abuse, lost in despair. Dark thoughts entered my mind when I normally pushed away the darkness and rode the waves of positive belief. Even this was too much for me.

In my senior year with only one semester remaining until graduating with a high GPA, I dropped out. No one could stop me. I couldn't run fast enough. I never looked back.

———— •◦•◦•◦• ————

Inside the loo down the hall from my office cubicle, after having endured the advances of Big Al and the botched sales closure on the warehouse deal, I came undone. I did nothing. What was happening? I breathed deeply and let go. I wandered into the labyrinth of myself, pleading for an alternative perspective. In time, a calmness overcame me. A flood of epiphanies rained down, quick and continuous. I repeated them in my head, lips moving rapidly. No one entered the loo to disturb my celestial practice. It was all mine. I relished it. It was the first serenity that I had felt in an extraordinarily long time.

I'd hit a roadblock. I was a victim of the inveterate goals of life. I was the victim of forces inside–and outside–of myself. I wanted more money, more power, more stuff (a better car, a better apartment, anything better). In my pursuit, I had experienced sexual assault. These were the narcissistic tendencies of my ego, but also because I had been naïve. Because of my thirst for power, nothing but pain had knocked on my door. I was out of my league. A lost girl from North Carolina. My soul was blocked. Joy and despair were reflections of how well I had done in life. And I possessed none of the joy. I lived in constant despair that felt like a lead blanket. I lacked insouciance: I did not laugh, sing, or dance with myself. I was wounded.

I felt an organ rip the inside of my gut. I had been wandering around, wallowing in the wrong direction. It was time for a new line of work. What, exactly, I had no idea. But I wasn't afraid. I had given this position as a commercial real estate broker my best shot. I had not anticipated the sexual assault. I would deal with that later.

Time to run. Time to get out.

"These boots were made for walking and that's what they're gonna' do." The lyrics came to me and brought me towards the light, and out of the darkness, giving me renewed resolve. I marched out of the granite stall of the loo and straight back to my desk. I was done with the Good Ole Boy network and Big Boys Game. After giving notice to Boss, I saluted the myriad of office cubicles and left.

I took the bus home. The bus passed through the area where I had left the Chevy, but I kept my eyes peeled forward, afraid to look. I would collect it tomorrow. Tomorrow was Saturday and freeway traffic would be light. Driving a busted Chevy–assuming it was salvageable–to a mechanic would be much easier on the weekend.

Once inside my lonely apartment, I lowered myself into a chair to grasp the reality of having no car, no job, and no money.

A trilling sound announced a caller on the phone.

"Are you Tina Carlson?" the caller asked.

"Speaking," I said.

"Ma'am, you need to come down and pay your tow of $200," the dispatcher, Officer Jenkins, reported.

"Tow?" I stammered. "$200?"

That was all I had left in the bank. My rent was due.

"Yes, ma'am. It caught fire on the freeway. The Fire Department, Police, and Ambulance services answered the call. The Department towed your vehicle to the Impound Lot on the far side of town. Your burning vehicle blocked traffic for hours," he said in a flat voice. "You might have been trapped inside. How were we to know?" A tone of admonition lingered.

He hung up after I assured him of my presence the following day. Before I rose from the chair, the phone rang again. It was my brother, Keith, offering his car while he sailed away with his wife, Nora, and her brother, Peter. It was early evening in Houston when I got the call from Keith. Just one phone call started the whole process.

"Can you fly to Fort Lauderdale and manage my car for a few years? I'm sailing around the world with Nora's brother, Peter. I want you to drive it," Keith asked.

"Is Peter's bride going too?" I asked.

"No, Peter called off the wedding. Something about having to don a Brooks Brothers blue blazer jacket on a tennis court. I don't know," Keith explained. "He's living aboard the boat, prepping it for the voyage. He placed an ad in the local newspaper looking for female crew."

Keith was the oldest of four siblings in our family; the other three were all girls. At six feet and 175 pounds, Keith could be pretty intense at times, but he had a magnetic personality that drew people in. His wacky sense of humor could dismantle just about anybody. At home when we were growing up, Keith was always designing things. He made planes out of plastic and cars out of plywood. He won design competitions. His creative talent led him into the advertising industry where he worked as a photographer. On his sailing journey around the world, he planned to shoot stock photos to augment expenses. Being the oldest of four siblings in the family, Keith always got his way. If I took on the VW Bug, I had to maintain it like a possessed alien obsessed over a compulsive cleaning disorder. His car was *unique*. It was a very cute neon-orange convertible. It was his pride and joy. Selling it had not been an option for him. He believed that cars were like boats. Let them sit and they die.

"Yes! I'll be there tomorrow!" I yelled into the phone. I was in dire need of reliable wheels. Maybe Keith's offering was an augury of better things to come.

Peter. A bachelor. Crew? My heart skipped a beat. I skipped into the kitchen, nothing but a small table and chair by the phone. This time, when I prepared my dinner of canned tuna and tomato, I stuck a used birthday candle into the top of the tomato.

I believed that angels danced when hearing expressions of appreciation.

Thank-you! I shouted to the Universe.

Little did I know, the angels would take me farther through those open doors than I ever expected. Angels sure had a sense of humor. On board Flight 368, Houston to Ft. Lauderdale, it occurred to me that this would be my second occasion in seeing Peter. Were the angels playing with me again? I smiled at the thought.

4.

OVERBOARD AGAIN

Florida

No, we're not dating, but he's still mine.

—*Anonymous*

The first time I met Peter was two years earlier when Keith married Peter's sister, Nora. The wedding took place in Lake Geneva, Wisconsin, the home of the bride. My two sisters and I were bridesmaids. As part of the wedding party, we shared a room in a guesthouse at the lake. Carol, my older sister, was striking. She had shiny black hair that hung in long ribbons down both shoulders. A former beauty queen of Boca Raton, Florida, Carol was tall. She possessed an incredible walk, with her head held high and her shoulders back in perfect posture. She resembled a model straight from a New York runway. Carol was one of those people who made everything brilliant the moment she walked into a room.

My younger sister, Lilly, was attractive, with long blond hair. She possessed an electric personality that bubbled over with fire. When she lit up, it was like she was on a Hollywood stage set. A tomboy like me, we were inseparable as young kids before we became teenagers and drifted apart. Lilly always blamed me for escaping the wrath of Mom's fury when caught in our misdeeds together.

The wedding of my brother to Peter's sister took place on a vast lawn in Lake Geneva. The green lawn lay like a velvet blanket across rolling hills. Beside it, azure lake waters sparkled brilliantly beneath the sun. Lavender delphiniums and scarlet poppies perfumed the summer breeze. Traditional wooden motorboats with colorful flags transited the waters, and the white canvas of sailboats dotted the large expanse of the waters. A magical essence wafted. You could not stroll down the hilly green lawn without pausing to sit and stare at the picturesque lake scene. The view caused one to reflect and dream.

The site was perfect for a wedding. Keith and Nora were scheduled to exchange their vows at twilight when the sunset on the lake cast shadows that were deep and long, and the color blazed pink and red with invisible love darts.

Since Peter was in charge of entertaining the wedding party, he invited any sailing enthusiasts in the party out on the lake for the afternoon. I was the only taker, despite never having sailed in my life.

Peter's boat of choice was a little Hobie, a catamaran known for speed. Members of the wedding party worked with complicated outfits and event arrangements. Refusals to join Peter for a sail smacked of: "My hairstyle takes time." and "The water was too cold." I opted for fun, casting flower arrangements aside. Maybe no one would notice.

I dashed back to the guest room to throw on a one-piece bathing suit for the sail. It looked faded, and a bit tattered, but it was all that I owned. Lilly strutted into the room. She paused in the doorway, placing a hand on her hip just so. Posing, she resembled Marilyn Monroe on a movie set, sizing me up. Lilly sauntered over to sit on the edge of the bed, leaned back and crossed her long legs.

"Now aren't you a looker," Lilly said.

She smacked her lips like she had just downed an ice cream cone in a hurry and wanted more.

"You'll stand out like a bag lady in that get up. It's quite the turn-on," she said, her tongue so forked it could double for fine dinnerware. Her sassy ways would have crucified that bozo back in Houston. In one sentence, she would have stripped Big Al of his ego. I wished she had been with me in that Texas boardroom. She could have given me some pointers on how to destroy bullies.

"I got it at the Goodwill in town. No one told me to pack a bathing suit," I said, petulantly.

"A wedding. On a lake?" Lilly said. "What part of 'lake' confused you, exactly?"

She kicked off red high heels. They landed in a heap with the other six spikes in the corner of the room. She shook her head at me. She had perfect hair, her blond ponytail flipping from side-to-side like a metronome. Several hairs had escaped and fallen in front of her face. She raised her eyebrows at me, waiting for my snappy comeback. I did not have one.

"Your point being?" I asked. I turned my back towards the full-length mirror to view my spreading butt. "At least I have one top-quality, world-class derriere. I try not to brag."

Lilly started laughing, a sound that reminded me of moose mating on the Discovery Channel. She pointed at the edge where the suit met my thighs.

"At least tuck in your flab. You've got more dimples than a teenager with chronic acne. Where are you going, sweetie?" she asked.

I loved it when she called me sweetie.

"I'm going sailing with Peter," I said.

Lilly suddenly stopped short and broke out in song.

"WHEN I FAAAALL IN LOOOOVE WITH YOU-OU-OU-OU-OU-OU," she belted.

I looked at her. She stopped, sashayed over to the mirror, and stuck her face into the glass.

"When I sing that way," Lilly said, "it feels like I'm on stage with Celine Dion in a duet." She kissed the glass, leaving a ruby red lip stain.

"Yeah," I said, "on the Gong Show maybe."

I made a noise like I was gagging on a Popsicle stick. And then I furrowed my eyes at my dour swimming suit. The navy blue had faded to a lighter hue, hardly a blue anymore, and the white had turned to a dull grey.

"Don't be dazzled by my fashion prowess, but that suit is not making the cut," Lilly said. "Fashion is one of my hidden talents. You probably never knew."

She moved fluidly from the mirror and semi-glided out of the room. I loved her wild, crazy ways. Boring was not in her dictionary. *Saucy wench*, I thought.

I sighed. From the pit of my battered suitcase, I grabbed a sarong and wrapped it around my swimsuit to create flair. My confidence was waning fast. Before I changed my mind, I strolled out of the guesthouse towards the hill that led down to the lake. I stopped when I reached the hill. The stunning beauty before me was mesmerizing. The lake below sparkled with a curtain of glittering diamonds. Leading down to it was the vast lawn that lay like a velvet carpet. At the water's edge, colorful flags snapped like gunfire in the breeze.

I unraveled the sarong from my body, clutching edges with forefingers and thumbs, casting aside gauche concerns about designer labels and hip swimsuits. I spread my arms wide like a flamingo and flew down the hill. The wind pumped up the flanks of the sarong like malformed wings. My toes gripped soft grass and in my mind's eye, I soared over a rain forest deep in the Amazon. I darted to the right and then the left, scooping low over serpentine rivers. I swooned with joy.

At the water's edge, I stopped, sensing Peter. He looked up from the boat that tugged on its mooring lines. Peter greeted me with a smile, the corners of his mouth twitching with amusement at my child-like display of antics.

Oops. A real class act you are, Tina, I berated myself.

Peter helped me into the little boat, parking me at the back, near the side.

"Hold onto this netting, Tina. You'll be just fine," Peter said.

I settled in the corner, willing myself to stay out of the way and out of trouble.

He tossed the ropes back onto the dock, and we were up and away like a rocket. Out on the lake, the Hobie Cat scudded beneath a stiff breeze. Waters were rougher than I had imagined. Rooster tails of spray shot from between twin hulls, flashing tiny rainbows. I watched the kaleidoscope of color against the clear blue sky, marveling at the rainbows' magic. Peter tweaked the sails, swooshing me to opposing sides whenever the boat tacked and changed directions. My long locks plied across my face. In my haste to meet Peter, I had neglected to bring anything to tie back my hair. My cute little hat was long gone by now. The wind had whisked it away.

Hats and Peter were always cast in the same sentence throughout my life with him. Either he was donned in one, or me. By the end of the day, one of us would be chasing down a hat, either his or mine. In the tropics, melanoma protection was a strict code of law to follow.

I hung on, amazed at our swift speed. The Hobie crested a wave and lifted into the air before slamming back down again. It pitched across short chop. Waves crashed across the trampolines. I laughed every time a wall of water doused the boat and us. It felt like riding the bucking bronco back in Dallas at the bars with my sisters, the only fun I ever had back in that forlorn place.

Sailing was euphoric.

"You're doing great," Peter said.

When he smiled at me, my pulse quickened.

"Want to hike out?" he asked.

He described the process of 'hiking out'. His cursory details signified to me that it was a simple maneuver. It hardly seemed complicated. In fact, it sounded like fun.

"Sure!" I said.

When Peter strapped a harness around me, I felt the warmth of his firm physique. My eyes shot to his wet biceps that bulged like baseballs. The SPF-45 sun lotion on his tanned shoulders was so oily that it reflected the sun. A hot flash came to my face when he clasped the buckle tight against my navel. The fleeting brush of his fingers against my belly made my knees go weak. I curled my toes reflexively and stared down at the belt to hide my embarrassment. I held my breath, reeling in my belly tight, so it looked flatter. Once he moved his hands away, it took me a moment before I could marshal the courage to draw in a breath. The belt left me nearly gasping for air. I breathed in short, little breaths to steady my nearly writhing body.

Peter added a few more instructions before the final liftoff.

"Just put your feet here, then lean out," he said. "Hold on here tight with your hands. Slide down until your right toe gets a grip there. Then stay close and wiggle over to the left."

He flashed pearly whites at me. The instructions sounded more complicated than a little "hiking out."

Instructions complete, I stood and leaned out with far less confidence than I felt, placing my feet at the edge of the boat exactly as directed. My entire body weight was suspended from a hook at my navel, placing the bulk of my weight around my hips. It felt secure and tight. Though I was not entirely confident of this exercise, I wanted to impress Peter with my natural affinity towards water sports—which was nil. Even so, I was a willing participant. I prided myself on being game for just about anything in life, assuming no harm would come to me.

Nerve Tina. You've got to keep nerve. I commanded myself down from near panic.

"Ready. Set. Go!" Peter shouted.

I sprang out.

Just as I leaped out, one foot slipped against the side of the boat. I felt it loosen, missing the grip entirely. In an instant, my hand reached back for a shroud. I had missed a step somewhere, somehow. But there were no ropes to grasp. No ropes at all. My eyes widened in disbelief. I plunged into the water … head first, upside down. Cold lake waters enveloped me. I felt the belt tighten across my hips from the fierce pull of the boat. The lines gave me a sense of false security. At least I wasn't floundering. The lines led to the boat. And those lines were attached to Peter.

The harness lines held, but they quickly became entangled around my body. My arms flailed. I clawed at the surface, but the boat ripped through the water too fast. It felt like I was being shoved down a water chute at high speed with a fire hose at my back. Any sane person would have detached the harness belt and lines, but I was unable to seize the clasp. Every time I reached for it, rushing water peeled my hands away like monster claws. Sunlight streamed overhead, slanting sideways through the water with ribbons of iridescent light. Strands of my hair twirled and twisted across my face, blinding me. My body flipped around, rotating in fast circles. Over and over, I spun. At the vortex of each rotation, I saw a blurry Peter silhouetted in bright sunlight through tangled strands of hair.

The world underwater looks like this from the view of a fish, I thought.

I held my breath, piercing my lips against raging waters. I was incapable of screaming for help. And it worried me, slightly. I am a strong swimmer, but not strong enough to alter the force of the pull of the lines. The funny thing was, I was not afraid. I had confidence that–in time–Peter would reel me in. I tried not to think about why this was not happening at this very moment.

Don't panic.

Rushing waters clawed at my swimsuit.

Oooh, please don't give way now!

My swim suit had ripped apart before during a particularly bad wipe-out while water skiing. I could not bear the humiliation again.

I grew worried when the neck tie of my swimsuit top started to loosen. The chastity belt of the harness encapsulated the bottom half of my swimsuit, so no worries there.

Part of my brain was berating me–foolish to do this without more formal instruction. Most of my brain, however, had kicked into survival mode. My adrenaline went haywire from lack of air. Maybe my body knew what my mind would not accept: this was about survival. I could very well die down here. Why was it taking so long to be pulled back aboard? My chest started to pound. I was dizzy. My heart beat hard. My lungs burned. My former reverie turned to genuine fear.

People ask survivors of bad accidents what their last thoughts were before they thought they were going to die. I can tell you this: *nothing but being rescued.* I needed to calm myself even as the terror tore a hole in my chest.

Suddenly, I felt the Hobie Cat round up into the wind. The boat stalled, and towlines started to shorten and then slacken. Peter grabbed my arms and yanked me aboard. I collapsed on the center pontoon, sucking air in vast gulps. My pulse raced.

Peter stared at me. I was trembling like a lost puppy, the result of the cold water immersion. He gathered up my sarong. Leaning across the pontoon, he coiled it around me and hesitated. When I smiled between gulps of air, he flashed a smile so warm and friendly that it split his face in two. Genuine radiance beamed back at me, maybe from relief that I was okay. I couldn't tell. And then the most delightful thing happened, which surprised the heck out of me. I broke out in a fit of giggles. Nervous giggles, maybe, but hey, I was alive. Peter sure had a bag of tricks to keep a woman entertained.

Later that afternoon before the wedding, Keith walked with me to the home of his future in-laws, located on the hill in front of the lake. Keith's future father-in-law opened the door. From behind him, Peter's mother beelined toward us with a radiant smile. Her arms reached out, implying that she hoped to do more than shake my hand. She wore a smile that turned her ordinary features into something almost celestial. She was a beautiful woman with a fleshy face and loosely curled hair. She wore a fashionable pant suit. A pair of half-moon reading glasses hung from a chain, resting on her chest. She had heard of my near drowning escapade out on the water with Peter. She enfolded me in her arms.

"You're such a brave sport," she said with a sweet sounding chuckle. I liked her immediately.

5.

BEACH COPS

Yacht Antilles

If you're going to love someone or something, then don't be a slow leaking faucet—be a hurricane.

—Shannon L. Alder

Two years after my brother's wedding, my second encounter with Peter unfolded in Ft. Lauderdale. Peter was still a bachelor. I forced myself not to think about him. Or how it had felt when he smiled at me across the Hobie Cat when he pulled me out of Lake Geneva. Or how animated I felt when we had chatted together. Or how tender he had been after my fall overboard. Or how soft his touch felt when he had unbelted the harness straps from around me.

Keith met me at the Ft. Lauderdale airport so that I could collect his VW Bug. I planned to stay only a couple days before driving his car back to Texas. He was excited about sailing around the world with Peter and Nora. Having a car greatly improved my outlook on Houston even though I was unemployed. Quitting my job may not have been the smartest move—since I had no other plans—but it had felt right at the time. Besides, I was doing Keith a favor. The VW Bug needed to be driven. I was one lucky girl. Once back in Houston, I vowed to put my life back in order.

Keith and I drove along the scenic beach road of A1A, bordered by stately palm trees. As the palms swept by, Keith filled me in on the maintenance procedures for his VW Bug. We parked in front of a house on the Intracoastal Waterway. I followed the grassy path to a dock where the *Antilles* was being outfitted for her global circumnavigation. Since Peter was skippering the vessel, he was busy onboard analyzing and testing the ship's systems. Keith and Nora were serving as crew members, and renting an apartment nearby. They planned to move aboard on the day of departure, set for two weeks. The islands of the Bahamas would be their first port-of-call.

The *Antilles* looked glorious in her classic wooden style. The foremast steepled into a clear blue sky, followed by a shorter mast, aft. A varnished toe rail swept from bow to stern, glistening with little fire lights of sundrops that accentuated her dainty sheer. A long boom covered with white canvas lay stretched lengthwise across the ketch. A small team of workmen moved about her decks like an army of ants. A cacophony of sound filled the air: *bam, screech, saw.* Chain links lay coiled around decks like snakes.

Peter popped up from the aft cabin wielding a massive paint brush in his ham-sized hand. He was brown and suntanned as nutmeg. He wore a white T-shirt and blue jeans. I blushed at his bulging shirt sleeves. Tendons and muscles pulsed against the cotton fabric. Dark hair lay disheveled atop broad shoulders. A three-day stubble signaled a casual approach to hygiene. *Like a cowboy*, I thought.

I followed Keith to the boat. Peter extended his large hand when we reached and led me into the cockpit. Those eyes again. Those white teeth. I was overwhelmed by his radiance and moved with lumpy grace, snagging my big toe on a steel cleat. *Ouch*. Blood leaked onto white decks. Nora grabbed a rag. *A lovely impression, Tina*, I thought.

Once aboard, I lowered myself onto a wooden bench, topped with a canvas cushion of oyster-gray. In front of me, a bronze binnacle covered an enormous compass that whispered of former ports-of-call to foreign lands. I breathed deeply to mask the toe throb, all goggle-eyed with Peter sitting across from me. I couldn't stop grinning.

After a brief conversation, Keith offered to show me around below-decks. We made our way down a steep wooden ladder and into the sleek main salon where an earthy scent wafted up from ancient beams. Inside was a nautical museum in miniature size. It took a moment before my eyes could settle on any one thing.

Cherry mahogany dominated the salon. Varnished surfaces gleamed. Suspended across mahogany bulkheads were black and white photos of the *Antilles* anchored in Bermuda, the Bahamas, and Newport. Above, brass lanterns hung gimbaled from the ceiling. I half expected Admiral Nelson to clamber down the companionway ladder in a dripping slicer and yellow boots.

After a time, Keith and Nora left for the evening. They agreed to meet with Peter in the morning for compass calibrations. I offered to help paint the bottom half of the mast for the duration of the afternoon. The boat was a beehive of activity. I wanted to be part of the progress so jumped right in. Brandishing a two-pound brush in my palm, it occurred to me that I was in for a whole new learning experience. I'd never handled a paintbrush. Peter stood before me with a paint bucket and rag and gave me rudimentary instructions on how to paint a boat mast with skilled technique.

"Keep your line moving; keep it wet; always go in one direction," he said with patience.

I stroked the wooden mast with the brush, back and forth, and up and down in a monotonous, but pleasant rhythm. The sky was bright blue and hot as fire. The sunshine was invigorating. All around me, stately palms swayed from an onshore ocean breeze. A song pushed up in my throat.

"Birds fly over the rainbow, why then, oh why can't I, I, I, I, Hhhhhooooooooo?" I sang.

I let the sun roar down on me and belted out to my heart's content as if it were karaoke night at some bar. A party all to myself. It felt tremendously liberating.

My disquiet from the loss of my job in Texas slowly began to thaw. My soul healed with each passing hour. I felt my body relax. My mind opened. My heart warmed. As I took in my surroundings, it struck me that one of my dreams had already come true: I was beneath a blue vault of glorifying sunshine, unencumbered and free.

Watch out what you wish for, wafted the sagacious call on the wind.

As an orange orb fell into the city, waning pink light cascaded across the decks of *Antilles*. Once the lower mast gleamed with fresh paint, I cleaned my brush and showered from a garden hose on the dock. I still wore the swimsuit, the same Chinese junk one-piece that I had donned in Lake Geneva two years ago. It smelled of lake water and moss. My fashion sense was lacking. I had to do something about that.

"Are you hungry?" Peter asked. "I know this quaint Cuban cafe on the waterfront. They've got killer black beans and rice."

"I'm starving! Love to!" I shouted back.

We clambered into his battered Audi and headed into an old part of Ft Lauderdale, popular with the Hispanics and sailors. Inside the cafe, a whiff of aromatic spices seized my appetite: cumin, curry, cinnamon. Over an exotic dinner of spicy chicken, plantains and black beans, Peter enthralled me with stories of his former ports-of-call—the Mediterranean, Bermuda, the Bahamas. He sported a slight grin across a perfectly chiseled face. My eyes grew wide from his close gaze.

His yarns captured and held my attention. My mouth hung open. Once, a catamaran he once crewed for ended up under house arrest by the Greek Gendarme. Another time he was picked up while hitch-hiking and wooed by an Italian princess. Then there was the time he cruised the canals of France as crew on a catamaran. And the time he lived in secret caves with Greek smugglers. He hitch-hiked through Europe on nothing but baguettes, apple cider, and a pocket of coins.

Salsa music resounded through the quaint café as foreign sailors drifted in to indulge the pretty waitress. Peter's voice was soft, and a faraway look penetrated his eyes. He slowly pulled me into his world. My life felt horribly blasé in comparison.

A man with long locks of shiny hair and pudgy cheeks bounded onto a makeshift stage. He whined through the air with grief, his face twisted by a painful ballad of love. The air pulsed with his passionate voice.

Women in tight bodices tapped their feet around us. In time, a young woman next to me wrenched out a hanky to daub at her eyes, lined with black kohl. Did she remember a former lover? The bereft woman surrendered, becoming the singer's first victim.

I was right behind her. My heart was full of bliss when the singer dipped his head at the end of his song. Two guitarists took his place and sat down on the edge of the stage, black hair pulled back into shiny ponytails. Their fingers stroked strings. Knuckles knocked guitar faces as if wooden drums. A filigree of high notes punctuated the night air. I entered their music with all of my soul.

At a break in the set, our flan arrived with more wine.

"I am sailing to the tropics of the Caribbean to explore distant lands, and see the world," Peter said.

He stared at me mischievously, batting twinkling eyes. His bronzed arm lightly touched mine, and I nearly fell off my bar stool. The blanket of reason that had vigilantly guarded the door to my heart had been pulled away, leaving me feeling naked and vulnerable. I was being swept away by the ecstatic riptides of love. *This guy can't be real*, I thought. *Give him a wide berth. He's dangerous. I have my career to think about, even if it's floundering at the moment. I have a normal life. What was a normal life? How could one define that exactly?* With Peter, my every movement was charged with restrained energy.

After tiny cups of espresso, we left the pulsing café to walk back to the car. We drove to the beach and strolled along an esplanade beside a white beach fringed with coconut palms. A postprandial lethargy had taken hold, so we lowered ourselves onto a wooden bench at the water's edge. A dog barked. Above us, a vault of sparkling diamonds spanned the night sky. Boats bumped the tide inshore. Offshore, four container ships from places like Panama, Gibraltar, and Singapore were lit up like Christmas trees, lights winking a staccato as if signaling a boarding call. The pungent aroma of honeysuckle and gardenia perfumed the night air. We whispered of dreams and foreign places.

We talked about going places. Not about why we were here. Just about places to go. The soft clatter of palm fronds heralded a full moon. As it rose in the east, a fat Chinese gong appeared nuclear-orange on the horizon. It segued into bright yellow on the ascent. We watched transfixed as a thin corona formed round it during its transit of the sky. It looked empyreal—formed of fire. The moonlight washed waters in shimmering silver, illuminating a small reef near the shore. Beneath palm fronds, the moon shadows danced lacy patterns across sands.

"Oh wasn't that glorious! Moon! Stars!" Any serious discussion on my part degenerated into my effusive outbursts once the moon rose.

The beauty of it brought me to tears. I leaned in to feel Peter's hot voice.

"I sent all my old girlfriends packing. I wanted you to know. All of them wanted a station wagon, 2.2 dogs, and a split-level house. I have planned to live all my life aboard a boat," Peter said.

His intonation made my heart vibrate like a hummingbird in my chest. Peter ran to the unfamiliar. He was his own man. Many of my friends and family members said to me later that he had gone rogue, which I found terribly appealing.

"Why do your journey so far?" I asked.

I wanted to know more of him. Who was this godly merman? This person of a pure bohemian spirit?

"It's not the journey I've sought after, but more of what happens from one port to the next. It's the unplanned. It's the people. It's what happens between the lines," he said.

Our connection alighted when we shared our favorite philosophers: Kierkegaard and Thoreau.

"Do you ever get lonely or homesick?" I asked.

"Home is where you make it. I travel to make my dream world real," he said. His eyes sparkled. "In the adventurous and restless life at sea, one has no time to be bored or lonely."

In time, we started walking again, not going anywhere, just up and down the glowing sands, still warm from the tropical summer day. When he kissed me, I felt my ground give way. There was a surge and then a release, a letting-go like I had never known before now. It was the type of a release where I was very still, surrendering to it. My heart pounded against my rib cage. My pulse raced. My knees grew weak. Every part of me relaxed and happily gave in. Afterwards, we smiled, and then I cried. He kissed my bare shoulder.

We collapsed onto the warm tropical sands to gaze at a cerulean sky above. Stars shot cirrus veils. A satellite transited west. A planet pulsed with green, blue and red. The galaxy held us transfixed. Peter pointed up, naming a variety of constellations, drawing invisible lines between them. We listened to the surf crashing at our feet. We heard the music and laugher and hum of the city. I breathed the scent of pollen. Blue evening reflected into the water, penetrating our souls.

Out of the corner of my eye, I saw something. I could not have pinpointed when, exactly, I knew we were not alone. I had been slowly passing in and out of reverie, taking the beauty in around me. I was breathing in Peter when my neck hairs began to prickle. It felt as if a rivulet of sweat had been reduced to salt on my neck by the night wind.

And then I was blinded. A bright light illuminated our bodies, entwined in a supine wrap. My irises shrunk from the beam. Yellow butterflies swirled before my eyes as if embracing an eclipse of the sun. I froze, unable to orient myself. We disentangled our bodies. I clawed at space over me, fingers grasping air. Suddenly, I felt sand trickle down into my face and eyes. My eyes felt like sandpaper.

A barely audible sound came from my left. I turned my head towards the shuffling echo. A sizeable black boot lay planted in the sands near my cheek. Another boot joined it, and two more until four were lined up. The sight of a brigade of boots made beads of sweat wick all over my scalp. It took a moment before I could marshal the courage to draw breath. When my hand stopped quaking, I pulled myself upright and shot a look at Peter, puzzled as to why he had not moved.

He lay prostrate in the sand, a monstrous hand clasped against his right shoulder. The brown hand —Latino maybe or Greek or Italian— was the size of a small dinner-plate. The man placed another hand, holding Peter down as if he was planting a tree. Rustling sounds came from behind me. I spun around to see two large men looming over us like a pillar of cloud in the bright light, their big bodies casting us in momentary shadow.

"ID!" A man shouted.

An unfamiliar, gruff voice screamed into our ears. As the light shifted angles, two police officers clad in riot gear marched from out of the shadows a short distance away, their waists bulging with pistols and batons and radios. They sauntered over to join the hunting party, brandishing major attitude. After a bit of police talk, I gathered the boots belonged to—what appeared to be—a gaggle of undercover cops. Searchlights momentarily swept away for me to study one of them.

The undercover cop at Peter's shoulder was a tall man. Reflector sunglasses rode high on his nose, and he wore tattered jeans and a black T-shirt. His tight jeans accentuated his bulk. His thighs looked swollen, like those of a weight lifter. He was bald with a shaven head so oiled that it reflected light and shone like a bulb on a Christmas tree. A sizable tattoo of a snake curved on the left side of his neck. A jagged scar ran the length of the side of his face, stopping at the corner of his lip. Pinched by the scar, his mouth never fully closed. I imagined the facial wound was sustained in a street fight during his smuggling days as a teen before turning undercover for the cops. He kept pushing up his sunglasses, as they slid down his sweaty nose in the tropical night. He watched anxiously, sweeping the entire width of the beach with wary eyes as he held Peter down. Fear rose and spread over me like goose bumps. My back was warm, as if their light beams would roast me.

Mr. Sunglasses began peppering Peter with questions. I choked on flying sand as boots shuffled about in nervousness like they had someplace to go, and quick. In brusque tones, Sunglasses demanded answers.

"Where do you live? Where were you born? What were you doing here?" Sunglasses barked.

"I don't have any ID. My wallet is in the car," Peter said flatly.

Peter was calm and respectful. He judged his timing carefully, waiting for the indignant cop to ease up. His take-charge manner gave me confidence.

He was not pleased when Peter failed to produce prompt and proper identification. Brows knitted as the small army deliberated, their hunting party extremely upset with our tête-à-tête on the beach. They demanded we visit Police Headquarters.

My mind started racing.

"For what, exactly?" I demanded, taken aback. No way. I felt the heat rise to my head. Ever since that Houston bozo bullied me, I promised I would stand up for myself. Fight back.

My palms were sweaty. I unknowingly clenched them, nails digging into flesh, upset with the intrusion. What was going on here? Peter gave me a telling look. His eyes were squeezed slightly without closing, brows knitted together. In our brief time together, his gesture held a meaning that only I knew.

The hunting party was unaware of the coded communication transpiring between Peter and me. It was as if Peter was telling me, "Let's not allow this to get out of hand. Let's let it go. Let us be on our way as quickly as possible." Or, more to the point, "hold your tongue, woman."

I did. But I was not happy about it. I'd had enough of bullies. It was as if these big boys had sprinkled on a little extra testosterone with their evening coffee. I imagined myself saying, *back off, all of you.* But I thought better of it. Peter seemed to be doing a far better job than my prickly self.

In a deferential tone of voice, Peter ruefully explained that his friend was new in town, and he wanted to show me the ocean.

"We were just on our way back to my brother-in-law's house," Peter said. "I intentionally left my wallet in the car. I only take greenbacks to cafés."

He further explained he was willing to produce ID and apologized profusely for troubling the Police. His voice inflections carried a note of calm composure. I thought of soft butter on warm bread. As he held the small army captive, I watched as the ends of Peter's toes curled and flexed with tension in the spotlights.

Two police officers escorted us to the Audi, where Peter unlocked the glove compartment, dug out his driver's license and handed it over with measured alacrity. The police officers called in the number. Once assured of Peter's clear record, the officers relaxed.

"Best if you two stayed off the beach at night. A report of a rape came in over the radio involving another girl. Her boyfriend received multiple contusions and cuts trying to ward her attacker off," the officer said.

"Another girl? Multiple contusions?" I mumbled.

"Yes. There have been attacks on girls. We were hot on the trail of the serial rapist before we ran into you tonight. We have been hunting him for a month," he said.

The officers went on to explain the complexities of their beach detail. They reiterated that we stay away from the beach at night, as the area was very unsafe.

My throat went dry. We had interrupted their sting operation and gotten in the way. I fell into a respectful hush. I was thoroughly shaken and appreciated their dire warnings.

As a child, I recalled how disturbed my parents were when a close friend of the family succumbed to a violent rape after a High School prom in a park. Her boyfriend was gravely injured. The victims' families never recovered, nor did our family. From that night on, I swore off prom nights, reliving the nightmare of hearing my parents' dinner conversations about the pretty girl, a former beauty queen. She would have to live with enough emotional and physical scars for the rest of her life.

It was a moot point since I never received an invitation to either prom night during high school. I was always the new girl in town.

Once the troops left, Peter appeared flustered. In the Audi, he took my hand in his. We drove back to the boat in agreeable silence, the stillness growing between us. The car felt small. Peter's presence expanded. I thought of how well he had handled the officers. His insouciant manner was admirable.

We exchanged glances beneath a street light at the boat dock. His smile corkscrewed right through my heart. After the passage of respectful silence, the victims of crime had passed. We suddenly started to giggle. The possibility of us ending up in jail on our first date was laughable. Musings fluttered across my mind like a banner pulled behind a Beechcraft that read: *I do not require a station wagon. I do not even own a car. I do not even have a dog.*

On the boat, we stayed up deep into the night lost in transparent exchanges, sharing details of our lives. In hushed tones, he told me of how I had penetrated his dreams over the last two years. I felt my pulse race.

In time, I took the berth in the main salon, and he retired to the aft cabin. The sound of creaking wood and the lap of water against the hull lulled me into a sweet lullaby. When pink morning light glinted through the hatch, bringing me awake, it took me a moment to orient my place. And then I smiled. It seemed I had always known Peter, that he had been a part of me over the last couple of years in our casual meetings with our immediate families.

We shared a breakfast of canned baked beans and eggs in the cockpit, laughing again at the previous night of adventure. And then the most amazing thing happened.

"Would you like to sail with me to the Caribbean?" Peter asked.

Did I hear that correctly?

"Though we've only been together for one day, it seems we have known each other for a long time," he said.

Peter's sleeves worked the forearms like tourniquets. He flashed me a gleaming smile. I shook my head.

"Even if I said yes—which I cannot—I thought you already had a crew," I said. I did not want to seem too hasty. I had life plans.

"I've interviewed a few ladies, but none match your abilities. 'Course, we'll have to do something about your clumsiness. Do you always stumble into things?" he asked with a chuckle.

I thought of my first day onboard the *Antilles* when I had stubbed my toe. I thought of my falling overboard during our sail together out on Lake Geneva at my brother's wedding.

"If you ever felt like you needed to return home, I'd fly you there," he said.

"Even if I agreed to go along with this cockamamie scheme, what about my university bills, my job—OK, nonexistent job—and my apartment?" I asked. It was a big offer.

"Life is more than school and work and a job," he assured me.

I thought about it long and hard. I looked at him with longing.

"I owe a lot of money. I worked as a medical transcriber through college and had scholarships, but I still owe $2,000," I said.

"Of course. I will help you there. I can loan you the money. We'll draw up a contract. You can pay me back later," he said earnestly.

"I don't know. I cannot just wander without goals. I have ambitions," I countered.

Peter's plan seemed surrealistic and yet, so right to me, though. The hairs on my neck tingled. *Sometimes, you have to take a leap of faith*, I told myself. My mind buzzed.

"All life was an experiment," he added reflectively. "The more experiments you made, the better life became."

"Ralph Waldo Emerson," I added. Something was happening here. The possibility of a real moment of synchronicity occurring was laughable or was it? Were we part of another collective coincidence? I smiled and giggled at the magical thought.

"Why are you laughing?" Peter asked.

I thought of the invisible envelope on the table that announced: big clue inside. I hoped for a miracle here.

"Look, I want us to be together. I would be lonely on the ocean without you. We could talk about kids," he said.

My knees turned to Jell-O. I loved kids. One of my goals in life was to have a loving family of my own. *But how can you have a family on a boat?* I wondered. My first feeling was the sensation I felt at the top of the roller coaster when the car clattered past the apex on its downward fall. I had known something momentous would happen with us. Right now, I was giddy with the reality of it all. *You started this. You co-created it with intention.* I felt dizzy from it all.

The day after I had quit my job in Houston, I had drawn up a list of the qualities I sought in a man of marriage material. It was soul searching time, and I needed a plan. He had to be someone I could have fun with, go places with, and share great ideas with. I taped the list on the back of my closet door in my Houston apartment and carried a smaller copy in my wallet. My wallet was usually pretty thin for the lack of bills, but that one piece of paper was all I needed. It grew shiny from the constant review. So when Peter showed up in my life, I was not so surprised. *What took you so long?* I thought. "Wait. Whoa, let's not get ahead of ourselves. And yes, I'll go!"

But I knew the kids would come … much later, of course.

And then I leaped into his arms, arms that seemed so familiar now, as if they had always been waiting for me. I mused quietly, not knowing what my fate would be once the boat left the dock. Was I throwing my career away? What would happen out there on the ocean? I still had zero sailing experience. The only time Peter had taken me sailing, I had fallen overboard. Why was that, exactly? The knowledge came to me instantly: *Don't worry. You have no control. It's happening already. Keep your eyes forward.* I trusted, plunging in with all the mojo I possessed.

That night on the boat at bedtime, I opened my philosophy book. I treasured the book and always carried it with me. Its pages had carried me through some rough times. Though the pages had yellowed, and the hardback cover was frayed at the edges, it was my gold talisman. As I turned towards it now, I was struck mute when the book opened with a quote from Albert Einstein: *There are two ways to live your life. One is as though nothing is a miracle. The other is as though everything is a miracle.*

I smiled at the comfort of those words and turned out the kerosene lantern. I entered into a deep sleep, one I had been longing. I slept as if I had not rested for twelve months. Rarely did sleep come to me when I worked as a commercial real estate broker in Houston. It felt like layers of hardness and despair were peeling away like the paper-thin layers of an onion. I felt happiness enter my soul, linger and stay.

Our Huckleberry-Finn life had begun with a moment of synchronicity after several moments of collective coincidences. Just by *one* single phone call. *Thank-you, angels!* I thought as I drifted to sleep.

6.
NEW BOAT

Yacht Scud, South Africa

*Only those who will risk going too far can possibly find out
how far it is possible to go.*

—*T.S. Eliot*

We stood in the St Francis Shipyard gazing at *Scud*, our new 44-foot (13.4 m) catamaran. We could hardly believe she was ours. A small army of African workers swarmed across decks, popping in and out of boat cabins with tools, charts and bits of fabric. Inside the vast warehouse that housed the catamarans under construction, the twin hulls of *Scud* gleamed in the ambient light. Finishing touches were being applied. It'd be another two weeks before she was ready for launch. During that time, we would take a driving safari inside of Kruger National Park. We would return to move aboard our new catamaran after the safari.

Before we entered the enclosed hangar, Peter gripped my hand and stared intently into my face.

"We brought the bag of Krugerrands from the resort, right?" he asked.

"I think so. I think I stashed them in a duffle or something. I'm sure I didn't leave it lying around in the room," I said with concern. But I knew I was horribly wrong. Where *had* I hidden that bag of gold?

When I first saw the Krugerrands, they resembled the chocolate coins wrapped in gold metallic paper that I relished eating as a child. When I lifted one of the coins to bite, I knew it was the real deal when it weighed heavily in my fingers.

Surely the bag of gold is under the bed mattress where I usually hide valuables when traveling. I tried to remain calm.

"I think it's still under the mattress. Right. I'm sure of it," I said.

"Just remind me to take it with us before we check out," Peter said. His eyebrows stitched together in a look of worry.

Every sailor transiting the globe carries a cache of cash, in case of an emergency. Banks and ATMs are not just around the corner. Every South African we met in the Bahamas had hidden their life savings in their bilges. During Apartheid, Afrikaners were leaving in large numbers. The best way to take your bank roll out of the country was by boat.

On the *Antilles* when Peter and I were first starting out sailing before the children were born, we had stashed our cash inside rolls of marine navigational charts suspended from the ceiling of our stateroom. Thieves in Panama in the early 1980's stole the cache of cash. All of it was gone. Dressed as NARC Agents (USA Narcotics Enforcement Agency), they boarded and raided the boat—ostensibly in search of drugs. We weren't even aboard as Peter and I were clearing Customs. When the NARC Agents buzzed up to the *Antilles* in a go-fast boat, our friend, Jim, was onboard as crew. As a former Navy navigator, he was well versed in maritime law. He insisted the agents board the boat when the captain was onboard.

"It's international maritime law. You are required to board only when the captain is onboard," Jim said flatly.

They would have none of it. While stamping their black boots and wielding weapons, they clambered aboard to search the vessel. Three agents disappeared below-decks to search the cabins, closing the doors to inhibit open viewing from the cockpit. Our friend was held hostage in the cockpit.

The agents lifted other items along with the cash: a watch and a pair of my earrings. They were never recovered even after making a formal visit to the US Consulate to file a police report.

"How do you know it wasn't your friend who stole the cash?" the Consular General had asked.

"Because he's an old friend and doesn't need the money," Peter answered.

"If you insist on filing a police report for the theft, I caution you. Your wife might be threatened. They could plant contraband on your boat. I don't advise it," he said.

"But it's a lot of money," I said, frustrated. *Threatened? Contraband?*

"Well, I've never heard of this happening in all the years I've lived in the Panama Canal Zone," he said, throwing his arms up into the air.

We filed the report anyway.

Once having transited the Panama Canal, word reached us of another boat search where heirloom jewelry of great value had gone missing. The owner filed a complaint, greatly upset as the jewelry had belonged to her mother. To everyone's surprise, the jewelry was recovered.

When I caught up with the woman later, she told me the Consulate had claimed that her theft had been a rare event in the history of the Panama Canal Zone. She was also advised not to file a complaint.

This time aboard *Scud*, Peter decided to store the bag of gold coins in the ship's safe.

"Gold coins are a better investment than cash," he said. "By the time we need to cash it in for emergencies, the Krugerrand will have increased in value."

Keeping track of a bag of gold coins was worrisome. Their value at our time of boarding the international flight back in Atlanta a month ago was at the top limit a US citizen could take out of the country: $9,999. Since then, we had lugged them all around Africa. I couldn't wait for the bag to be secured aboard *Scud* so I could forget about it. We carried the small satchel of coins in case the banks failed or went on strike.

It had happened before when in Milan, Italy. We couldn't access funds because of extensive banking strikes. ATMs were not around yet. The banks were closed, and we were stuck.

So when Peter prodded me to keep track of the bag of gold and not lose it, I made a mental note. "Right. I'll make sure we don't forget to check out of our hotel room without the gold," I said.

Both of us had left valuables in hotels, rental cars, and taxis when in a rush, items we never saw again. This time we hoped our lousy history of losing things while traveling would not catch up with us.

───◆◆◆───

When we entered the marine hangar to study our new catamaran in the St Francis Yard, Dick Lethbridge's large hands swallowed mine in greeting. He was the CEO of the St Francis Marine and Shipyard. His fingers were calloused from years of handling sails and building materials, and a toothy smile spanned his tanned face. He was angular and fit with graying hair at the temples, punctuated with sun-breached blond streaks. He spoke slowly, enunciating his words with careful intention. I liked him right away.

Dick was an avid yachtsman, having sailed competitively over three decades. He knew the perfect design to enhance speed in a catamaran. He knew about bad weather, having served over two decades with SASAR (South African Search and Rescue Organization). The Cape of Good Hope and South Africa had some of the roughest waters in the world. It was little wonder the East Coast was dubbed the Shipwreck Coast and the West Coast dubbed as the Skeleton Coast.

As he led us around the shipyard, Dick's enthusiasm and passion for boat building was evident. Pride exuded from his warm personality. He had started the shipyard when he was unable to locate the kind of catamaran he wanted to take his family cruising around Africa. He hired a keen yacht designer by the name of Angelo Lavranos to design a catamaran built to handle the rough weather at the tip of Africa, but comfortable enough to please his wife, Karen. Angelo Lavranos designed a cat that paid minute attention to detail for safety, comfort and speed.

"Our company theme is grace, space, and pace. It says it all," Dick said, beaming.

Dick led us around the spacious and modern shipyard, introducing each of his tradesmen. He explained how each craftsman contributed a certain flare of style or technique to the St Francis cats. The shipyard was immaculate, not a bit of trash littered the grounds or inside of the warehouse. Even a well-tended garden bordered the office as we entered to sign papers and assume ownership. Inside, a gold trophy announced "1st Place Cape-to-Rio" for the multihull division. The St Francis 44 MK II convincingly beat all other catamarans on the South Africa to Brazil race.

Peter was pleased with the professionalism of the factory. The mast of *Scud* was tall, but even with its height, *Scud* could easily sail beneath the highway bridges that crisscrossed the Intracoastal Waterway along the US East Coast. The rig looked powerful. Peter liked how Angelo Lavranos had distributed the buoyancy of the hulls.

"The widest or most buoyant part of the hull is 2/3 forward of the mast, which precludes the potential for pitch-poling at sea in high winds," Dick explained. He went on to explain how the well-designed hull buoyancy also prevented the bows from digging into blue water, a term referring to waters in a deep ocean where storms suddenly develop and sailors learn to reef sails early. The hull buoyancy kept the decks dryer. The engines were set amidships to center the weight, which reduced pitching and kept the stern lighter for good performance.

The workers looked happy. They lent an air of confidence and appreciation to the company, possessing no obvious grievances. In a country where racism was a prominent social issue—many black Africans lived in poverty during the Apartheid era—these workmen appeared content.

Before we left the shipyard, a large *Braai* (barbecue) was given in our honor. Every staff member and craftsman attended the event, where the key to *Scud* was officially handed over to us. As the succulent aroma of pork ribs, steak and chicken wafted, Peter and I went down the long line of workers, shaking their hands and thanking them for a job well done.

I felt we were finally beginning our life goal of sailing around the world. From now on, I would be living in comfort, no longer coping and gripping white knuckled at rail handles in an outdated monohull while bashing into seas.

My musings took me to a time when we were battling headwinds to make our way down the Windward Islands of the Caribbean in an earlier *Scud*, a monohull. It was a light wind day, but seas between the islands were still fifteen feet. Our boys were ages 8 and 10 years-of-age,

51

and they seemed to be having the times of their lives down below-decks. Every time we hit a big wave, the boys leapt off the large v-berth forward, crashing into a laughing heap of tangled limbs as we surfed down a wave, landing with a crescendo into a trough.

I struggled in the small cockpit to keep my breakfast down as Peter made his way forward to reef in the genoa as roller furling genoas were not a marine luxury item then. The sound of breaking glass in the bilge promised a messy clean-up upon landfall. Condiments in cupboards would have spilled, flour and sugar bags torn open from bashing seas. *There goes the celebration*, I thought. No matter how well I stowed gear, breakage happened. The back of my neck pains me today as if I had endured a litany of whiplashes during our dozen passages through the Caribbean chain. It was like gritting my teeth, getting from point A to B without fun along the way.

No more though. Aboard catamaran *Scud*, it would be a whole new way of passage-making. I could indulge in all my favorite pastimes underway. It would be a safer way to passage too: no more dangerously canting decks.

That night, we dined at Dick's palatial home. Karen, Dick's beautiful wife, greeted us at the door. She looked resplendent in a flowing dress. A traditional Mediterranean style of décor created an ambient atmosphere. A large foyer led out onto a veranda, where a chef dressed in white was busy grilling various types of meat and fish on an outdoor grill. Standing on the veranda, I looked over a brick wall that lay suspended over a hill, overlooking a body of still water.

While we had drinks with Dick and Karen, Adam and Warren disappeared to play darts in the game room next to the bar. After a gin and tonic, we joined them. Dick did an excellent job of putting the boys in their place with a deft twist of the wrist in flinging the dart into the bullseye.

Looking at the fine interior, I was pleased I had asked Karen to choose fabrics for *Scud*. It was especially gracious to meet and get to know the owners of the St Francis Marine and Shipyard. I felt we were off to a great start together. When we expressed concern about rounding the infamous Cape of Storms, Dick offered to help in selecting the most opportune weather window and insisted he join us as crew for the two-to-three-day passage. The offer struck me as particularly impressive.

"I'll be sure to send down a couple of baked chickens and bread for

Dick. He tends to become seasick when under sail," Karen said with a look of concern. "As long as he keeps something in his belly, he'll be fine."

The next morning, an employee of the shipyard drove us to the Elizabethtown Airport for our flight to Johannesburg. I was excited to see my mother and niece. They were flying in from Atlanta to meet us for the driving safari in Kruger National Park.

Once onboard the flight, I took Peter's hand in mine and breathed in an excited breath. "You got the bag of Kruggerands, Babe, right," I asked, casually. Seconds passed before Peter spoke. My hand was let go.

"Wait. What? You don't have it?"

"Me? Why me? You were supposed to remind me."

"I remind you? You know I forget stuff. A lot is going on now. I'm distracted. Anyway, I just figured you checked the room before closing the door."

"Where is the bag of gold then?" I asked. My hands grew sweaty.

"Still in the beach villa? In our checked luggage? In the driver's back seat? Think, Tina."

"Could be in the grocery cart too, for all I know. I'll phone the villa when we land."

In the J'borg airport while Peter checked in to Hertz Rental Car, I phoned the beach villa. "Did you find a blue bag in our room? No? Can you please check under the mattress, inside the mini-bar frig, in a drawer? Yes, I'll hold. Ah, no then?" *Shit just happens sometimes. Best to move on, girl.* I shared the news with Peter.

"Some lucky person has it now. I'm sure he needed it more than us," he said.

"Travel collateral damage," we said in unison.

7.
DEATH IN THE WILD

Pregnant with Eve

Part of your heart dies with the child that goes.
—Kiley Hanish

The fantasy of lunching out in the field with our family on a blanket in the Park vanished the moment I picked up a news article at the J'borg Airport. We were awaiting the arrival of Mom and my niece, Brittany. They were joining us on the safari in Kruger National Park. Family survival in the bush had not been on my mind at all until now.

"MAN DEVOURED BY LION" was splashed across the front page of the local newspaper. Curiosity got the best of me, and I read on.

A lion in Marloth Park had devoured an unknown man in a small township that shared a southern border with Kruger Park. Only the man's head and one foot inside a shoe were all that remained. Identification of the body could not be completed. Andre Lubbe, clerk of the township, suspected he was an illegal immigrant from Mozambique. It was easy crossing the border—just a mere twenty-mile trek from the east.

I was shocked to learn that, in this region of South Africa, immigrants were routinely eaten by lions. *How about tourists?* I wondered. Every day, illegal immigrants made their way across the Mozambique border through Kruger Park to find food and work in South Africa. Kruger Park was guarded heavily by paramilitary guards who patrolled in helicopters, airplanes, vehicles, and on foot during the day. Tight security was a deterrent to poachers, who were eager for the valuable rhino horn. It forced the illegal immigrants to walk under the cover of darkness when man-eating lions hunted. The immigrants could not use flash lights in case guards might spot them. Some lucky souls survived the trek by following telephone and electrical power-lines, and using the Drakensberg Mountain lights as a guide. The poor fellow in Marloth Park probably never even saw the lion pounce until it was upon him.

Fodder for thought—in case we had a flat tire during our family safari.

Though our sons possessed a rather cavalier attitude about the threat to human life by large animals, including sharks, I knew about lion attacks. A fatal attack nearly struck down our young family one day, while hiking the North Inlet Trail in the Rocky Mountain National Park. At the time, Adam and Warren were ten and eight-years-old. On a parallel trail close by, a young family hiked with two young children. The six-year-old girl bounded ahead in pursuit of her older ten-year-old brother. As she rounded a bolder, a cougar pounced and dragged her into the forest. Her parents found her behind a fallen tree, dead of asphyxiation from vomit. Abject fear was the killer. There were no puncture wounds on her lithe body. It was horribly tragic. I never got over it, and I couldn't imagine how her parents felt.

That ghastly day remained fixed in my mind because, after just two hours into our family hike that morning, I had insisted we turn around. Something just was not right. I could feel it in my gut. I was uneasy and edgy. Sweat rippled down my body even though a cool mountain breeze wafted across the trail, deep in shadow from the canopy of Douglas fir trees overhead. It was uncharacteristic of me to feel adverse when in the beauty of the great outdoors, especially in the stunning mountains of Colorado.

Together our family had logged many miles of mountain trails. But that day, I knew something was wrong. The kids were grumpy too. We practically ran back to the trailhead to the car. We instantly locked the doors as if being chased by a freakish alien. It was an otherworldly experience. From then on, I always paid attention to my intuition.

When we passed through the Park Ranger's exit gate, I leaned across Peter and stared intently at the female Park Ranger.

"Can you please tell me if anything happened on the trails today?" I asked.

She stared back at me, her face masked in grief. It was a face that was wet, settled in a stony silence.

"An ambulance just drove out of here with a young girl—fatal attack by a cougar. Nothing like this has happened since 1915. We're all in shock," she muttered.

Her attempt at stoic composure collapsed, and she buried her face in her hands. Her chest heaved from gasps of pain. Tears began to rain down my face as we pulled away. All mothers grieved as one. I knew what it was like to lose a child: we had lost our first baby by DIU (death-in-utero) at twenty-three weeks of gestation. It was purely a natural loss—not by a raging lion—but by the threat of a tiny animal that weighed a mere 2.5 milligrams.

It had started in a jungle in Central America when Peter and I were living aboard the *Antilles*. Once married, we had begun making our way towards our dream of sailing around the world and were en-route through the Panama Canal to the South Pacific. We planned to stay in Panama for two months, using the extra time to visit the remarkable San Blas Islands nearby. Both Panama and the San Blas Islands consisted of dense jungle regions, rife with malaria-infected mosquitoes.

We were advised to follow a strict regimen of anti-malarial prophylaxis. I needed to remain on contraception. The drug had commenced three weeks before we reached the jungle, to build up to satisfactory blood levels. Once leaving the endemic region of Panama, we needed to continue the drug for several weeks. Side effects were blindness, loss of hearing, mood changes, and seizure.

Peter and I debated back and forth whether to consume the poison. We wanted to dump our cache of anti-malarias down the drain, but in the end, we capitulated. It was a fatal mistake. It was one I lived to regret.

We were at the end of our jungle transit through the Panama Canal. No more jungles. The countdown to the end of our anti-malarial pill regimen intake was now down to four weeks. In the cockpit, we were about to sit down to a dinner of Spanish mackerel and potatoes to celebrate our arrival in the Pacific Ocean. I turned back to retrieve a love poem I had composed as a gift to Peter— something about us having a baby—and returned to retrieve it from a secret spot behind my perfumes.

"Oh-my-gawd!" I screamed.

"What's wrong?" Peter shouted.

"It's gone!"

"What's gone?"

"My thing! It's nothing but a big hole now!" I wailed.

"What THING? What hole? What are you talking about?"

"My diaphragm!" I choked on the words. "What are we going to do now?"

I stared in horror at my contraceptive cap that lay on the floor. What once looked like the rubbery lid of a jar was now nothing, but a circle of wire encapsulated in rubber, partly chewed. Threads of ruined rubber dangled. Teeth marks punctuated the rubber in places. The wire was gouged and stuck out in odd directions.

"Magic!" I shouted.

To my horror, our schipperke (a Belgium canal barge dog bred to guard boats) had eaten my vaginal diaphragm. She had ratted it out, tearing it to sticky fragments of rubber. This would have been funny had it not been my only spare in a Catholic country. The next morning, I dashed all over Panama in taxis and buses and on foot in search of a replacement. Every time I requested a diaphragm, laughter followed my tearful exit out the door.

"Why don't you want children?" the women peppered me in Spanish. "Babies are good! God loved babies. You need babies!"

They did not fathom why I was in tears. How could I explain that I was going to sea for several months? How could I make them under-stand there were no doctors in remote ports of the world? Would they understand we were sailing on an endless ocean into the South Seas? Would they understand that I was on anti-malarial prophylaxis?

Weeks later I gave up in locating a replacement diaphragm in Panama and we decided to sail on to New Zealand. If we did not leave soon, it would be too late. Cyclone season would be upon us. We left Panama and sailed to the Las Perlas Islands, a day sail away. There we sat.

I grew ill and depressed. My mind was fuzzy. Concentration was difficult. Headaches plagued a languishing spirit. Normally, I was not given over to headaches. When the agonizing aches began, I flew to the ships mini-pharmacy of emergency pharmaceuticals for a strong dose of acetaminophen. What greeted me held me in absolute shock. A once organized medicine cupboard was now nothing but a confetti of pills that spilled from decomposed containers. The tropical heat had wreaked havoc: rubber bottle caps had melted away, little pink pills spilled from open containers, printed labels had faded.

Let's not panic now!

Refusing to identify this as catastrophic, I hastily reorganized the messy heap of pills, guessing—wrongly—which pills matched which bottle, and relabeled them with a magic marker. The pink acetaminophen pills looked exactly like the pink chloroquine (anti-malaria) pills. In my hazy confusion, they became one and the same.

We explored the Las Pearlas Islands: attended a festival, hiked into the hills, and watched the weather in preparation for a departure. My headaches continued, but I tried to maintain a positive outlook by jumping overboard for a swim to cool the pain in my head. To ease the throbbing, I took the imagined acetaminophen. I was puzzled over the ineffectiveness of it. Headaches continued and grew worse. To ward off pain attacks at night, I took more—three at a time now.

Unknowingly, I was building my body up to a dangerous level of toxicity of chloroquine that can be fatal. I suffered from all the side effects: anxiety, depression, headaches, extreme fear, and hallucinations. Peter wanted to abort our voyage to the Galapagos. I refused, insisting we carry on.

I became pregnant. It would be weeks before I discovered my condition. During this critical time for good health, I continued the ingestion of toxic chloroquine, believing it to be acetaminophen. The morning of our departure to the Galapagos, Peter asked me to walk with him up a tranquil creek bed into the rain forest. He sat me down, took my hand in his, and peered into my eyes.

"Babes, do you truly want to do this," he asked. "Sail into the Pacific?"

Love spilled out of him.

"Yes, but something is not right," I wept. "I have terrors like those of a mind tortured by malaria fever. I feel trapped in an endless nightmare from which there is no escape. I cannot experience the relief of waking in the sweat of terror and knowing it was only delirium. What the hell is wrong with me?"

It was the deadly overdose of chloroquine. This voyage had meant so much to us. We had labored over the dream, fitted all the details together that required such a trip. We had worked hard to put the boat in good operating order for such a serious voyage. But something—I could not put my finger on it—was not right.

"I think we should turn around," I said.

I could not stop crying. But I trusted in the divine way of things. I just could not see the big picture at this moment. After much consideration and talk, we agreed to abort the voyage to French Polynesia. The thatched huts and waterfalls would have to wait. We turned away from the giant tortoises of the Galapagos and pointed the *Antilles's* bow back to Florida. Our crew, Jim, flew out from Panama, quite angry with the change in plans.

Peter sailed us home. I dumped the anti-malaria pills into the sea, sick of pills, sick of the confusion, too sick to think otherwise. By the time we dropped the anchor in a Florida bay several months later, I had discovered the reality of my pregnancy. In time, my doctor told me my baby had died of heart failure at twenty-two weeks of gestation, death-in-utero. I was stuck numb at her news.

In driving home, I climbed behind the wheel in despair. Tears rained down my face. I drove on auto-pilot, unaware of my surroundings. I never saw the car that I pulled out in front of, sending my car into a tailspin, totaling both vehicles. Luckily, neither of us were hurt very seriously.

Later, Peter and I walked down the street to my OB-GYN. Her office was equipped with state-of-the-art fetal monitoring. As a sailor, she had become a close friend. Our friendship allowed her to treat me medically in a more intuitive, personal way.

She saved my life. Peter saved my life by aborting the sail to French Polynesia.

From the accidental toxicity of the anti-malaria pills, six grapefruit-sized cysts had grown around the fetus. In time, the fetus became hydrocephalic (water on the brain, resulting in an enlarged head). The baby was a girl. A specialist in St Petersburg scheduled me for emergency surgery to remove the dead fetus, poisonous cysts (septic, if burst), and ovaries. It struck me that the hysterectomy would leave me barren. I could never have children again. I was bereft, psychologically drained from the difficult unfolding of recent events. The six month voyage to Panama and back, the disappointing withdraw from our sailing dreams to passage in the South Pacific, the long and troublesome pregnancy. But I always landed on top, once I looked to God for guidance. I could not see my way up this time. So I waited.

The moment before going into the operating room for a hysterectomy, Peter snuck away to call Dr. Linda. The nurses ushered her to the phone right away at her OB-GYN office. In a concerned voice, Dr. Linda told Peter to bring me back to Sarasota for a less intrusive medical procedure. I would deliver the dead baby naturally. The cysts would recede in time with medication. It was as simple as that. I could have more children. I felt joy lift me from the depths of the black hole I had been living.

I looked at the lifeless baby girl in my arms as the young nurse stood next to me. We had named the baby Eve. I whispered to her that I was sorry and promised to do better next time. I felt like a failure as a mother. I blamed the dog for eating my diaphragm, the Catholics in Panama for not promoting birth-control, the anti-malaria pills. Most of all, I blamed myself.

In time, I forgave myself through Peter's love and constant nurturing.

"Shit sometimes happens, babe. You can be pregnant in no time," he said.

His words comforted me, but he couldn't understand the pain. Only mothers can ever truly relate.

One day, when refilling our ship's medical chest for another voyage, I came across the empty container of chloroquine. The prescription warnings of the malarial prophylaxis announced: "DO NOT TAKE IF PREGNANT" on the first page.

Who reads these pages?

An acquaintance, Jane, paid an uninvited visit two days after surgery.

She appeared at my front door early one morning where Peter and I had settled into a clapboard house on a Florida barrier island to seek relief. The tranquil scenery promised to deliver me into calmer waters, but it was not to be anytime soon. Gnarly vents were stirring, and I was not in the pilot seat.

When Jane arrived, I supplanted crumpled pajamas with a garden dress and stumbled into the kitchen. I gathered a set of battered teacups harvested from the local Thrift Shop and limped out with far less confidence than I felt. All I wanted to do was sleep. Jane and I were not friends. She excelled in high society and was a legend in her mind. To her, Peter and I were social dropouts, modern hippies. We had rejected social constraints by adopting a "narcisstic lifestyle" (her words, not mine), instead of seeking career paths and work. Surprisingly, vitriolic outbursts concerning our independent free choice were standard fare at gatherings. But Peter handled it with aplomb each time. With him, I quickly learned how to become a free spirit. I just needed to overcome this tragic chapter in our lives.

Peter had brought me the world on a platter, filling my passports with enough foreign stamps until additional pages were needed. He taught me how not to bind my actions based on religion or gender or custom or most of all, fear. My ability up until now to act on my free will, formerly affected by belief cognitive structures, had formed my experiences and societal perceptions since as a young child. With Peter, the quest for venturing had banged on my door loudly. Gone were the white gloves and nylon stockings and patent leather shoes. I grabbed and held on for the ride.

Seated before Jane, I gazed at her intently. She wore mousey hair in a bob, accompanied by gray eyes, the color of ditch puddles on a cloudy day. She was a wooden woman, never laughing uncontrollably. Her aura field needed some serious fluffing. I wanted to reach out and pluck imaginary—possibly real—dark particles that orbited her body. I held back, knowing she would shout, "Devil act, devil act!" Jane revered herself as a hubristic Bible Thumper.

When Jane learned our baby was hydrocephalic and we had the option to abort at twenty-two weeks, she was furious. Dr. Linda had spent hours helping us reach a decision. In our minds, a deformed fetus brought into this world was a selfish act. The child would suffer tremendous hardships: always poked, prodded, and tested for the latest treatment.

It was a tremendously difficult decision. We stayed up all hours of the night weighing moral issues. In the end, it was a far easier decision for Peter, as he had worked with disturbed children and witnessed their daily suffering, fully comprehending the burden parents carried. Our decision was labored over in pain. It was an especially tragic, emotional and devastating experience for me. Finally, our resolution was a moot point, for God intervened with the verdict in taking Eve home into His loving arms instead of mine.

Jane's harsh judgment of us having consented to an abortion before the advent of the fetus' death spit like snake poison. Sipping my tea, I prepared myself for a stern look or even a sermon, never suspecting anything worse. But today, it was her daughter who held my keen attention. I stared at her with fascination.

Jolie was four-years-old, a juxtaposition of light and joy that belied her mother's wilted spirit. Blond hair cascaded down her tanned body. Her little hand glided over a handcrafted greeting card and placed it on my lap. It was painted in brilliant colors, splashing wildly in all directions over a poster-sized page. A small bouquet of wild flowers accompanied the card. The warm gesture moved me to tears. I grasped the flowers and held them to my breast, breathing in the sweet scent. Water droplets from my eyes splashed onto the painting, causing the colors to blend.

In Jolie, I saw the daughter I had lost. I knew then that my daughter's little hands would never reach out to me for hugs. I would never kiss her booboos. Never teach her to swim. Who knew if I could ever have normal children again?

Dr. Linda's dire warnings still echoed through my insomniac mind at night, warning me to prepare for the worst, but also to hope. I held on to the latter, but my gut still coiled in terror whenever I saw babies in the arms of mothers. It was years before I could tolerate the cry of a baby without welling up in tears. Once, I nearly accosted a bad mother in Wal-Mart for smacking her toddler.

"You don't deserve to be a mother!" I shouted.

In a rush to take Jolie to the bathroom, Jane popped up while I was in the kitchen preparing another pot of tea. She took the liberty to walk through my marital bedroom to my private bathroom instead of choosing the guest bathroom nearby. Jane knew the layout of the house well.

Inside my shared love pad with Peter, Jane paused to study a small medicine bottle of white powder on the night stand. Satiated with her analysis, she later hissed to friends and family members: "Cocaine! Heroin! She killed her baby!"

The bottle was cornstarch, used in conjunction with a vaginal diaphragm to prevent pregnancy. It would require two full years before my body healed from the intra-uterine fetal death of Eve. If I became pregnant too soon, birth defects were an imminent risk. Acute abnormalities still lingered in the female reproductive system from the malarial prophylaxis and needed to be fully extricated.

Jane's poisonous dart was almost more than I could bear.

My soul was broken. If I failed to forgive Jane, I knew shrapnel would wound me in the end. It was like being shipwrecked on the moon. Her emotional pyrotechnic was the tool of a psychic vampire.

I went into a lengthy period of depression. We moved back onto the boat. I hated the house for what it had taken from my wound. I wanted no more of houses and dead babies. I needed a clean start.

But I could not turn away from the wound. My heart, now broken, began to beat slower. I woke in the mornings, crying. I went to sleep at night, crying. My tears wetted the sheets. Peter offered loving support in the beginning, but when the depression dragged on, I pulled away from him.

After a long time, I realized I had reached enlightenment when I came to feel more embarrassed for Jane, than by her. The healing wasn't complete, but I was making progress. I would never, ever, be her victim again.

* * *

One morning, needing to make peace with the demons in my soul, I headed for the Bay waters just a stone's throw from the back of the house. The Bay was famous for its changing hues: the way light moved across its surface in shades of sapphire to aquamarine. Standing atop the seawall of stone, I dove beneath the surface. Shafts of light beamed through clear waters, creating a cathedral-like atmosphere. I was in my Xanadu.

Manatees relished the nutrient rich feeding grounds of Bay waters. They inhabited the coastal waters of Florida and migrate north during hot summer months. I had come to love the elusive creatures. Peter and I knew they had come to feed when we saw wide eddies, much like whirlpools, moving on surface waters. Today, I hoped the matriarch in residence with her young calf would make an appearance.

During my last swim, my heart thumped audibly in my chest when twin noses broke the surface with a resounding whoosh of air being released close-by. Transfixed, I treaded silent strokes to watch intently at a respectful distance. Apparently I passed inspection. The manatees never hesitated. Coasting straight towards me with enormous forelimbs out-stretched, they veered off at the last second. They swept past almost at arm's length, their great eyes benevolent but curious. Their puppy-like snouts glided through waters, long whiskers glistening in iridescent hues of the morning sun. The mother nuzzled her baby down to graze on a bed of seagrass, gliding with infinite grace. Taking a deep breath, I dove down with them, grasping young shoots of mangrove roots on the seafloor to prevent from rocketing towards the surface. The manatees were awesome: a vast and gentle presence on the seabed.

The mother's body resembled that of a hippo or elephant torso, looking to weigh roughly 1,200 pounds. Her ten-foot long body tapered to a flat, paddle-shaped tail that fanned to propel forward motion. I smiled inwardly at her wrinkled face that resembled one of those Chinese Shar-Pei dogs. Twin flipper-like forelimbs fed. Like the elephant, fat fingernails that had yellowed with time studded them. I wondered what they would look like if painted a little girl's pink. Their low rumbling sighs assailed my ears, and a stone welled in my throat. I wanted to cry.

Memories of my dead baby and Jane's scandalous words poured through me, engulfing me into an emotional nadir. Suddenly I felt terribly depressed. The beauty before me elicited passionate emotion: either dramatic joy or despair, depending on how my day was going.

The manatees glided on, and I remained behind, not wanting to follow them. They had graced me with their presence, and now I wanted to let them be. I wandered in the labyrinth of myself. Zen masters had told me: *you cannot see yourself in running waters, only still.* So I floated.

Gazing up at the wide-space cumulus clouds, I saw how they languished in shades of white and blue as shadows traced a contoured horizon. In my mind, I retrieved a time when, as a child, I lay like an angel in the backyard with my younger sister to study cloud shapes. Our faces were awash in the reflected light of glorious innocence, lacking pain. I wanted to be back there in that time and space, to just let go.

Find release. I could not tell where my body stopped, and the sea began. I wanted to break this spiral of despair. I rasped a message.

Help me.

I stroked back to the seawall and collapsed on a tiny stretch of sand visible only at low tide. Goose pimples ran like a rash on my arms and legs. I stretched out to warm, eyes dilating in sunlight filtered through trees. Dante's words flooded into me.

"God is not merely a blinding vision of glorious light, but that He is, most of all, *l'amor che move il, sol e l'atre stele* (the sun and the other stars)." I melted into a void and dozed.

I woke when waters lapped at my heels with a returning tide. Where memories were once harsh and indelible at sunrise, ruminations had at last faded. All that remained were a mere scrim in my mind.

Now I know differently—I was a victim of forces outside myself. My ego. It had blocked my soul light, leaving despair to be a reflection of how well I fared in the world. It sought to divide and separate. Spirit brought unification and healing. Now I would choose differently.

No more pain.

I would seek healing perspectives in times of agony—whatever it took to cast off the darkness. It was just too bleak to handle it alone. No one wanted to share it with me. I didn't want to share it with anyone else. Who could relate to losing a baby and being accused of killing it? Peter had considered Jane's devil tongue as normal operating behavior for her—a gossipy, social pariah. I looked for peace. At last it settled over me like a mantle. From here on out, I would trust God implicitly. It was a matter of pure survival. Nothing else.

One day I turned to Peter and gave him a look that meant I had survived the death of our first baby. Our baby girl would always be with us in spirit—forever.

When our two sons came into our lives, I guarded them carefully, needing to keep my family whole from the start. A single event of tragedy had not sensitized me to familial loss. I vowed to protect Sam and Gary, our forthcoming crew, with the same fervor as if they were my own. The boys' parents, were our dear friends. Their mother found it a painful decision to place her sons in our care on a vast ocean with no medical help for nearly 3,000 nautical miles. I wasn't sure I could ever do the same after having lost a child.

8.
INTO THE BUSH

Charging Elephant

In the end, it's not going to matter how many breaths you took, but how many moments took your breath away.
—Shing Xiong

Africa drew me in by hook, line, and sinker.

"Why the fence?" I asked a wiry man. He was from the Xhosa tribe. Bent over double, the African cut grass with a rusty *panga* (cutlass) in front of me. Tall with soft brown eyes, he had a pleasant smile set in origami creases of weathered skin the color of warm walnut.

A stout fence rose behind the Xhosa gardener, barring entry to a serpentine river. The brown waters were fringed with thick woodland and studded with boulders.

The gardener paused and looked over at me.

"It keeps out hippos," he said with a chuckle. "The Sabie swarms with a hoard of 'em. They forage at night in the woods—used to wander into camp. Buggers ruined my grass!"

His lips smacked, releasing a sucking sound. The soft cadence of his tribal voice lent a light rhythm to the air. His words were interspersed with short clicking sounds; the sound resonated when the tongue flicked the roof of the mouth. He snarled at the river and its invisible occupants.

We were in Kruger National Park, one of the largest game parks in the world. Going to Africa and not going on safari would have been like going to the beach and not swimming in the sea. A final coat of bottom paint was being applied to our new boat, so we had time to explore hidden corners of South Africa. We would stay in remote bushveld huts in the Park while searching for the Big Five: elephant, black rhino, African buffalo, leopard, and lion.

Yesterday before entering the park, we had met my mother, Charlie (short for Charlcie), and niece, Brittany, at the J'borg International Airport. As a traveling companion, Mom was an asset. Her fat passport was studded with enough international stamps to tattoo a body. Best yet, she was capable of enduring rugged journeys, having been reared on a Kentucky farm.

My niece, Brittany, was a high school basketball star in Missouri. Her effervescent personality and easy ways were a complement to our rambunctious sons. She possessed a quiet demeanor and was smart, contributing flare to our family banter. As she spoke, a loose ponytail swung across her left shoulder, and her eyes were bright. A brown leather band, studded with spikes, encapsulated one wrist. An array of body piercings sparkled.

Mom and Brittany's flight had failed to arrive on time because of continuing security issues post-9/11. Everyone was edgy about hitting the freeway before dark. By the time we clambered aboard our rented Landcruiser, the haze had begun to shut out the sun even before it dropped below the horizon. Wielding a miniature map in my lap, I guided Peter right, no left . . . Stop here, no, go there, until, finally, we were hopelessly lost.

Looking down a maze of roads, we could see people going about their business on foot and on bikes in all directions. It was nearly twilight before we found our way to the freeway. On the N4, we pointed the Landcruiser down the road to Nelspruit, a service town for Kruger Park. Once we left the hum of the sprawling J'borg metropolis behind, the freeway narrowed into a two-lane road and became barren, devoid of traffic. We drove towards the Drakensburg Mountains as an orange orb fell onto the vast terrain, turning the sands a fiery ochre. It reflected into our vehicle mirrors, turning them into flaming torches. Traveling in such a mystical country put us in an expansive mood. We buzzed with the alacrity of excitement.

Twilight segued into night. The evening's crepuscular charm diminished when the road became devoid of ambient light—no illuminated exit signs, no illuminated residential dwellings, no moon. The white dividing line in the middle of the road faded to a near pearl gray and lacked reflective paint. It was like cruising inside a black chasm. After a time, a single headlight in the center of the road signaled an approaching motorcyclist, and we pulled more closely to the side to give the motorcycle ample room.

Peter was avid about keeping a sharp lookout for motorcycles. He had driven a BMW bike for a decade, relishing the sensation of the open road. Peter sold the BMW after we were married, terrified I would tumble into the gutter. I constantly fell asleep on the back end, lulled into sweet slumber by the smooth rhythm of the finely built machine. Just as I was about to topple onto the tarmac, he would feel me sway, and then rouse me by pinching my thigh until I pulled upright again. More than once, he saved my life. My sleepy ways put an abrupt end to our motorcycle diaries on the road.

Even now on this lonely stretch of road, our hearts alighted with the awareness of sharing the road with humanity—even if a complete stranger. When an anticipated motorcyclist resolved into a battered car with one broken headlight that pointed up and to the left like an unblinking eye, we fell into a sense of foreboding. We avoided colliding at the last second. Peter ran into the dirt on the side of the road. We collected our breaths before we started back on the road again. This time, we were intent on pulling far to the right with any sign of a single headlight, lest it be a Mack truck.

The ghost of the battered vehicle seemed an augury of worse things to come.

Road trains loomed behind us. Each train pulled four Afrit wagons on sixty wheels, each wheel the size of a compact car. Lit up like Christmas trees, they resembled mile-long trains and were driven by a single operator loaded on Benzedrine. The beams of their headlights swept the sky over the earth like search lights, revealing an expansive, empty terrain that lay scorched from the dry season. Leaves of trees were gone, and branches pointed at the sky like a thousand gnarled fingers of witches.

The semitrailers carried assorted staples from South Africa to Zambia, and further still to the Congo. They drove at breakneck speed. They shot past our vehicle. The force of their transit as they passed us created mini-tornadoes that violently rocked our Landcruiser. Once, two truck-trains racing side-by-side clawed up the tail of our vehicle. Peter abruptly pulled off to let them pass. My gut went sour as they whizzed past in a blur. Rocks and stones flew from behind them, pinging our windshield.

Other hazards kept Peter and me alert while the three children slept. A wave of humanity was making its journey home alongside the road from places we never saw. On and on they came. Our headlights had swept over their dark figures often before we noticed them. In our distorted vision through the harmattan night haze, our headlights swept over wiry women donned in *kitenges* (a colorful African print wrapped into a makeshift skirt). Strapped to their backs were infants draped in folds of cloth. Alongside the women lumbered men, bent double from the weight of water jugs. Some of the women carted heavy jugs atop their heads, balanced by circular cloths placed on the crown.

The highway was devoid of shoulders, so there was no place for them to seek refuge if the need arose. Their dark figures flashed pink palms in our headlights, signaling an appeal for a lift. They looked forlorn and somnolent. I pressed my face into the windshield to aid Peter in driving. I announced their approaching figures, terrified a weary soul may stray into our path. Even at a snail's pace of 50 mph there was not enough time to react. The lack of visibility haunted me. I felt sad about the women. *Like sighing angels,* I thought.

"Can't we stop and help them? Give even just one of them a lift?" I pleaded with Peter.

"We just can't," Peter insisted. "Don't you remember what the J'borg car rental agent told us about driving at night? She warned us to never,

ever pick anyone up alongside the road, however innocent, lost or appealing they may look. So we just cannot take the risk. Besides, where would we put them? We're loaded to the gunnels already." He released an audible, poignant sigh.

"Couldn't they stay on the roof of the van . . . Or something? Somewhere?" I begged, my voice wavering. But I knew it was hopeless. Though I had seen it done in other developing nations, I knew there were not any racks to support the women atop the Landcruiser.

By late evening, we entered the Numbi Gate of Kruger Park, having scheduled a late arrival time to ensure an opening. Kruger Park Gates were like chastity belts: gate openings and closings adhered to strict rules of engagement. Beneath a sliver of a crescent moon, we made our way to Paul Kruger's former hunting lodge. On the veranda, ghostly shadows of moonlight filtered through branches of the eternal acacia trees, casting an eerie gloom. Inside, we entered the great room, where a history of past grandeur announced itself. My mouth fell open at the sight of several pairs of eyes staring down at me. Glassy-eyed and opaque, the eyes belonged to heads of lions and rhino and gemsbok. Dead animals were suspended from walls of grey stone everywhere. Overhead, wooden beams spanned the ceiling that ended at the hunting rifle of Paul Kruger's, founder of the park. Every time I looked at it over the fireplace, I half-expected the legendary man to stroll through the door. I sniffed, imagining a faint whiff of cigar smoke. Paul Kruger was not sitting in the corner wearing a smoking jacket, but he should have been.

The kids raced to find their rooms down the long hallway. Peter and I lowered our weary bodies into oversized chairs to take in the scene. Paul Kruger and his men had gathered here next to roaring fires over a century ago, slugging back whiskey and boasting of their hunting accolades. I envisioned Paul Kruger crowing about bringing down the vicious African buffalo—arguably the most dangerous animal known to man, next to the hippo. The African buffalo was known to inflict more human deaths in Africa than any other large animal. Before we left the park, we would have our own anecdote to share about the unpredictable beast. That night, I tried to fall asleep to the call of hyenas and the grunt of hippos as goose pimples rippled up and down my arms.

I drew awake as a rind of a sun flooded up over the horizon, releasing a slash of bloody-red and molten-copper through cabin windows. I kissed Peter's ears until he stirred. Together we descended a hill in back of the lodge before Mom and the children were up. We followed a dusty path down to the Sabie River, pausing to lower ourselves against the bole of a large baobab tree. Its branches were thick as a fat woman's thigh. We reveled in the picturesque vista before us. Muddy river waters twisted round and round, until disappearing into the expansive darkness beyond it. A rising sun gilded treetops bright with gold and river boulders were shiny with dew. Ever so gently, the morning mist drifted away from still waters. A myriad of bird calls enlivened the air. We were in Africa—at this time and at this moment—and we felt a palpable sense of wonder.

Abruptly, a boulder moved in the misty shadows. Our reverie was cut short when what appeared to be a boulder reared up suddenly. My eyes went wide when a fire-hose of spray jetted up like a violent geyser. Massive jaws protruded from formidable tusks attached to a hippo head. The head split wide open. Jagged jaws tore at the sky. The barrel-shaped body looked like it weighed as much as two Mack trucks. The hippo retreated into the waters, sides reflecting like mirrors from morning sun rays.

Another bull's roar resounded through the scrub, flooding the woodlands. Its echo brought the children—Adam and Warren and Brittany—bounding from out of the lodge. They charged down the hill in a heated race with Mom rushing after them. At the river's edge, we gathered to watch the killer herbivores caught in a fierce challenge. The violent show cut short when the bull hippo uttered a low grumbling noise. It slid beneath parted waters to rest on the river bottom, settling onto hidden haunches. Only two tiny ears and the tip of a giant muzzle peeked above the shadowy surface.

We relaxed, thinking it was all over and got up to go, but abruptly the waters ripped apart again. It was if a small tornado had descended with fury. In a flare of temper, another hippo leapt from the water. A frenetic frenzy set in when the hippo bellowed fiercely, challenging the old bull. Like a duel, the two lunged at each other with gaping jaws and razor-sharp teeth. Inside their open jaws, I saw dentition strong enough to tear apart our family dog, Robin. The rough hides of the two hippos scraped, sending an audible sawing noise reverberating across waters. Powerful geysers gushed from gaping mouths. We were mute, riveted with the sudden display of a violent battle.

A voice came from out of the mist.

"They're two rivals fighting over space and territory," a man said.

I turned to see the wiry Xhosa gardener.

"The river is too shallow this year, because of the lack of rain. It's the dry season. Tempers always flare up," the gardener said.

"Has anyone been killed by a hippo?" I asked curiously.

"Hippos have not attacked anyone in Kruger Park, but outside the park enraged bulls and nursing females have lifted boats out of the water and put holes in them. Hippos and buffalos kill more people than any other animal in Africa," the Xhosa said.

"What about crocs?" I asked.

"Oh, the river is chock full of crocs," he replied. "They eat whatever— and whomever--they want, but a croc won't eat the hippo. The river horse can slice the reptile in two if bothered."

He gave us a look of knowing. Our sailing itinerary led us near African rivers. Two more teen boys were joining us as crew later. The curiosity and rambunctious ways of the four of them together— all childhood buddies—made me shudder with both unimaginable and probable possibilities. We said goodbye to the Xhosa, rushing out the front gate as the sun climbed higher.

Peter pointed the Landcruiser down a sandy track through the untamed terrain. Everything felt like a fresh start. It was May when the grass had turned brittle, and the streams were dry with the onset of African fall. Wildlife viewing was at its best this time of year. There would be scant cover for the big cats—lion, leopard, and cheetah—to hide beneath.

We rumbled along at the speed of a horse lope. Large trees—Mopani and palms and eucalyptus –dotted the dry landscape in green hues. I let in the rich aroma of the African savanna through my window. The air was chock full of wild bird calls. Coupled with the evocative backdrop of the grassy plain and the sounds of the bushveld, I felt ebullient.

"Where's your pith helmet?" Peter said with a wide grin.

His smile shot out like a beam of sunlight. I relished his funny ways. I flashed an electric smile back and handed him a cup of steaming hot tea. I had prepared a breakfast picnic before leaving the lodge. I passed back another cup of hot tea to Mom. She sat behind me, occupied with Brittany in animated conversation. Between three rows of seats, six of us were evenly divided. Adam and Warren stretched out asleep in the far back row. Brittany helped pass around the mobile breakfast of boiled eggs, cereal, and boxed pear nectar. We traded banter between rows.

"The Numbi Gate employee told me that a rambunctious group of juvenile elephants pounded down a fence and feasted on a village cornfield not long ago," I said.

"Where's my lioness? I've got my leash ready!" Mom said. She gave a sweet chuckle, flicking her petite wrist in mock battle pursuit. Red, green and blue gemstones studded her slender fingers, winking back at me in the morning light. Dressed in a pretty safari suit, she looked charming at eighty. Curly brown hair peaked from beneath the brim of a gabardine hat that was tilted jauntily to one side. A leopard print scarf was tied in a bow at her neck. She was an excellent sport in all great endeavors, having traveled the globe with my father before his death a short time ago.

It was my mother who made a traveler out of me. My predilection for international travel was seeded on Saturday mornings when, as a young girl Mom dragged me—in initial protest—to the public library. Inside a labyrinth of shelves of books, she gathered up an armful of historical fiction, autobiographies, and travel essays. She entered me into reading contests. Because of my mother, I eccentrically mooned my childhood over volumes of books and nature magazines. I curled up into the top tier of a bunk bed and lost myself in imagination.

I began to fall in love with a foreign world. I formulated dreams of going native with Maori tribes in New Zealand and the Hindus of India and the tribes of Africa. I scoured photos of ethnic peoples, comparing traditional dress with my own. I sniffed for the imagined scent of their homelands, straining for the accompanying sounds.

I jerked upright when Adam shouted, "Watch out!"

A colossal shape bolted from out of the bush and rose. It loomed over the vehicle like Godzilla. Peter slammed his foot on the brakes. The Landcruiser jerked forward. I was filled with instant terror when I looked up and saw what was coming. My hackles rose. I gripped the door handle for impact. Behind me, bodies collided. I heard a moan.

I stared in shock as a reddish-brown beast filled the frame of the windshield. It looked to be five-feet high from the shoulder to the hoof and had long daggers of horns that spiraled towards the clouds. A longitudinal white stripe ran along the middle of its back, and several transverse white stripes ran down each side. It bounded across the hood of the Landcruiser with hooves the size of dinner plates, inches from my face. With a piercing thud, it landed on the other side and darted away. As it retreated, a white tail flickered like a candle flame. The figure grew more spectral with each leap into the distance until the bushveld closed around it.

"Is everybody alright?" I asked

I turned around in my seat and stared at utter chaos: knapsacks and cameras and maps littered the floor, juice cartons had spilled their contents, and a kaleidoscope of Cheerios blanketed the seats. Brittany was a limp heap on the floor. Warren and Adam were disentangling limbs in back. Mom appeared stunned: her mouth was agape, and the whites of her eyes large as saucers.

"What was *that*?" cried Warren.

"What *was* that?" screamed Adam.

"The heck?" Brittany said, puzzled.

Colliding with a deer in Colorado was one thing, but colliding with a horse that sprouted spiraling horns and was five-feet long and resembled a unicorn? Adam tore open pages of field guides and park brochures. At last, after much discussion between us, he identified the large beast as one very fine—and very large—kudu. Kudu. Who'd ever heard of such a thing?

"We nearly collided with it! I can't bear running over something so beautiful. It could have demolished the van. Someone could get hurt!" I shouted. "We've got to slow down!"

After a brief break to gather wits, Peter keyed the ignition, and we idled forward at a snail's pace. We rambled into the dry highveld where we trained our eyes to focus on the unseen: camouflaged animals in distant fields, spaces between trees, the underside of bush, and tops of trees. We could easily pass an animal and never know one was ever there. It was an arduous effort.

Where animals had once been invisible, we began to see shapes. In the distance, a pair of elegantly patterned tubes of necks loomed. Giraffes were on the run, towering over acacia trees and looking like ambulant skyscrapers. When we rounded a bend, two young giraffes appeared at the side of the road. They were trailed by three adult giraffes a short distance away. The adults served as rear-end protection from predators, like the elusive leopard and cunning lion. The family of giraffes loped in long strides with slow-motion grace.

The Xhosa tribal members called them *indlulamith*, or "he that surpassed trees." A giraffe stood nearly eighteen feet tall. So tall, I imagined looking out from a second-floor office window and seeing a pair of liquid brown eyes gazing back at me. Lined in Kohl and fringed in long lashes, they resembled the eyes of Vogue runway models.

The giraffes mounted into a gallop on our approach. We watched their leggy gait: front feet lifted together; then the back feet lifted to supplant the forefeet while the neck moved backwards and forward to maintain balance. At times, it was hilarious and simultaneously puzzling to figure out. But galloping at 35mph, they quickly overtook our turtle pace. We stopped to watch them pass. Their majestic, eloquent dance moved us to silence. The kids spied another band of giraffes in a grove close to us.

"Come on, Dad. Reverse!" Adam said

Peter rumbled back slowly, not wanting to spook them. We knew they saw us: their colossal height and acute vision afforded the giraffes the ability to spot predators from afar while simultaneously maintaining a sharp lookout for family members. The giraffe possessed an early-pred-ator-warning-system. It was so acute that other prey, like hyenas and warthogs, followed them. Soon, we rolled to a stop where a juvenile giraffe nibbled leaves a hundred yards away.

"It's a male because he's feeding on the higher branches," Brittany said. She trained the binoculars more to the right. "There's a female feeding on the lower branches beside him. Her tongue looks like a fist. She's stripping leaves. Her teeth are huge. Wow!"

Brittany had been honing up on her facts during the drive. Our homeschooling class had become "no-schooling," a far better way to teach at this moment. The boys' interests were piqued.

Warren turned the page of the field guide and chimed in. "It says here, no one pattern of skin spots was the same on any other giraffe. They're all different, like thumbprints." He began flipping pages with keen awareness, full of wonder and amazement. Questions rapped out in rapid fire succession, bright and penetrating.

"Could there be a grand design happening here?" I asked, hoping to encourage philosophical reflection and erudite consideration.

An audible sigh rose from the back rows.

"Perhaps a divine plan existed for the universe, perfect to protect and enable survival?" I asked.

These kids had studied science and biology, but the real evidence was unfolding before their eyes. I was pleased these kids were getting to know the African bush in a real live Charles Darwin experience.

By midday, sun rays bore into the hood of the Landcruiser. The kids grew fitful and napped intermittently. Soon rumblings of "what's for lunch" reverberated in the back. Like our breakfast, lunch would be eaten within the confines of the Landcruiser. Park authorities had routinely instructed us before we started out on safari.

"Never leave your car. No matter what happens. Don't become alarmed if lions stand and stare," the park guide said.

We crested a ridge and paused before a golden grassy wind-scoured plain that stretched endlessly and was flanked by hills. Grass blades rippled in the breeze like an immense silk cloth. Tall candelabra aloes grew on the upper slopes while further down the aloes became even denser. There were strangler figs with bark like elephant hide, grey and wrinkled. The astonishing purring of the cicadas was as loud as the roar of a freight train.

A sky the color of old bruises hung low over a grove of trees off in the distance. We watched as it rolled in with ponderous dignity across the dried plain towards us. The kids sagged in slumber from the rhythmic rumble of the van.

Peter and I gazed at the wonder before us, lost in the immensity of the plain. Once again I looked up at the sky. A slight prickle rose on my neck. The low cloud was no longer rolling in the same direction.

"What's that dark line in front of us?" Mom asked, looking puzzled.

"…a dust storm?" Brittany said, stirring. The boys came alert, their minds registering a hint of possible drama.

"Nah, it's locusts or a bunch of wild horses," Warren said.

"There aren't any wild horses in Africa," Adam said.

We left our lofty vantage point of the ridge and descended into a miniature valley. There, in time the black cloud met us. We collided in the scene as black-and-white striped horses emerged out of the African haze. The zebras slowed to graze on the guinea grass that fringed the sandy track of road. Their infinite herd of stripes merged and molded into a complex puzzle. It was dizzying to study. Which stripes belonged to which zebra? Much pointing and debate arose from the kids. They completed one zebra puzzle piece, then moved on to piece together another. In the end, each zebra had a different and unique stripe pattern. Only the white bellies, devoid of stripes, offered clues to its master in the end.

We watched transfixed as two male juveniles collided to jostle over a mare. They snorted, ears lowered. One reared up to challenge his larger rival, emitting a loud whinny. But the stallion refused to give way, and they began to bite necks and legs. Desperate kicks—all four feet off the ground —ensued. Only a fierce kick with a cocked back leg driven into the side of one ended the battle.

Our lunch spot was beneath the umbrella of a large baobab tree. Outside, the brilliant highveld sun threw shadows black and crisp like paper cut-outs beneath the trees. Noonday swooned in the heat. We talked over peanut-butter crackers and oranges and chunks of cheese. We rolled down our windows, caked with a patina of red Sahara dust. Arms and legs stretched through open windows, draping down sides of the Landcruiser like colorful banner flags.

Just when we had relaxed, chaos unfolded in the treetops above us. Adam stretched his head out of the open window to peer above. *Plop!* Something soft landed.

"Yuck!" Adam wailed, bumping his head on the way back in through the window. "What the ... ?" A primitive, foul odor penetrated the space of the van. Our eyes burned and misted as if we'd been hit by a rotten egg. I held the bottom of my shirt to my nose.

"Dude! What's wrong with your bowels, Man?" Warren said, laughing in uncontrollable guffaws.

I looked aghast at the lime-green ooze that lay across the crown of Adam's head. A Milky Way of splattered stools, looking like spoiled yogurt, streaked down his face. Raindrops of green goo dribbled onto his arms. When he reached up to finger the eggy mass, his face grew white.

"It's like ... warm! Sick!" he wailed.

"Oh, dude!" Warren guffawed.

"Geez, you look awful," Brittany said with a laugh. Her braces flashed in the sunlight, streaking from the open window.

Adam gagged and grabbed clothes to wipe the foul feces. The first sacrificial item was Warren's shirt.

"That's my new t-shirt!" Warren wailed.

Brittany spun around, grabbed her new t-shirt, and quickly stuffed it in her seat to thwart the attack. I secretly grabbed mine too. Sweet Grandma relented, passing back hers.

Curious, Adam steeled himself for another look by slowly edging out to test the unforgiving skies. Nothing. He drew his entire torso out of the big window, perching on the sill. Nothing.

"Go ahead. I dare you," he yelled to the invisible invaders. A hailstorm of green golf balls rang down. "Aargh," Adam yelled out. On the way back in, he let loose a litany of highly creative language. "Just don't say a word," he said and yanked on his hat, fully extending the brim. He crossed his arms and sat stoic, immersed in a fit of fury, still as stone.

Looking forward, I stole a peek through the windshield and gazed up into the maze of branches. "Pull up, Peter," I said.

He inched forward until the upper tree canopy ballooned into view. There, a troop of roughly thirty baboons whirled at play. They whizzed through leafy branches with a loud clamor: juveniles wrestled and pin-wheeled, scampering over a sleeping male.

Hoon, hoon, hooooon, a baboon called from his elevated perch. A silvery-brown matriarch, the size of a dog, sat on her haunches grooming ticks and fleas from her infant. Nimble fingers parted hair, plucking insects from the roost. Their long furry tails were entwined and dangled from thick branches. An older sibling tried to nuzzle its way between them for attention, but the matriarch pushed him away.

Suddenly the infant was seized by a large male with a menacing look. Canines bared, he gestured wildly, staring with feral eyes. The matriarch panted and grunted loudly to win back her infant. I held my breath, counting the seconds until the captured infant would fall from the tree. I locked eyes with the matriarch, feeling her yearning for her baby to be returned. I waited with abated breath, half-expecting the infant to fall to the ground. I couldn't bear to watch. But the deliberate grab was a ruse. To my relief, the little one was released from captivity. It quickly scrambled back to safety onto its mother's lap. I let out a deep breath of relief.

We waved our furry friends goodbye and moved out. It was three o'clock: time for the big animals to awaken from their afternoon naps and stir from the bush in search of water or prey. But after an hour of pointing our noses down the sandy path, the wilderness seemed devoid of visible wildlife. We grew groggy from the heat. Eventually, I succumbed to the call of a catnap like everyone else. Occasionally, I forced open an eye to peer into the bush for animal signs: the movement of a branch or leaf, moving shadows, fresh spoor or scat on the road. It seemed the whole of Africa was at rest on this warm day, except Peter. The solitude of driving was a metaphysical state of awareness for him.

We came to the Olifants River. Awake now, six pairs of eyes peered into the Mopani forest—favored food of the elephant. With our trained eyes, we peeled away the layers of foliage, trying to pinpoint a moving target.

"There's something there!" Brittany pointed.

"No, over there!" Adam said.

We passed binoculars and cameras left, and then right. "Where?" I asked.

Down to a crawl, Peter approached timidly. It was the unpredictable and unexpected that we became attuned to, searching with our pair of 2nd eyes. We came around a bend, and there before us were mountains of steaming feces filling the road. Each pile looked to weigh nearly 50 lbs. If we barreled through it, waves of feces would rise like the parting of the Red Sea. Peter edged closer to study its contents: chewed bark and twigs and nuts of wild fruits.

"You left something behind, Warren," Adam snickered. "Man, you stink!"

"Sick," Brittany chimed in.

They bantered back and forth with humorous fluidity. I stole a glance at Peter and caught the merry twinkle in his eye. He'd grown up with five siblings, and banter was music to his ears.

Dung littered the middle and the sides of the road. We drove off-road to navigate around it as if driving through an obstacle course. After Brittany got broadsided by a glob, we kept the windows up. Tires became encrusted as we passed. There were enough dung heaps to supply an African village with butane fuel for an entire year. But where were the owners of these piles? I wrapped my fingers around Peter's arm, feeling hesitant. My breathing slowed.

"Babe, let's turn around. This doesn't feel right," I begged. I had a feeling of being watched, although there were no eyes around. There was no sound. But I knew something was there.

"Tina?" Mom said in a choking sound. She felt it too. We shared a joint awareness that she penned as "gifts of the spirit." I called it "psychic ability."

"Dad?" Warren said shakily. It was our first pause of near panic in the African outback. I had the impulse to grab the wheel and backpedal.

"Go on, Dad," Adam snorted. "Find him!" Once a unified team, we were breaking down on opposing sides. We studied the scene, peering into the bush.

"What do we do? Where should we go? Back up? Go forward?" I stammered.

Besides the evidence of elephant feces, other signs of a recent passing were there: trampled saplings and uprooted trees and strips of bark peeled from trunks. A complete swath of woodland lay in ruin, looking like a newly bulldozed highway.

It struck me that we were without emergency communication devices: no mobile phone, no public phones, and no two-way radio. No one would ever know if we died. The animals would get to us before the rangers did.

We heard him before we saw him: the blasting of a thunderous trumpet. It resounded across the bushveld so forcibly that I drove my nails into Peter's arm. I leaned forward to peer through the filthy windshield. It was like peering through fog. The windshield was streaked with wiper skid and coated with bug carcasses, dung, and dust. I strained my eyes to see the unseen, but nothing was there.

The piercing call of the wild came again. But still, nothing came forward. A wild animal scream usually indicated intense anger or fear, so it was only a matter of time before the elephant showed himself.

"Never approach wildlife," park authorities had told us. It seemed we were doing precisely that, although we couldn't see him.

"Lock your doors and roll up your windows," I shouted. I was so distracted by focusing ahead that I failed to check on whether any of the kids had done as told. Locking myself inside gave me a sense of security, however false it was.

Then we saw him—a giant bull elephant. He stood sentinel, looking regal, silhouetted against a late afternoon sun. He was broad-shouldered and broad-hipped. He loomed over our Landcruiser on pillar legs. Dried mud clung to his thick hide, and colossal ears fanned out from a head checkered with wrinkles. From the head protruded a pair of tusks that were six-feet long, curved to murderous cutting edges. Ears as big as tents fanned back and forth to cool an overheated body. Liquid brown eyes— the size of tea cups and fringed in long lashes—gazed back at us. I sobbed inwardly in appreciation of his majestic form.

Beside him stood a female. She tugged at lianas in treetops and inter- mittently soothed a calf with the caresses of her trunk. When the bull raised his trunk, the base of it was as thick as a man's torso. His pink fleshy mouth looked to be as soft as a child's blanket. The trunk writhed, assessing our scent. When the female gave a low-pitched rumble, the juvenile came hurrying. The little elephant looked to weigh nine tons.

"Little fella looks like you, Adam," Warren giggled. "Poor kid, he'll have no luck with the Sheilas."

Adam harrumphed and threw his hat, meeting the intended mark of his brother's head.

I'd read that elephants communicated through infrasound, sending out alarms in frequencies over many miles, too low for the human ear to detect. The long-distance vocalizations kept family members bonded and warned each other of impending danger. A roar and a scream from a distressed calf could wreak havoc as all available family members rushed to the rescue. It struck me that because of the large number of dung masses lying around, the big tuskers were already here. We were ruining their family picnic. Bull rocked forward and back, whipping his trunk from side to side, upset with our intrusion.

"Get closer, Dad. I want a better photo," Warren urged. Peter shifted into first gear, inching forward.

"I don't think so, Babe," I said. We rumbled forward. My face grew ashen. We had no right to disturb this family setting.

Bull began to stomp the ground, unsure of our intentions. Dust flew from feet with pads the size of basketballs. When he brought them up, deep fissures ran like rivers through soles. The female bobbed her head from side to side in alarm. I was rigid with anticipation. *Please, don't upset the baby*, I thought. "Peter, don't!" I reached for the wheel, but stopped short when implacable eyes gazed back at me.

"I just want to say hi," Peter chortled. Blood roared in my ears.

"Closer, Dad. He's not in full frame yet," Warren said, clicking away with his camera.

Peter inched closer. Words stuck in my throat. I stared dumbstruck at him. It left me with the unshakeable impression that our sons had the ability to palaver their father into reckless behavior. I had no influence.

The wobbling of Bull's trunk intensified. Trunk pumped air. Pads pummeled dirt. Bull lunged forward and back again in fury as if prepping for a marathon race. The female took off with her calf into the Mopani forest. They disappeared behind a billow of dust. Now it was just us and Bull.

"Peter, elephants have the right of way. Don't argue the point," I wailed. I shot him a sharp glance, but he didn't hear me. Tears welled in my eyes. I imagined newspaper headlines of "Big Tusker Tramples Family" and a photo of us next to our children, shot in happier days. I gave Peter a serious wide-eyed stare of incredulity. He had gone mad. I had no control over any of the men in my family. How was I going to sea with this bunch of lunatics?

And then came the *coup de grace.* Bull trumpeted a cry so full of passion, my blood ran cold. Time thickened like wet cement. If elephants can send out low-frequency alarms inaudible to human ears, what other messages had we missed? Was Bull calling in his buddies, the Green Berets of the big tuskers? Any minute now, an entire support herd of elephants would eat up terrain to protect their comrade, and trace the missing mother and baby. It was nearly sundown—the time when ultra-violet noise lessens, the ground cools, and the calling range across the bushveld triples in as little as two hours. We would be road kill for the vultures. Their shiny black figures perched atop barren trees, looking like black angels in Halloween costumes sitting atop Christmas trees, waiting patiently for death and … us?

"Tina!" Mom cried out. I spun around in my seat and looked in terror at Warren. His entire body extended out the open window where he sat perched on the door frame. Both hands were busy with a heavy single lens reflex digital camera (SLR). His only lifeline to the Landcruiser was Brittany's grasp around one of his ankles.

"Warren, get in!" I called out. But he hung there, intent on rapid fire shooting. The camera clicked and whirred. Cold chills sprinted up my spine. I couldn't breathe. Suddenly, everyone started yelling at once.

"Get in! Idiot, get in!" Brittany grabbed both of Warren's legs and yanked him into the seat.

Peter's eyes were crossed in a myopic stare. I knew that expression—he was calculating, juggling with time. What happened next unfolded in slow motion.

Bull charged.

Peter's face grew etched with sudden horror, realizing his tangle with wild things had gone all wrong.

"…thy rod and thy staff protect me!" Mom prayed. Her hands whirled above, performing hand signals as if calling in all the celestial forces she could muster.

"Sweet Jesus, Peter! "Back off!" I screamed. I pounded the seat to get his attention. It was mere seconds now before Bull was upon us. The monstrous bull could topple over our little van.

"Yeah, yeah. Okay!" he shouted. Sweet capitulation. I went limp with relief. Then the most horrible thing happened.

Peter ground the shift lever incorrectly, confusing the American with the South African position. We jerked forward, and then violently backward as he tried to correct. Our heads bucked from mini-whiplashes. And then the gears jammed altogether. He hammered it into reverse again, getting it right this time, but all going wrong.

"HURRY!" I screamed. "He's coming!"

"By the stripes of …!" Mom prayed, even louder now. She pounded a fist towards the heavens as if clutching a staff and calling off the demons chasing us.

Several tons of bristling flesh bore down. The kids hollered. I was mute. There were no words left.

Suddenly the engine bellowed triumphantly, and we surged into reverse, slipping on loose dirt. After a few terrifying seconds, the tires gained full purchase. We shot onto the road, kicking up roots and rocks behind us into rooster tails of spray. Bull pulled up short ten feet away, confused by the noise and commotion. But he stood his ground, rocking back and forth, wildly trumpeting as dust billowed around him.

Peter fired into a rapid three-point turn and sped away, leaving the beast behind. Once our getaway was clean, he flashed me a pearly white smile.

"Wow, that was a doozy," he chuckled.

I was livid. I was crossing an ocean with five male teenagers, one of which was my untamed husband. "Shall I drive?" I asked.

"Nah," he said with a feral look of high adventure in his eyes. "But I'll take more of that Coca-Cola." It was the last can. I loved my Diet Coke like an alcoholic loved gin. I fixed him with a penetrating gaze.

"Sorry, all gone," I said. I kicked the single can beneath my seat. We didn't need any more caffeine addicts on the road. It was all mine or Mom's, whoever needed it first to keep from killing a testosterone-fueled man.

Silence inside the van ensued. In time, Brittany broke the stalemate. "One big check for elephant. Only four more big animals til the big five." She jostled the field guide with pen and notebook as she settled in next to Warren.

"Five bucks to the one who sees the first big cat," Peter blurted out. His effort at redirecting the stale atmosphere was admirable after our little tiff. All eyes went to the windows as we descended into the tabletop openness of the vast plain and came upon a herd of several hundred springbok grazing . They looked like a fine dust of cinnamon powder across the pale earth. A fawn nursed from her impala mother, quivering on matchstick legs as her playmates frolicked nearby. Another impala shot up into the air in a graceful leap, its red-brown skin resembling silk.

A glint of lyre-shaped horns sailed by attached to a lovely creature. It bounced away so lightly that it seemed to be flying. Some of the antelopes were lordly, and others were as delicate and graceful as ballerinas. The herd drifted elusively, looking like swirling smoke. Near a patch of trees by the Crocodile River, we watched as a herd of sable antelope entered the Mopani forest. Their heads were held high, tipped with curved scimitar horns and their snowy breasts against black bodies were a dazzling contrast of color.

We were warned by park authorities to be on the lookout for the black rhino. Next to the elephant and hippo, rhinos were among the biggest and heaviest land animals in Africa. I remembered reading that, until the late 1800's, rhino had freely roamed throughout Africa. But unrestrained hunting had caused their numbers to decline to near extinction. Powdered rhino horn mixed with dried lice was once used by the Zulus to treat jaundice. They believed it held magical powers and that vapors of burned horn chased away evil spirits.

Legend had it that black rhinos were ill-tempered and charged without reason. "See it, before it sees you," park authorities had warned us.

I once sat stupefied while viewing a documentary as a child in which a rhino entered a campsite at night to scatter the smoldering logs of fire, and then peacefully waddled away. Many trophy hunters believed their erratic behavioral charge was merely an attempt to investigate. During an attack, a rhino could suddenly halt, distracted by a slight detail in the bush—a smell or a sound. The hunters wrote of how their territory had been invaded by rhino that raced alongside trains, sprinting at speeds of 35 mph.

"It's nice to know these things when you start out," I said. "In case we have to walk back to base camp for some odd reason, like from a failed engine or elephant charge. Think we should climb a tree if we get chased by a rhino?" I asked, hoping to engage the children in conversation.

"Mom, just yell 'on guard!' Try to look mean. Throw your arms up over your head. Look bigger than your shrimpy size," Adam teased me.

"Bro, your butt's big; you couldn't run fast enough to make it into a tree," Warren guffawed.

Brittany giggled. She had squeezed in to sit between her two cousins. Her calm presence kept their banter at bay, but barely.

"Be sure you run in a crooked line to the tree. Rhinos have trouble zigzagging because of large hind quarters," Peter said.

We were a team again. No more opposing sides or near death experiences in the bush. I hoped it held and breathed a sigh of relief, believing it would, but knowing it wouldn't.

Outside a grove of Natal mahogany, we stopped to admire a troop of baboons fingering brown sludge for loose twigs and blades of grass. Pale green tendrils rose and swirled on the lazy air from what looked to be a pond. But upon closer inspection (and a fight over the single pair of binoculars) it turned out to be a gargantuan pile of dung. The three-toed spoor of a rhinoceros encircled it. The spoor resembled the Ace of Clubs, the mark of territory by a male.

"I see a rhino!" Adam shouted. Armed with the trusty binoculars, he found the prehistoric looking beast nearby in the woodlands. "Check out the shiny tree limbs. There's hardly any bark left," Adam said.

He recognized the effect from our family walks in Rocky Mountain National Park where tree limbs had grown shiny from the rubbing of elk antlers during summer months. Inside Kruger Park, fallen tree limbs had grown shiny from the rubbing of the rhinos' rumps that could itch from parasites or ticks. A yellow-billed oxpecker scampered on the rhino's wide back, prying ticks and fleas with sharp claws from the thick hide. I remembered reading that the Swahilis called the bird *askari wa kifaru*, meaning the rhino's guard. Just then a shrill alarm went up from the starling, high on alert from our intrusion.

"The rhino is getting up," Adam said.

"Busted!" Peter shouted.

Rhinos have poor eyesight for distance, so either he'd caught our scent, being downwind of us, or the oxpecker busted our cover. The rhino's saucer-like ears rotated in our direction. His elongated horned head turned left and then right, but he was unable to see us directly in front of him because of his sideways-facing eyes. He looked lethal on short pillar legs. Two enormous horns projected from his snout. They stabbed at the air, looking like auguries. The front horn was nearly five-feet long.

We drew in our breaths when the armored mammoth gave a grunt and loud puffing sound and then lumbered out of the trees with a ponderous gait. After stomping over to the dung heap, he sprayed a powerful jet of piss backwards, then rolled in excrement until thoroughly blanketed with a shiny new coat. It was his personal calling card to other rhino. It announced, "Find me, Sweetie! And stay out, Bub!" to competing rivalries.

We drove alongside a grove of bush willows. A little warthog darted out of the bush by the side of the road, his long tufted tail held high. It sprinted at nearly 35mph and looked to weigh two-hundred pounds. It had the most remarkable features I'd ever seen, with big eyes set high across a flat face on a head with an elongated snout. Warts of all sizes adorned the squat body on pillar legs. Two sets of tusks (one, semicircular, the other worn to a cutting edge) emerged from his snout. A bristly mane completed the look.

Panic stricken, it charged back into the thicket to escape the invisible demon chasing him. Pigs ranked high on the lion's list of a favorite entrée of the day, so I suspected it wouldn't be long before a lioness came calling. "Follow that hairy dude!" Warren shouted.

He was buoyant. Our spirits lifted after the slow morning crawl. Mom took charge, placing everyone in battle position. "Adam, you and I will search the thickets and tops of trees to the right. Warren, you and Brittany scour the savanna to the left," she said.

We rounded a bend, and I prickled with pleasure when there, out of the blue, were four blasé lionesses stretched out in the middle of the road. They languished like tourists. An audible gasp arose from the kids in the back. Park authorities later told us lions were fond of the feel of their bellies against the warmth of the tarmac during winter months.

Peter slowed to a quiet stop. The lionesses eyed us snidely, and then returned to grooming paws from a recent kill. Across the whisker-studded muzzle of one lioness stretched a sickle-shaped scar. Beside her, another lioness bore a vivid wound across her forehead and a nick in one ear. When she yawned, an ample jaw revealed a broken tooth—possibly a kick from a fleeing zebra. Leaning on her back was the chin of another lioness. Now and then, the great felines showed acts of bonding. They rolled near each other, touched muzzles, and rubbed, acting like social animals. Their languid morning respite had transformed them into a feline version of a bunch of golden retrievers acting coy.

After an hour, it was time to move out. There was only one problem: the lionesses blocked our route. We couldn't go around their kingdom because of the dangerous spiky bristles of the Oxtail Buffalo Grass that fringed the tarmac. Punctured tires meant a walk back to camp, which would certainly lend a zing to my African travel anecdotes, but it wasn't an option. It struck me that the lionesses' noses told them that a car was not good to eat, but what about us?

"Shoo!" Peter shouted from his open window. Unperturbed, a lioness tilted a tawny head in our direction, squinted an eye and went back to dozing.

"Woof!" Warren barked. Nothing. Not even a glance. Peter tooted the horn. Still, nothing. Time was getting on.

"Give them a push, Dad," Adam said.

"Yeah, a wee bit of a nudge might get them going," Peter said. He keyed the ignition and inched forward, startling the pride. The largest feline announced her annoyance by looking up with a start and growling in a low rumble. Her sisters complied by pulling themselves up from supine positions and moving warily. A slow prickle rose from the base of my neck.

"Roll up the windows, everybody," I shouted. Park regulations required it. A few years after our trip, a woman was bitten on the arm by a lioness through an open window. She bled out and died before she could reach a hospital. We inched up our creaking windows.

Our weak attempt at feline removal was comic because the lionesses simply lay back down and dozed, bored with our intrusion. The sun climbed. We began to swelter lightly in our tin can. Soon, it would be unbearable without a breeze pushing through open windows. To pass the time we ate, read paperbacks, and shot more frames. The kids began to quarrel. Surely the sun would drive the lionesses into the bush for a respite before long.

After what seemed an eternity, sweat began to flow in rivulets down the tawny sides of the lionesses, and the felines got up the juice to leisurely rise, satiated with their nap. They sauntered off, their pretty white bellies swaying. The last lioness in tow paused to spray urine, broadcasting her eligibility and indicating the pride's territory. She was probably in estrus.

Her hormone-loaded urine would attract male suitors from far and wide. They would come loping along very soon, hot on her trail.

"Just two more predators before we hit the Big Five!" Brittany announced.

The African buffalo should be easy to spot, but the elusive leopard would be a challenge.

Time passed in relative calm, compared to the hullabaloo of the lionesses earlier. The tarmac gave way to a sandy road, and the old Landcruiser bumped along the scorched sepia plain. Baobab trees stood bare and tall out on the plain. The spreading branches looked like roots sticking up into the air as if the trees had been planted upside down. The Bushmen called them magic trees because, when they die, the tree rots from the inside and suddenly collapses, leaving only a pile of fibers. The tree disappeared when it died, according to the Bushmen. Void of leaves, the trees stood out like barren scarecrows across the plain. The ubiquitous hooded vultures crowded its branches, sometimes in numbers of up to two dozen. We rounded a bend, and there they were, ugly black creatures bunched up at the bole of a tree. They hissed and pecked, claiming places at the dinner table with their serpentine necks. They departed in a swirl of whooshing wings, and we got a clear view of the carcass—a yearling zebra.

"Oh, poor thing," Brittany said. Vultures consumed all: paws, teeth, and fur.

We drove deeper into our Eden, becoming mere specks against a broad plain, marked by a feather of dust we threw behind us. Africa was a country of unimagined splendor. As the sun rose higher from early morning, colors washed out to ethereal eggshell browns and greens, and finally faded altogether in the heat haze of midday. Now they reappeared in the lateness of afternoon in a suit of different colors—pale pinks and ash of roses, ripe plum, and delicate apricot. Long shadows danced across bushwillow, jackalberry and umbrella thorn.

A river before us carved through a valley, dotted with ancient hardwoods: mahogany, baobab, and marula trees. Undulating spear grass carpeted the valley, now dry from lack of rain due to the dry season. It provided an open landscape for spotting camouflaged carnivores. We turned towards the hills and traveled more slowly, not much more than a running pace. To the right were scattered herds of antelope that scampered about in clusters, merging and then drifting apart to fuse into a new group. We climbed out of the valley, skirted a ridge, and then sped out across the plains towards a low rise studded with date palms. We saw more game now: small herds of springbok far out on the dry savanna that resembled a patina of gold dust on pale earth and reached almost to the skyline. Such an abundance of small prey meant one thing: predators. Our curiosities piqued. We drew in close to the impending event of a leopard sighting, casting MP3 players and earphones and field guides aside.

My mouth went dry, and my heart froze for a long moment and then raced wildly when my eyes alighted on the most stunning creature I'd ever seen. *Leopard!*

Warren was onto the sighting before I could sound the alarm. "Quick! On the left!" he shouted, bursting out of his seat.

Bodies slammed into the left side of the van, faces mashed into glass panes to sight him. A slight movement caught my eye. I peered into a maze of acacia thorn trees next to a riverbed. There, a big cat was in silhouette against the blue sky, enjoying the breeze atop a rocky knoll. His beauty was so magnificent it moved me to tears, like stepping into a cathedral and feeling the presence of God.

Black spots on a base coat of pale tawny yellow stretched across a sloping back with smaller rosettes covering the flank and head. A row of spots spanned the neck like black pearls on a necklace. The entire under part was fluffy white fur. As he stood to move from a crouched position, a long tail snapped the air. He blended in perfectly: a master of concealment. It must've been a male, for it looked to weigh 135 pounds.

"Where? I can't see!" Adam hollered. The light was poor this late in the afternoon as branches met overhead in a canopy.

"He's coming down the side of the hill, out from the boulders!" Peter said.

The leopard's footsteps were inaudible. As he came down from the knoll, large pads lifted up, tilting up into the air before clamping back down again onto the earth. It was an elegant dance of moving forward effortlessly. Across his sloping back were shifting shafts of light cast from an overhead thatch of leaves. He moved with grace that belied his massive shape and size. It was nearly sunset, and he was on the hunt for a meal while the light was low and heat diminished.

When he stepped out in front of our Landcruiser to cross the road a mere ten feet ahead, we could barely contain ourselves. In hushed tones, we whispered high-pitched notes of pure rapture, lost in nature's perfect creation.

The leopard moved languorously onto the road, pausing to stare at us with liquid brown eyes. And then he let out a primal call so full of passion that hairs tickled the back of my neck. It sounded much like a sawing noise. I'd read his call could be heard as far as two miles, possibly directed at a female in estrus nearby. If other males invaded the leopard's territory—established by the scenting of trees with urine or feces and renewed often—it would not be tolerated, and a fight to the death could result. The leopard padded across the savanna and then loped into the distance, disappearing in an instant. The sight of his tawny spots against the backdrop of the dry savanna was as serene as any watercolor.

The Landcruiser exploded into screams, cries, and high-fives. We were undone, wild with pleasure.

"Did you see that?" Brittany screamed.

"Oh, my!" Charlie exclaimed.

"Dude!" Warren and Adam hollered in unison.

"It was simply amazing!" Peter said.

I was too moved to speak. I placed my face in my hands and wept, thinking: *How could anyone kill such a gorgeous creature?* And then, I turned around in my seat to relish the children's joy.

We stared into the spacious void of the bush, hoping the leopard would parade back across the road. We waited.

It grew warm inside. Mom was the first to pry apart her rolling door for more air. We awaited the leopard, trusting him to appear in the bush, hoping he would cross the road again. Brittany moved to sit on the window sill. Warren leapt out to sit on the door frame. Suddenly, Peter was out his door, bent double over the cab of the van, staring into the bush. I sprang out the door with the zoom lens in tow before anyone could squeak a rejoinder. I ran like an Olympian sprinter around to the back of the van, continued a distance, stopped and turned, praying that this would not be how I met my death. *Click, whir. Click, whir.* The family photo of exposed bodies stands sentinel at the threshold of our door at home.

We were racing nightfall to make the closing gate on time. We pulled over beneath the canopy of a baobab tree and crouched over a rudimentary map, searching for a shortcut back to camp. In time, a pickup truck skidded to a stop alongside and a man leaned out of the window.

"Did you pass a cheetah by any chance?" the man asked.

He was a strapping, sun-and-dust-tanned man: "Ranger Douw Grobler, Park Headquarters" was announced across his shirtfront lapel. He was following up on a report of a cheetah with a hurt leg. When we pulled back onto the road, the kids' faces were instantly attached to grimy window panes in search of nature's fastest cat, the cheetah.

We got lost due to absent road signs. We turned left and then right, ending up beside the same gnarly baobab. This time, we drove straight through the four-way crossroad and jolted down a dirt track across the relatively flat terrain. In time, the open plain gave way to thickets of buffalo thorn upon open woodland.

The buffalo thorn puzzled us. I told our group of amateur scientists that I remembered reading of trophy hunters who once sought out the buffalo thorn in search of bovine giants. Bovine giants like the African buffalo—not a good sign. "No one survives a buffalo attack" was the tribal chant up and down the safari bush line. Raconteurs of Kruger Park told us bulls were mean and noxious.

"African buffalo charge unrepentantly for no apparent reason," Kruger Rangers had said. We heard it in hushed tones in the Bush Camp lobbies, kiosks, and cafes. The little-known herbivore was as big as an ox and among the nastiest creatures around, rumored to have killed more hunters than any other creature in the wilds of Africa.

"They have been known to chase people up trees, staying there for days munching grass until the poor guy came down, only to be gored to death. Even if a buffalo ended up wounded, it still circled around, stalking the hunter. The buffalo waited to charge," said Mlengu Mwachofi, an African native who worked at a kiosk.

Foxtail Buffalo grass—favored food of the African buffalo—thickened between acacia trees alongside the road. We drew our breath up short when we saw buffalo spoor in dried mud in the middle of the road. The footprint was a foot deep, the exact impression of a hoof pad cast in plaster of Paris with each crack and fissure of skin imprinted on the sole. A series of them ran together, resembling a line of pot-holes. Suddenly, our tardiness in returning to camp was forgotten, supplanted by a wicked sense of high adventure.

We passed into the evanescent stipple of the forest and entered the mystical. Light shafted theatrically through the leaves, and a silvery mist swirled on the cooling temperatures of late afternoon. A fecund aroma wafted, redolent of earth and dung and animal hide. Riding the breeze was the loud trilling of female cicadas, their drum-like membranes buzzing loudly in hopes of attracting male suitors. The quiver of anticipation was palpable inside the van.

We were more than halfway through the forest when we came upon them: several hundred African buffalo. The number of them was staggering. We approached hesitantly, creeping to a rolling stop to gape in awe. They languished like a herd of domesticated cattle chewing their cud, ostensibly nonplussed with our sudden appearance. Their size matched the vast buffalo herds of Montana, in a time long past, and I half expected John Wayne to ride up and tip his ten-gallon hat in salute. Though the road was unencumbered ahead, the bovine masses widened to both sides of the road around us, filling an area the size of a stadium. My heart galloped at the sight of them.

To the right, females lay in the dry grass. To the left were the great bulls, their thick necks pulsing from massive shoulders. Trumpet-shaped ears and enormous horns nearly a yard long protruded from a base in the head that formed a thick helmet, looking like battle gear. The buffalo emitted a lugubrious air. An audible hush arose from the kids, and we held our breaths in total fascination and watched with delicious terror.

Now and then a calf bawled, bumping its mother to pull on a teat for milk. Juveniles horned up in mock battle as a light mist twirled from snorting nostrils. Mothers called out to their wandering calves with deep grunts that resounded through the forest. When the little ones recognized the signature cries, they trotted back into the safety of the herd. The bulls groaned, and the only movement was the lazy flick of their tails. Stinging flies swarmed over their giant flanks.

Then a movement caught my eye, and I blinked to clear my vision. An enormous bull—the herd's patriarch and commandant of the harem— stood sentinel in front, on watch and guarded. When his horned head swung in our direction, implacable yellow eyes stared back at me. They were sinister looking: pig-like eyes that calculated with murderous intent. I cranked up my window, leaving a crack for the lens of my SLR.

I instantly chided myself. The bull responded to the distraction by lifting a colossal hoof, then began to shamble our way. His horned-head swayed, and hooves thundered on the slow approach, shaking the earth, and carrying the demons that possessed him. He lumbered up to the side of the van and stood glaring at me from twenty feet away, emitting a bovine reek so rank that my eyes watered. He was big as a mountain and black as hell. Dried mud clung to the stiff black hairs of his back and streaks of drool three-feet-long dangled from black lips. From one sharp horn hung wet blades of grass.

We heard teeth grinding on cud and a puffing sound from a wet muzzle. Twin nostrils the size of teacups flared like giant commas. They wriggled and writhed, assessing our scent, puffing in and out, in and out. Hot steam shot forth from them, accompanied by a loud snort and a grunt. When he lifted a front hoof and pounded it into the earth, I grew alarmed. Was this a warning signal? Another loud snort echoed through the dark forest. A shiver shot up my spine. "Peter, back up," I said. "Very slowly. Don't spook this guy."

"I can't."

"What?"

"Look behind us," he said.

I turned my head to stare aghast through the back window, where standing sentinel, was a buffalo with a pair of two-yard-long horns. The deadly horns bobbed up and down as he chewed the cud. His frame filled the expanse of the rear window, and it occurred to me that I was a matador without my red cape. He seemed harmless enough though—it was the fella at my door that held me in a tangle of nerves. My knuckles were white from gripping the door handle. "Do a U-turn off to the side!" I said. I leaned forward to press my lips to Peter's ear, not wanting to frighten the kids. Up to now, we had kept the panic in our voices to ourselves, but now they were on to us.

"What are they doing?" Adam asked with alarm. The black masses swelled, closing in on our toy-sized vehicle.

"I'm not sure," I said. We sat transfixed, considering what to do.

"Move!" Peter shouted at the buffalo. *Beeeeeep!* He blasted a long toot that reverberated through the dark forest without success. There was no reaction from the herd.

"Woof!" Adam shouted from his open window.

"Scoot!" Brittany yelled.

"Get out of the frigging way!" Warren heralded more loudly.

Each of us in turn sent violent echoes forth without any due effect. The herd was oblivious. Their deep raucous groans bore into the very bones of my soul. *Oh, my gawd. we're going to die out here. No one will ever know.* I felt depleted of gumption, all bravery cast upon the African winds. "Push them out of the way!" I roared. I'd had it. But when Peter started up the engine and inched forward, the bull stood frozen, refusing to budge. "Now what?"

"We wait until something changes. Maybe they'll move on soon," Peter said. The light faded, and the orange orb of the sun dropped into the tree canopy that now lay in deep shadow. Crepuscular chill lent an unpleasant air inside.

Something did change as time passed. The merging of the herd was furtive at first, a slight movement here, a shuffle there. The lead bull signaled his harem with an invisible call, so primeval it was beyond comprehension.

Adam was the first to see it happen. I was the first to hear it. I heard a snap. A branch trampled by a fifty-pound hoof … and then another. The masses folded into position as if the dinner bell had rung, and we were the first entrée. Next when I looked, two hundred bovines had surrounded us. "Dad … look," Adam murmured.

Together we all gazed in horror at the two hundred reeking bovines that enveloped the van in the middle of nowhere in the waning light. I turned my head left and then right, peered forward and then aft, and still, the herd filled the depths from all degrees of the compass. It seemed utterly implausible. I imagined we were on a Hollywood set, awaiting a director to yell, "Cut!" It struck me that I was not prepared for this safari business. "Just jam 'em outta' the way!" I implored. I was tired and wanted to go back to the lodge *now*.

"I tried pushing them. It didn't work. Remember?" Peter said, frustrated. Alarm etched his otherwise calm face that was stiff from the strain. As the more sanguine of us two, he rarely got flustered. His alarm was infectious and raced through the van like an electrical current.

Mom prayed. The kids had grown quiet, a genuine sign of fear. And so we sat in waning light as a spectacular red blaze of the African sunset floated across the dense forest like a wishful augury of better things to come. When the sun finally fell into the earth, the night dropped like a blanket. Headlights beaming, we huddled inside the tin can, watching wide-eyed at big faces and glowing green eyes around us. We were utterly flummoxed. Stars slowly began to emerge.

An hour later, along came an ugly, but adorable warthog. The warthog darted out of the thicket and made off down an animal path like a quarterback through a crowd. He ate up track as fast as his stubby legs could carry him, a cloud of dust billowing in his wake. With his spiky tail held high, the hairy figure ran a short distance, and then dashed back into the forest.

We wondered what had spooked him when all of a sudden our breaths were caught up short. A lioness sprang out of the forest after him. Apparently the warthog had blundered into her pride. Our headlights silhouetted the lioness as she converged on the hapless warthog. We sat mesmerized by the scene unfolding before us.

The warthog zigzagged in and out of the forest in an attempt to throw off the lioness. The big cat closed to within a few yards. Her enormous canine teeth glowed yellow-white in the glare of our headlights. When low growls emanated from the forest alongside us, we peered right to see four neon-green saucers floating mid-air, looking bizarre in the moonlight. Two lionesses shot forth like a rocket from the green dots and landed before us in the loom of our headlights. They appeared more ragged than their leader.

Abruptly the lionesses joined forces and accelerated after the warthog. Squeals of terror rode the night air. It made my skin crawl, and I found myself rooting for the warthog. What if it had offspring hidden in a ground tunnel, and was enticing the predators away from its hidden family? The scene pulled at my heart, and I had a difficult time attending to the violence of death.

Always, my thoughts go to the babies. Once you lose a child, it's inevitable, agonizing. My musings took me back to the time, but I pulled back center to focus on the now. The boys were enthralled with the parlay of death: life was still pretty to them. They had yet to suffer through the trials of adulthood. But I gazed over to see Mom less imbued with the realities of Africa. She had lost an infant sister as a young girl, a harsh reality for anyone too young to understand. Even today, Mom still speaks of her lost baby sister, Caroline. I wondered if I would be speaking of Eve when as Mom's age.

The cacophony of sawing growls from the lionesses echoed through the night. Deadly teamwork had enabled the pride to ambush their prey with shrewd skill. The attacking cohorts sneaked in from the sides, clawing the warthog by the haunches. It broke into a fast walk, yelping, emitting another chilling squeal of terror that rang through the air as if on loud speakers. The next lioness pounced, lunging at the throat to inflict a suffocating bite. The final lioness clamped her jaws into the warthog's windpipe. At that, the warthog issued a squealing crescendo so profound that I winced. Afterwards, all was quiet on the forest floor. Death had come quickly.

Two more hours later, time passed into eternity. The night, left to destiny, would fail us, surely. But my heart did a flip flop when headlights loomed from behind us like a beacon of hope. They filled the frame of our rear-view mirror, swelling, until the light overtook us.

A white 4WD came into view and pulled alongside. A man leaned out of an open window.

"You need help?" He shouted with a thick Afrikaans accent as sparkly teeth flashed white in the green glow of his dash, winking like a lighthouse. A lasting radiance fell from his headlights onto the side of the vehicle's white door where green letters announced: "Kruger National Park, Wildlife Management." He was Douw Grobler, the Park Ranger we had met earlier that morning when he was on the hunt to aid an injured cheetah.

We nodded mutely.

"I'm just off work, and you're past curfew, so I'll phone your camp. Follow me," Mr. Grobler said.

From the corner of my eye, I caught a grin on his face. I was taken aback when he moved ahead of us and edged into the buffalo herd with the confidence of a prize fighter. If the big bulls refused to move, he nudged their portly rumps with his fender.

I gaped at Peter and in the dim blaze of the dash, our eyes met and held. We were flabbergasted. So full of the wonder of it all, I sent a kiss into the indigo sky and laughed salaciously. It was a wild maniacal laugh, full of hysteria.

We hastened back to base camp. In a tide of jubilant spirit, we were lost in our thoughts as we followed Mr. Grobler down hidden roads, dark as death. A high moon, partly veiled by swift-rolling clouds, dusted the road yellow-brown. At the Kruger gate, we rolled down windows to thank our savior.

"Are buffalo dangerous?" I quickly asked before the moment was lost.

"Oh yes," Mr. Grobler answered. "They are known to possess an unabated fury with a fierce spirit. It's lucky for you that I came along. I wasn't planning on taking the forest road but chose to at the last moment. I really can't say why."

With that, he lifted his hat and sped away. I wondered and turned around to look at Mom. She flashed me that knowing gaze. I smiled. We were all in this together. At the cabin, we wandered into bed in a heightened state of awareness.

9.

BUDDIES ARRIVE

Landfall at Twilight: Sam and Gary.

Walking with a friend in the dark is better than walking alone in the light.

—Helen Keller

After the safari, we drove back to the Johannesburg airport, kissed Mom and Brittany goodbye and caught a flight to Port Elizabeth. Dick met us at the airport and drove us to the Port St. Francis Marina where *Scud* was waiting for us.

"Let me show you what *Scud* can do! Let's put her to the test," Dick said. It was time for a sea trial.

Right away, I fell in love with the boat. In the main salon, I could lounge in the roomy dinette and peer through an array of windows to all degrees of the compass. Catamaran designs had advanced in marine architecture in the last decade. Today, catamarans regularly crossed oceans, having been designed to handle rough weather and newly outfitted with advanced marine technology. Statistically, multihulls dominated the sailboat market. In any given port during our cruising years, more than half of the private yachts were multihulls.

I began stowing items in preparation for the sail into the Indian Ocean outside the marina. It was blowing a steady thirty knots. It would be lumpy. When I picked up a bouquet of flowers on the main salon table to place in the galley sink, Dick placed his hand on my arm and looked at me with a twinkle in his eye.

"You can leave it there. It'll never move," he said. *I've got to see this*, I thought.

I left the flowers in the center of the table where everyone could see it. I thought about taking bets on whether or not it would stay put. It would surely be one fine mess to clean up if it crashed onto the floor.

I knew it was rough out in the Indian Ocean because the fishing fleet had remained in port due to strong north-easterlies. It made me nervous. But *Scud* shot through the narrow cut and into the ocean like a bullet, bolting like a steeplechaser at the starting gate. A whirling chaos lay before us. The scene was a tumultuous blur of wind and waves. Peter gripped the helm, his face in the throes of ecstasy. One heavy eyebrow went up on his handsome face, and his cobalt-blue eyes widened. He flashed me a smile of sly profundity. "Pretty cool, huh Babe?"

I gave him the thumbs up, feeling his pride.

On a beam reach we flew. Spray jetted away from the bows as they made a clean cut through the waves. We were under full main and genoa. I thought we might be overpowered and should reduce sail. But no, *Scud* handled it like the steeplechaser she was. In time, Dick moved to show Peter how to handle the reefing system. He released the helm to Adam— we would all eventually have a go at steering.

Levers and lines were pulled and pushed until soon, one slab of reef remained in the mainsail. Peter ran over the reefing procedure with Warren. Each line was a different color for quick handling. A novice could easily release a line or lever and bring down the entire roller furling if caught in an emergency.

Winds were howling at thirty-five knots, greater that I had expected. Rooster tails of spray studded with little rainbows danced from the boat's sugar-scoops (the name given to the aft end of the hulls) as the boat raced across the bay. Dick stood on the port bow with his feet splayed, large hands clasped behind his back. He studied the sea intently and moved with grace.

On a beam reach, *Scud* was in her element. It was the right amount of wind and sail area. At no time did I feel threatened. The high freeboard held back the common slap of the sea beneath the boat. The wide bows allowed *Scud* to overtake waves comfortably. Reserve buoyancy prevented them from burying into seas that could cause, in severe weather, a lesser designed catamaran to pitch-pole. All these features would allow us to sail around the world in safety, style, and comfort.

By the time we had sailed back through the narrow cut leading into the marina, everyone felt jubilant, eager to head back out again to begin our maiden voyage. From the cockpit, Dick pointed to the front of the boat. "The windows in the main salon are bulletproof. A violent sea could smash into them without incurring any damage," he said.

Would it come in handy when facing off pirates off the coast of Somalia? I wondered. We would be transiting the Red Sea, eventually. Our bulletproof windows gave me a sense of comfort.

"Your flower vase, Madam," Dick said with a grin as his hand swept over towards the vase that still rested on the main salon table.

It hadn't moved an inch. Remarkable! In fact, I felt emboldened enough to purchase a scarlet geranium to adorn our cockpit table. Never once did it slide off on our Atlantic crossing—a testament to the sea-kindliness of our new St. Francis 44 catamaran.

The next day we began preparing the boat for the passage: provisions were purchased and loaded, gear checked, and weather gathered. Nestled in the Port St. Francis Marina, *Scud* tugged at her dock lines. Every evening at sunset, Peter and I walked the docks to study the fleet of fishing boats: chokka (squid), hake, and pilchard fleets of vessels. The marina was the hub of the South African fishing fleets, which remained at sea for weeks at a time as sea based factories.

In these parts, calamari is also known as squid, chokka, or, simply, *white gold*. South Africa exports the majority of its white gold to Europe. At night, we saw the vessels lit up like Christmas trees in the bay, the winking lights reflecting like bush fires. The sight often took me back to my first night on the beach in Ft. Lauderdale with Peter, when we'd watched the freighters just offshore and when we'd almost been arrested because the undercover police thought we were a rapist and his victim. Massive deck lights illuminated waters to lure in squid caught with a hand line or jig—a colorful lure comprised of a multi-hooked head and a meter of fresh fish chum.

When the chokka vessels returned to port, we awaited the fresh delivery of squid to the marina café and then dashed over to dig into hot calamari rings. Over a tablecloth of newspaper, we gorged on hot fried rings.

It was the fishermen who taught us to understand the local weather. They took a liking to Adam and Warren, since they helped in hauling heavy loads of fish up the canted walkway. We often chatted up the fishermen, hearing about their days at sea and learning about weather patterns while they repaired nets on the dock.

Sometimes the chokka vessels were forced to remain in port when conditions were too dangerous to exit through the marina cut. Once the weather had moderated, the boats hesitated until a break between the swells. Engines ran at full throttle on the final approach as if their life depended on it. Weather in South Africa on the high seas was an arduous task even for the experienced sailor, and certainly not for the novice yachtsman. The weather was worst during the winter months. As luck would have it, we were departing in late autumn. It struck me that we would encounter winter weather, and the thought sent butterflies through my stomach.

Early one morning, a loud crash sent me charging up from the galley and into the cockpit of *Scud*, colliding with Peter and the boys. Standing sentinel on the dock were Sam and Gary, our new crew, surrounded by a mountain of duffle bags bulging with gear, including a long surfboard and a boogie board. The two boys had the glazed eyes of sleep-deprived insomniacs, red with grey shadows that clung to the skin below them. They had traveled for two days, from Iowa.

"Permission to come aboard?" Sam shouted with a grin.

Standing six-feet tall and weighing roughly 225 pounds, his large frame and thick arms made him look like a football linebacker or wrestler. Both attributes would be an asset at sea when the going got rough. Every sailor knows the sage cliché: "stay at sea long enough, and eventually shit hits the fan."

Gary stood next to his older brother, donned in scarlet red foul weather gear. Reflective patches spanned the sleeves—handy when needing to locate him in the blackness of night on the foredeck. Gary possessed an amicable personality. He was easygoing and polite—a lot like his mother, Sybil, a good friend of mine. I could still see the strained look on her face in my mind's eye when she'd agreed to send both of her sons on the ocean voyage. It was like sending your sons off to war and not knowing—but praying—they would return in one piece.

Gary jumped onboard and landed in the cockpit with a thud. I knew he would work out just fine. His sweet presence lent peace in spaces around him. I hoped his calming influence would balance his brother's more bellicose ways.

Warren thumped Gary's back with a hearty welcome. Standing side-by-side, you could almost imagine Warren and Gary as twins because of their similar size and blond hair.

Sam jumped in after him, trailing an oversized duffle that bulged with an eighty-pound fisherman's anchor. It would be our life saver when in unprotected anchorages, exposed to an unforgiving swell. Sam strained with the duffle in getting it aboard, and just as Adam leaned in to give him a hand, the handle parted from the bag and the duffle gave way. The giant anchor landed with a loud clunk onto the cockpit floor. Sam stared in shock at the solitary duffle handle left in his hand. His eyes went wide, and he looked up at Peter sheepishly.

"Oops," he said. "How in the hell did that happen?"

"Whoa, dude," Adam said. "You nearly lost your foot there."

"You okay?" I asked.

Peter and I were mute with shock. The double flanks of the anchor were sharp enough to have severed a toe, if not a foot. The anchor was considered a storm anchor due to its heavy size and advanced design. It easily dismantled into separate parts, making it ideal for a boat with limited space. We planned to use it in the open roadsteads of St. Helena where seas from far away as Africa and South America wrapped around the single island, wreaking havoc in the anchorage.

Nervous laughter echoed between us. Peter appeared less sanguine. His brows were knitted together, and a frown soured his otherwise happy countenance. He bent down to hoist the heavy anchor and get it out of the way less someone got hurt.

The boys hustled into the main salon as my eyes swept over Peter. He stood still with a look of dismay. Where the anchor had been was a large hole. A new owner brushes even the slightest bit of sand from surfaces or wipes away hints of impending rust. A new boat is like a newly acquired Renoir—you protected it with the fervor of a maniac.

"Nice to know we got the first blemish on *Scud*. Now she's just any other boat," Peter said with a chuckle. His ready smile brushed away the previous frown. I was glad the sorry bum who left the hole wasn't me.

With the arrival of Sam and Gary, the four boys settled into a busy, but a pleasant routine of working mornings to prepare the boat for the 6,000-mile passage to Grenada. Once we left the African coast, we would not have access to modern ports for provisions until we reached St. Helena, an island located in the middle of the Atlantic Ocean nearly 1300 miles away. As each day passed, the list diminished. Water tanks were filled, provisions purchased and loaded, extra fuel jugs acquired and filled, and sailing gear reviewed. The boys were eager to lend a hand and help get the chores completed so that afternoons were open for surfing.

There were several surf spots within walking distance of the marina. Given the geological location of Cape St. Francis, it is susceptible to swell year round from large low pressure systems that form between Antarctica and the southern tip of Africa. When a large southwest swell wrapped around the coastline of the region and the prevailing offshore winds came up, the surfing was as good as it got.

Surfing film pioneer Bruce Brown hunted the world's perfect surf spots in the 1960's cult film classic, "The Endless Summer." He put Seal Point on the map. On any given day, the quality, consistency and difficulty of the surf had the four lads bounding off the boat as soon as chores were completed. Because of chilly temperatures, they were donned in wet suits and foul weather gear. I sent them off with granola bars and a liter of hot chocolate for the two-mile trek through the Seal Point Private Nature Reserve.

One evening after a long surf session, Warren spoke of the trek.

"Mom, you and Dad should take some time off and come with us to the Nature Reserve. Just follow the St Francis beach across the street. The path winds across wooden walkways, and we saw a Red Bishop puffing out his plumage for his sweetheart. Jackass penguins, cormorants, and oyster catchers are everywhere! The bright red bills of the oyster catchers are awesome. And a blue crane was just standing there on the beach today!" Warren said.

"Yeah, and the spot is really peaceful," Adam said.

Both boys were avid nature enthusiasts. Some mornings, I'd find one of them nestled down in the cockpit chair watching birds, armed with a pair of binoculars and a field guide. Since they loved to fish, they kept a sharp lookout for swooping birds. If the waters ruffled, they dashed out with rods. Adam could often be found sanding rust from hooks, changing colorful skirts, and replacing weathered monofilament.

One day, after a long afternoon of surfing, the boys returned exhausted and ravaged, shivering. Together we sat down to a meal of freshly baked bread, three barbecued chickens, brown rice, vegetables, and salad. I loved to cook. Their appetites left me beaming. My mother had always had a spread for me and my three siblings when growing up, so I adopted the habit.

Sam was especially appreciative on seeing the spread. "That looks mighty tasty!" he said, digging into his plate.

I worked hard at keeping them well fed, comfortable and busy—best to keep their minds off lesser things like missing home or computer games or the lack of instant TV.

"How was the surf at Seal Point today?" I asked at the dinner table.

"Epic!" Adam said.

"Pumping!" Gary said.

"Quantum!" Warren said.

"Totally nectar," Sam said. He looked at Warren. "You were lighting it up on that wave, Dude."

"It was off the Richter, Man. I got Maytagged in the end," Warren said. "Afterwards I was noodled."

"We party-waved on that one. And I got hell-munched too," Adam said. "Dude, no landlords, either!"

I was relieved to hear this. The boys had picked up the colloquial name of "landlords" to describe great white sharks.

"Nar, nar," Gary said.

Sam looked at Gary, "Hey, you were a paddlepuss, Dude. Never left the shallows. What's up with that?"

Gary looked back at Sam, the whites of his eyes going wide.

"Dude, those were ankle busters, I know, but I was just checking out the gidget next to me," Gary replied with a chuckle.

"That quebee was a surf bunny to that kook who kept trying to cut in on you," Warren said. "Loser."

The four of them could have been speaking a foreign language. Peter and I reveled in their cheerful banter. I caught Peter's eye, and he flashed me a brilliant smile.

"Translation, please?" I asked, laughing.

"It was bitching," Warren said. "Most of the swell was generated from a ground swell with an angle from a south-southeasterly direction. An off-shore wind was blowing in from a north westerly direction ..." His eyes rolled back into his head as if shot by a gun, Clint Eastwood style.

"Right. We get it," Peter said, laughing.

Clean-up after dinner went to the boys. After much debate between them, they settled into a routine of alternating days for dish duty. After dinner clean-up, we gathered for what would become a family favorite— poker. Instead of coins to gamble, we gathered up a pile of red kidney beans. Later, these would be supplanted with the real thing.

The next day, we were up early to drive to J-Bay, a renowned surf spot for the fearless. An exposed point break along Jeffrey's Bay coastline, the site was favored as the ultimate wave ride. But today, waves were closing out, unfavorable for surfing. The surf was up at Bruce's Beauties Beach at Cape St. Francis though.

"Suit up, dudes!" Sam shouted.

"Oh, and keep an eye out for sharks, watch for urchins, beware the rips, and you'd better not snake out!" Warren yelled.

"Translation, please? Oh, never mind," I said.

I was delighted the four boys were having such fun. Their coded language baffled me but cheered me as well. Peter and I sat on the rocks watching the four boys ride the super tubes like the legendary surfers before them. Now and then whoops of joy and high fives were exchanged. Their thrills were infectious, and it lifted my heart.

It struck me that I was very tired. No wonder, we all had been working like boat slaves since our arrival at the marina. I made a mental note to retire early and skip the late night poker with the boys. It wasn't a game I particularly relished. I was lousy at it. A good book was more up my alley. Still, the unusual fatigue I felt gripped me differently than having endured a long day of work. It was as if my whole body ached. Just yesterday, I had lain supine on the foredeck as Peter reviewed the reefing system with the boys. I had been unable to stand through the litany of instructions.

I was fine. Wasn't I?

10.

CAPE OF STORMS

Cape of Good Hope, South Africa

Courage is being scared to death ... and saddling up anyway.
— John Wayne

Peter sat at the navigation station, bent double over weather charts, analyzing GRIB (Gridded Information in Binary) weather data. When I looked at him, he magnified a frown, getting his eyebrows into the act.

"It doesn't look good for leaving tomorrow," he said. "The isobars are squeezed—too much wind. Let's see what Dick says."

National Met Services (NMS) used GRIB code to store and exchange forecast data. Used by the US National Weather Service (NWS), they were popular with sailors. Early in the morning before the sun climbed into its zenith, propagation was good for downloading the data. Since I had my HAM radio license, we could exchange emails with our family and friends. The emails rode the airwaves along with the data. Despite being permitted forty-five minutes of download and upload time per HAM radio station, stations were few and far between, and we often ran out of radio time. GRIB files were long, leaving little— if any— download time for emails. We were forced to be selective in choosing what we downloaded. Since weather data was a priority, many emails were bumped.

Once the data was received, we analyzed it using electronic marine charts and navigation software with a computer laptop. Gathering weather data and analyzing it was the main focus of our days, now that we were ready to depart. Weather files were sometimes downloaded up to three times a day to ensure the safety of the vessel and crew, particularly in rough weather. Many GRIB files were cut off due to the time they took to receive and our limited access. When that happened, there wasn't anything to do but wait until the following day to gather more weather files. We could go for days without getting an email out, especially if propagation conditions were poor.

Later, I came to understand this caused much worry and consternation with Sam and Gary's mother, Sybil. She wanted to hear from her sons every day, but it just wasn't possible. On the odd occasion that emails got through, Sam and Gary's father wrote, begging his sons to get in touch, saying, "Your mother was deeply worried."

Her imagination created horrible thoughts of her sons gone missing if she didn't hear from them on a regular basis, which I understood. But Gary and Sam didn't want to bother. Whenever I mentioned the need for them to write home, they shrugged and continued with their current activity. Their mother's anxiety was the least of their thoughts. Since the two brothers ignored my requests for them to write home, I realized it was up to me. But I had my hands full feeding and caring for the crew, and taking my watch at night. Besides, there just wasn't enough radio time allowed for the correspondence. Sybil obsessed with worry. And who wouldn't be? Her sons were rounding the Cape of Storms—arguably the most dangerous waters in the world.

We would be sailing around the Cape of Good Hope, also known as the Cape of Storms. Thousands of shipwrecks lined the rugged coast. Because of navigational issues, shipwreck casualties on the South African coast were frequent. The Cape of Good Hope was the legendary home of the *Flying Dutchman*, a ghost ship that can never make port, doomed to sail the oceans forever. Sailors claimed to see the ship still today, glowing with a ghostly light. If any sailor ever tried to hail the *Flying Dutchman*, it was reported its crew would try to send messages to their loved ones back home. Tormented crew of the *Flying Dutchman*, damned as ghosts, were forever doomed to beat their way through the wretched waters without ever having succeeded in rounding the Cape of Storms. Any sighting of the ship was deemed to be a portent of doom in ocean lore.

I don't believe in ghosts, but odd events often occur at sea. I could not help but shudder at the thought of seeing a ghost ship at sea. We would be following in its wake. I vowed I would find a cross to wear around my neck at night when on dogwatch, when the imagination runs rampant.

While waiting for Dick's call for imminent departure, I took a walk along the wharf early one morning to watch the fishing boats come in from their night at sea. A fisherman stopped me one morning as he carried a load of white gold to his truck. He looked at me intently.

"Are you leaving today?" The fisherman asked.

"No, but soon. This week, I believe," I said.

"You watch out for that low pressure a comin'. I've lost a few o' me mates to the sea along this devilish shore. They're resting at sea with the mates of 2,300 other shipwrecked crews along this frigging coast since the early days. Before them, a couple hundred Arab trading dhows were lost at sea there too," he said in a thick Afrikaans accent.

The salty character sounded like he had a mouth full of marbles. (Afrikaans was a West Germanic language, spoken natively in South Africa by the early Dutch settlers.) I appreciated his comment and made a mental note of his warning.

"Dick was charting our route around the Cape," I said.

"Ah, right on ya thar. He's a good mate. Dick knows his ropes. You just make sure to be tucked in before that next low pressure comes in, lassie. She's a wicked one, that she is. Ride the favorable currents too. You'll save time. You keep a sharp eye out now," he said in earnest.

"You bet. Thanks," I said, a little shaky, and gave him a wave. His concern warmed my flagging spirit.

I knew the old salt was referring to a dangerous weather pattern that occurred when the low pressure cells moved in a northeasterly direction and ran against the strong Agulhas Current along the coast. Giant waves generated as a result. Dick had warned us about it.

The Agulhas Current ran northeast to southwest and followed the two-hundred-meter contour near the tip of Africa. In places, the current ran up to six knots. When a low pressure hit, the wind could suddenly change from a northeasterly gale to a southwesterly gale in a matter of minutes. It is the interaction between the southwesterly gales against the south flowing Agulhas current that created the monstrous freak waves. Great energy was released when they collided.

Our Admiralty navigational charts announced warnings. "Abnormal waves of up to sixty feet in height, proceeded by deep troughs, may be encountered in the area of the edge of the continental shelf and twenty miles to seaward thereof."

During favorable weather, large oil tankers (too large to transit the Suez Canal) rode the south flowing Agulhas Current, en-route from the Middle East around the tip of Africa. At the Cape of Storms, the Agulhas Current can sometimes meet contrary winds disastrously during unfavorable weather. Dr. Bengt Fornberg, a mathematician at the University of Colorado, studied freak waves. He described the Agulhas Current as focusing waves "like a magnifying glass concentrated sunlight."

"Three or four tankers get badly damaged there every year," Dr. Fornberg said at a conference.

After his findings, the South African Weather Service began to give "freak wave warnings".

But it wasn't freak waves that sent the American-owned tanker *Wafra* to the bottom of the ocean at the Cape of Storms. The *Wafra* went to the bottom right about where *Scud* would be soon—off Cape Agulhas. The tanker had struck a reef. It was February 1971. Not only do devils ride freak waves, but they also scatter reef for wayward sailors to snag.

Oh boy, won't this be fun, I thought.

———————

One day, Dick appeared on the dock at dusk while we were having dinner aboard the boat at the dock. When we heard his knock on the hull, we alighted into the cockpit.

"Be ready tomorrow at first light. It'll be a little rough the first day out because we'll be riding on the tail end of a low pressure system. It'll be lumpy, but only at first. Winds will be light and variable afterwards. We have a short window to Capetown, but we can make it," he said.

A low pressure system?

We sat down to dinner with a sense of foreboding and excitement. Riding my nervous anticipation was the fisherman's caveat of the *Flying Dutchman.* My stomach was tied up in knots. I didn't believe in superstitious tales, but stories of shifting sands, contrary currents, and gales had me worried. I had no idea what I was doing. I felt as if I was riding on remote control mode, but loving it too. How crazy was that?

"Scud," a woman shouted from the dock. I clambered outside to see a woman standing there with a fat loaf of bread.

"Hi, I'm Carol, a friend of Karen's," she said.

Carol had kind eyes and a smile that brightened her face. She was tanned all over, and announced herself as a sailor.

"I heard you were rounding the Cape of Storms with four kids. I wanted to give you this as a token of good luck and friendship from all the people here. I made it myself. We're all rooting for you," she said.

I jumped off the boat and stood beside her. The kind lady handed over a loaf, still warm from the oven. A bow of thatch wrapped its wide girth. I was overwhelmed with her touch of friendship and generosity.

"Oh my, thank you so much," I said.

Dick, true to his word, appeared on the dock at first light with two baked chickens—his sole fare for the two-day voyage to Capetown. He would eat light to refrain from seasickness. My nerves were a wreck. I had slept poorly, eager with excited anticipation and rigid with fear.

Out in the Indian Ocean, we hit gusty winds right away, but the seas were moderate at six to eight feet. *Scud* shot forward, meeting the sea with ease and confidence. On the foredeck, Dick stood by as Peter grappled with the reefing system, taking turns to work with each one of the boys.

We rounded Cape St. Francis feeling the rhythm of the sea as an orange orb rose above a distant horizon. Our speed rushed us toward Seal Point, where the boys had spent long hours surfing. I fell back as the Seal Point Lighthouse stood sentinel in swirling mist. It was under attack by a multitude of heavy seas that crashed at the base, looking like geysers. The wind whipped the ocean before us into a maelstrom.

"Stay at the two hundred meter soundings, three miles offshore,"

Dick said. "We'll have protection from the fierce headwinds from Cape Agulhas ahead."

He explained we were taking evasive action from rough seas by staying clear of waters seaward of the continental shelf.

"Remain inshore, inside the 200-meter line. The continental shelf is at the six hundred feet contour line, roughly three miles or less offshore. The Agulhas Current is strongest next to the continental shelf edge, attaining rates of three-four knots or more at this time of year. It's our rhumb line to Capetown," Dick said.

By afternoon, conditions had eased considerably. An easy afternoon of sailing segued into nightfall. It was my dogwatch, the 2-4 AM pre-dawn watch. Living in close quarters with five males often left me feeling claustrophobic. Taking the helm seat alone at night enlivened my spirit. Despite being considered the least favorable watch, I relished my personal time beneath a vault of glistening stars, listening to the wind and call of the sea. For me, it was a solitary time for reflection. I often sang to myself, lost in the wonder of being out of sight of land. Without ambient light, stars punctuated the night sky so heavily it felt magnificently magical. Afterwards, I fell heavily into bed, and into a deep snooze, feeling centered as if I had jogged five miles on an empty beach.

By midmorning, I awoke to slight seas. Curious, I stumbled out to see Dick picking at a breakfast of bread and boiled eggs. The sails were full. The sun was shining brightly against the backdrop of a clear blue sky. We were moving at a fast clip in light winds. *Scud* clawed her way southwards. She sailed like a witch.

Adam stood at the rail unwinding monofilament from a yoyo, a circular half-tube that looked like a doughnut. With 200 pound test, the fishing line was led behind the boat. Bright pink lures with skirts attached were a tuna's favorite dinner.

"Gearing up for a big one, Adam?" I asked.

"Morning, Mom. How was your watch last night?" Adam said.

"Oh, rather uneventful—no shipping traffic. No *Flying Dutchman* either, gawd forbid," I said.

I went over and wrapped my arms around him from behind in a love greeting. He turned around and put his arm around me.

"How fast are we going?" I asked.

"Ten knots! We picked up the Agulhas current this morning. It added four knots to our speed. Whoopee!" Adam shouted into the wind.

"Be ready on that reel too," Dick said with interest. "Soon as we pass over the Agulhas Banks, you'll see a bounty of fish. The warm-water current meets the cold water current and turns back on itself. It might even happen first at Cape Point. Just you wait."

By midday, winds were light and variable as forecasted. *Scud* roared along with both engines to maintain top speed. It was critical for us to reach Capetown before the next low pressure hit. They had been coming every four to five days. We did not need any freak wave warnings. One day while listening to the BBC via high-frequency radio, I heard an amazing statistic.

"One ship every week is lost at sea from anywhere in the world," said the broadcaster of a Science and Nature Radio Follow-up segment.

"One ship was cleaved in half," reported Captain Malloy in 1974 when describing freak waves at the tip of Africa.

The next day was exceedingly still. I came up on deck and greeted Warren at the helm with a hug, walking to the side of the deck to collect the morning harvest of flying fish. Two fat fish proved worthy of my frying pan.

Warren gave me a look.

"How can you eat that crap? They're already dead," he said, shooting a teasing snicker.

"Ah, but these fine fish are tasty with scrambled eggs, my lad," I said. "Makes hair grow on your chest." It was a common phrase my Dad had used whenever I refused to eat my Brussels sprouts.

Dick stood on the port bow, hands clasped behind his back. If I did not see him in the cockpit or main salon, I knew I could find him in quiet repose on the foredeck. Sam and Gary busied themselves at the salon table, folding paper airplanes to dive bomb the sea birds. A great many of them dipped across our stern, picking off pilchard and anchovies.

"Thar she blows!" Warren shouted.

Arm extended like a yardarm, he sprang up from the helm seat and pointed abeam of the boat.

Sam and Gary leapt up from the table; Peter and Adam came running up from below decks, having been sleeping off watch. The more one slept, the better for the whole crew. Peter insisted on not engaging the auto-pilot to ensure that wayward hands were at the helm and not busy with other distractions. Good sleep off watch kept one sharp when on watch.

"Over there! Three o'clock position," Warren shouted again.

A mile off to our starboard side, a distinctive V-shaped stream of misty vapor jetted from the surface. The geyser shot fifteen-feet into the air, straight up like a rocket on take-off. The whale lay lollygagging on the surface, seemingly unaware of our presence. The stout body was dark grey, resembling the underbody of an overturned boat. It shone, reflecting morning rays like a mirror. The whale lazily undulated in the sea as if it were asleep. We held bated breaths as one. We felt miniature in size next to its vast size and girth. The tail of the whale extended past our stern another ten feet. Fortunately, the whale showed no signs of aggressive behavior. Despite the whale's lack of interest, I had good reason to fret.

Not long ago, a South African couple had the fright of their lives when a southern right whale launched itself onto the deck of their sailboat. Sailing instructor Ralph Mothes and his partner, Paloma Werner, of Capetown Sailing Academy, were sailing the yacht *Intrepid* off the coast of Capetown when they spotted a whale breaching out of the water some distance away. Suddenly it got close to them, leaped out of the water and crashed right on top of the yacht. No one was hurt, but the sailboat was totaled.

"Maybe we should pull away, give the chap some room—say a couple hundred miles," I said. The eye of the whale was freaking me out. It appeared way too docile and confident around our little boat. "Throw him an Oreo and pray he dives for it," I shouted to Adam, who was standing at the rail.

The humor masked my concern. Other than dairy cows—the most feared mammal in the world *to me*— whales followed close behind on my list of "creatures to run from". Memories as a little girl of wandering into pastures with a bouquet of wild flowers and sprinting from charging bulls haunted my dreams. How did I know they were just curious, seeing hay and expecting dinner?

Gary looked pensive while he flipped through pages in a field guide, studying the whale as it finned alongside.

"Look here. This male has the largest penis of any other living mammal!" A smirk alighted on his handsome face.

"Lucky devil," Warren said. "He'll be a hit with the ladies."

Gary possessed a passion for the marine environment. Our floating universe around *Scud* was a laboratory. I was pleased we could give him this experience up front and close. I hoped our sons were getting it. A divine design was happening here again—just as in Kruger Park. Who could ignore such magnificence? It made me smile inside. We sailed in a virtual Eden. Charles Darwin was not here on the *HMS Beagle*, but he should have been.

"Nice, Gary. I like that," said Sam.

He slapped Gary hard on the back. Gary reeled and then fell into the life lines and onto the deck. My eyes went wide, considering the possibility of him tumbling overboard with the whale as his new traveling companion.

"Yeah, smart, Dude," Adam chimed in with a grin. He reached down to pull up a stunned but smiling Gary.

"It's a southern right whale," Dick piped up. "He's feeding on the nutrient rich waters of the currents: krill, shrimp-like crustaceans, snail-like mollusks. Named as the "right" whale to hunt because they swam slow and close to shore. Uncontrolled hunting contributed to them being nearly exterminated."

Suddenly the great shape breached, hurling forty tons of ponderous grace towards the clouds. As gravity took hold, the whale fell back down into a thunderous reunion with the sea, smacking the surface with a resounding crack like cannon fire. A storm of spray erupted in its wake. As it fell into the sea, the whale rolled to one side and dove, lobtailing the fluke of a tail that jutted from the surface. We watched, breathless.

The wind died and with it went the choppy seas, leaving us motoring in a milk pond. We soon discovered the attraction for the whales: vast schools of thousands of fish surrounded the boat. Immersed in a moveable feast of plankton, the fish fed on the nutrient rich currents flowing past. We had reached the great convergence zone where the cool and warm currents converged. It created a unique environmental setting for a startling diversity of marine life, resulting in a major upwelling of sea life.

I looked down into the clear waters and felt transfixed as sunlight beamed into the depths far below. Visibility was limited because of the highly concentrated sea life in the soupy sea. It was like trying to peer through a shifting blanket. Fish beneath the surface shone like meteors that darted back and forth in one fluid motion.

And then the skies filled with blackness. At first my skin prickled from the unusual sight and then we all rejoiced. Shearwaters, petrels, penguins, albatross, terns, tropicbird, and skuas took turns punctuating the sky. They arrived in masses, feeding on the great numbers of fish. On and on they all came. It was like watching the stage set of Hitchcock's legendary Hollywood horror flick "The Birds."

Marine biologists regarded these waters as a distinct biotic province: immense concentrations of the microscopic plant life called phytoplankton. This rich sea pasturage supported vast populations of zooplankton, small floating animals ranging up to shrimp-size krill on which the seabirds, seals and whales fed.

Ppphhtt. Pphhhhttt.

The smooth sound caught my attention from the other side of the boat. Adam dashed across the netting between the hulls on the foredeck, making it to the opposite side in two swift bounces on the trampolines. Dusky dolphins cavorted above the surface, riding the bow waves like gymnasts of the sea. They filled the horizon to all points of the compass. We saw hundreds— perhaps thousands—of dusky and bottle-nosed dolphins. Their aerial acrobatics held us mesmerized. If one breached, others followed suit, executing a series of graceful leaps and somersaults as beautiful as a performing group of ballerinas.

Beneath the surface, the dolphins relished a game of chicken. Two and three at a time sped towards the boat on a bee-line like a homing torpedo. Just before they hit the boat, the gaggle of juveniles veered off at the very last nanosecond. On show now, two dolphins posed alongside the boat like runway models, pausing ever so slightly for photographs. Just as my camera whirred, they streaked down into the depths of the ocean. My resulting image was nothing but ocean.

I laughed. *Those little devils*, I thought.

Despite the absence of a breeze, the water boiled from the swirling of immense schools of small fish—sardines, anchovies, and pilchard. The clouds of fish were so dense, they appeared as swirling rivers of glistening silver in the bright sunlight. Fish erupted from the waters, caught in the flushing of our bows. When one landed on the deck, it flopped back and forth, seeking its home back in the sea. Gary rushed forward to free it from instant death, flipping it back into the sea with a soft bunt of his toes.

A loud thwack boomed across the waters.

"Man!" Warren shouted, pointing into the distance. "Did you see that? A giant manta ray just catapulted! Its wingspan had to be at least ten feet!"

116

We turned our heads in unison, looking for more of the springing rays. As if on cue, a large manta shot from the depths of the sea and careened for the heavens at eighty miles-per-hour, the speed of an Olympian tennis player on serve for the final match-point. At the vortex of its height, the leviathan paused in mid-air as if for applause. Then it tumbled in a free fall, somersaulting and spinning like an expert diver immersed in an impressive high jump from a platform three stories high. It tumbled gracefully into the sea, as a crescendo of sound resounded across the surface louder than a bull horn.

The African penguins called out to their kind, making awkward noises like those of jackasses.

"The black and white coloring of the penguins is a vital form of camouflage called countershading. It works from above by blending the penguin's black back into the ocean bottom, and from below by blending the white belly into the surface of the water," Gary explained.

"That's amazing stuff, Professor!" Sam shouted.

Gary beamed.

We sailed close to the tip of Cape Agulhas, a sanctuary for birds and sea life. Dense vegetation and thousands of nesting birds made the cape stand out like oases in a boundless sea. From our vantage point, a raucous conclave of nesting penguins crowded the tip of the peninsula. Ill-designed for land, the penguins became the epitome of grace and competence in the sea. Their wings were useless for flight, so they became powerful flippers; webbed feet were like rudders. Groups of penguins hopped up the slanting ledges of rocky crags. They bounced from boulder to boulder like kids in a sack race. I was charmed by their deceptively doll-like appearance. Time and again, I watched the penguins leap from clear out of the water, and then slip back in again.

On my way forward from the cockpit to lounge on the dolphin seats, which were built into the bow pulpit (the forward tip) of each hull, I glanced curiously at a ripple in the water. A head popped up. We stared at each other. The fellow was more surprised than me. He stared curiously back at me. I made out the dark fur, round eyes, small ears, and tufts of whiskers as the sea otter's head bobbed up and down.

The sea otter rolled onto his back, craned his neck, and opened its mouth in a yawn, revealing a fleshy pink interior. Then he lay back to sunbathe. His thick, lustrous coat blended from reddish to dark brown. The luxuriant pelt was once his ticket to imminent death back in the days when fashion prized the coat. Today, the otter is an endangered mammal, saved from extinction.

Two surfaced together close by the boat. They snuggled, touched noses, and groomed each other in childlike play. They swam languidly, then porpoised methodically alongside to hunt. The larger one dove and surfaced with a writhing kelp crab. With nimble forepaws, it grasped the end and crunched as if munching an ear of sweet corn. The otter laid back to float after gulping it down, satiated with his catch. Its belly bulged and glistened in the morning sunlight. The other otter, tantalized by its mate, disappeared beneath the surface and brought up a flat stone and sea urchin. A prickly armor of black spikes shielded the tasty morsel. With its dexterous forepaws, the brown fellow floated on its back alongside his buddy and broke the urchin against the stone, eating the flesh with relish. Breakfast now over, they ignored a school of silvery pilchards nearby.

They were not wary of our slow approach. They appeared curious, but shy.

"Woof, woof," Warren howled, imitating their nasal bark of alarm.

The otters looked up and charged towards the boat, disappearing below the depths at the last second. Later, we knew otters were present by their snort of alarm. Often they eluded our search for them, as we clambered into the cockpit with binoculars, cameras, and video recorders.

And sure enough, despite my initial qualms to passage around this dangerous tip of Africa, we motored safely around the Cape of Good Hope, two miles offshore. Against the backdrop of Vasco de Gama Peak lay the rusty hulk of a shipwreck stranded on its rocky shoreline. Huge swells crashed over the rocky ledge against the cliffs where a bridal train of white froth streamed into the open sea.

The "Cape of Storms" was later renamed by John II of Portugal as "Cape of Good Hope," because of the great optimism engendered by the opening of a sea route to India and the East. Since departing two days ago from the marina, we had passed by Wreck Point, Storm Point, Needles Point, Flesh Point, Bull Point, and Danger Point. We motored past Martha's Reef, Atlas Reef, Miles Barton Reef, and Bulldog Reef. We motored above Six Mile Bank, Twelve Mile Bank, Rocky Bank and East Shoal, York Shoal, Hell's Gate, Judas Peak and False Bay. The vivid names caused me to shiver. Such wicked sounding spots. I studied the route on the chart with shaky fingers. The town names were equally interesting:

Hottentotshollandr, Kleinriviersberge, and Babilontoringberge. When pronounced, they sounded as if marbles swirled in my mouth.

As we neared landfall, I took the helm seat and was on watch when a large shape of an albatross glided past me overhead, casting me in a momentary shadow. Its impressive wingspan exceeded ten feet. Riding the wind, it circumnavigated the world in the southern latitudes without ever touching land.

"Oh look!" I shouted. Everyone came running.

"That's Albatross Island," Dick said, pointing ahead.

When we entered Table Bay, a thousand or more seabirds hovered over the wake of a large trawler. Their mass looked like a great cloud of white and shadowed the rusty hulk of the vessel. A cacophony of screeching resounded across the bay. Their antics of swooping down to pluck residual fish left in the inky waters behind the trawler transfixed us.

Against the backdrop of the vessel rose magnificent Table Mountain. It stood sentinel over the modern metropolis of Capetown. A flowing river of cascading clouds swirled in white masses and drooped over the summit. Pine trees clung precariously to footholds on each ledge. As we neared the 2,000-meter-high mountain, a black cloud swept by, filling a gorge with cottony mist. Then the sun came out and swept away the cloud, supplanting the dark mood of the mountain with a renewed cheery disposition. It seemed an augury of good things yet to come, but I had my doubts.

Big cities meant big trouble. The lure of late nighttime entertainment drew young men in like flies. I knew that Peter and I could keep our sons under wrap, but Sam was a different matter altogether. At 18, he could be a problem keeping on the boat at night. I was against him experiencing the excitement of Capetown, but I feared him drawing our under-aged sons into the night and off the boat without parental permission. Visions of discovering empty berths at 2 AM held me in a cold sweat. I feared the dangers they would face on land much more than I feared the dangers of the sea. Drugs and sex held male teenagers captive to their testosterone. South Africa's extreme poverty and violence were well established. I knew I'd have to do my best at being in charge of four teenagers who were dying to bust loose after having been at sea several days.

When the clouds over Table Mountain returned to blanket the summit in white cloth, my mood darkened with it.

We made our way into a narrow channel and approached a small bridge that served as a walking boardwalk for the marina. When we passed beneath the bridge, crowds formed by the wayside, gawking at our appearance. Normally, large fishing vessels plied these waters. A modern catamaran was an uncommon site, I surmised. I felt proud. We had rounded the Cape of Good Hope, a great accomplishment to be sure. A few cameras flashed amongst the crowd, and we all waved.

With ease, we entered a slip in the Victoria and Alfred Waterfront Marina. Just as we finished dressing the ship by coiling ropes and tightening halyards, Karen appeared to collect Dick. There were handshakes all around, heartfelt thanks and goodbyes.

At night, a horned moon rose within the frame of the hatch above us. I watched as a pale halo formed around it and in the darkness, I succumbed to a deep slumber like a drunken woman. A gaggle of footsteps resounded heavily on deck but receded into the distance just about the time I succumbed to fuzzy dreams.

11.

CAPETOWN CHAOS

Sea Point Surf Break, Capetown

*I put my heart and my soul into my work, and have lost my
mind in the process.*

—Vincent Van Gogh

The next morning, the boys worked with Peter filling water tanks and scrubbing decks. A gooey mass of salt crust had enveloped the rigging from the passage. Down below, a talk show host held my attention as I worked a fat piece of dough into bread.

"My baby will die from AIDS if I don't get my hands on some drugs! Why can't the government allow free drugs to save my baby?" a woman screamed on the show.

I cringed at her words. It was 2002. HIV/AIDS was a full-blown epidemic in South Africa: one in 10 South Africans and one in four mothers suffered from infection with HIV/AIDS.

"President Mbeki claims HIV doesn't cause AIDS," said the radio talk show host.

Suddenly Thabo Mbeki's voice wailed over the air waves as the announcer patched in a recording.

"HIV does not cause AIDS. Poverty, bad nourishment, and general ill health are the main causes of AIDS, not HIV," shouted Thabo Mbeki, the second post-apartheid President of South Africa. "Personally, I don't know anybody who has died of AIDS," Mr. Mbeki said.

I was flabbergasted and turned up the volume.

"You've GOT to be kidding!" I yelled and slammed the dough down hard on the countertop. Seven million people were living with HIV in South Africa.

At that moment, Sam ducked his head into the galley.

"Someone's gotta' shoot that man. He can't be living in the real South Africa," he said. His eyes went to the loaves in my bread pans. "Yummy! When will they be ready?"

Together we listened to the continuing interview with Tim Sebastian of "BBC Hardtalk" with South African President, Thabo Mbeki. I relished Sam's comments on the radio commentary. His keen interest in world affairs was infectious and I enjoyed our talks together.

Mbeki refuted scientific research, aligning himself with dissident scientists who rejected the link between HIV and AIDS. He insisted expensive Western medicines would not be the solution. Even the health minister, Manto Tshabalala-Msimang, was off her marbles. She proposed garlic, lemon juice, and beetroot as AIDS remedies. I figured that Health Minister Manto Tshabalala-Msimang, President Thabo Mbeki, and AIDS denialists must've all been drinking buddies in creating such nonsense.

Thabo Mbeki continued to rant. "Nonsense, absolute nonsense..." Mbeki retorted.

His denial of the causes of AIDS caused him to reject offers of free antiretroviral drugs, which would prevent the transmission of HIV from mother to child during labor, and grant money. Women revolted. Their babies were dying of HIV infection at an alarming rate. They called in to the show, demanding to voice their pleas for assistance. Some wept. Some stammered with indignation. All were irate.

Infection with HIV had once been a real threat to me. In 1983, an emergency blood transfusion was required after the death in utero of our first baby, Eve. Fearing tainted blood reserves carried the virus, my intuitive female doctor had prescribed intravenous B-12 (iron supplements). Her medical colleagues confirmed her suspicions, but the public had not been fully aware of the HIV/AIDS impending pandemic at that time, and many blood reserves were tainted. Not long after my hospital stay, the news media covered gripping tales of women who were infected from bad blood in the hospital. Only then were more strident measures finally adopted for screening blood supplies. I never forgot how close I had come to becoming infected. I've steered clear of hospitals ever since, unless an emergency.

I chilled at the thought of anyone onboard our boat needing to visit a hospital. I needed to maintain a sharp eye on the four boys, all of whom relished active sports. Preventing injury was a serious challenge, especially when they saw themselves as omnipotent. If President Mbeki denied the threat of HIV, I felt certain local hospitals were not screening blood donations for the virus. I needed to keep my guys safe.

According to research by Harvard University later in 2008, the AIDS policies of Mbeki's government were directly responsible for the avoidable deaths of more than a third of a million people in South Africa. I felt the acute stress of a mother hen in a country where not even the government looked after their people adequately.

Once we checked in at the marina office, we stopped to grab some grub and meet visiting sailors at a trendy cafe. While waiting for cokes and burgers, I noticed a middle-aged man with a teenage boy at the bar. I surmised they were Americans by the man's accent, so I wandered over.

"Hi, would you like to join us?" I said. I was eager to establish new friendships for ourselves and the kids.

"Great. Sure," the man said. "I'm Nick, and this is my son, Earnest."

Nick was of mid-height and stocky. He presented a nice smile and appeared sunburned. Bits of skin flaked across his nose and tops of ears. Probably from a recent sailing passage, I thought. His eyes were sunken with grey shadows. He didn't appear to be very active. The boy was tall and wide. Something about him gave me pause. He was slow to respond and walked with a slight limp when he approached our table. When they sat down, Earnest seemed physically and mentally challenged by his lack of people skills and muteness. My curiosity rose. Having such a handicap on an ocean-going sailboat was a real challenge, and yet I admired the father for it.

"I commissioned a forty-two foot catamaran to cross the Atlantic this winter. My son and I dubbed it *Running Wind*. We sailed south from Durban two months ago. Right now we're repairing gear that failed on the shakedown passage. I expect we'll be ready for sea in a couple of weeks," Nick said.

Over the next hour, we shared brief sailing histories. I was shocked to learn Earnest had no bluewater sailing experience. More surprising was the fact that Nick had little bluewater experience other than coastal cruising back home in the USA.

"I've hired a captain and 1st mate to help us deliver the boat to the US. I've never met them, but they came highly recommended," Nick said.

My concerns over how a physically and mentally challenged boy could handle rough seas eased somewhat. Hiring a strange captain and crew without having interviewed them personally nearly threw me out of my chair. What if they didn't get along? I knew of several yacht deliveries that quickly went sour with strange crew.

Once sailing away from the coast of Africa, Nick's next port was St. Helena Island. Located in the middle of the Atlantic Ocean, St Helena was so tiny and remote that it lacked a runway. One could only leave the island by mail boat back to Africa. What happened if the boy needed help or wanted to get off the boat? What if Nick wanted to throw the captain off?

We continued in animated conversation. Although Earnest was quiet, his eyes listened with attention. The boys gave him the respect he deserved and talked to him. It made me proud that they made Earnest feel comfortable and well at ease.

Whereas public school students might bully Earnest, our sons knew such abuse was not acceptable. Bullying did not exist amongst their homeschooling peers who lived aboard boats. When a new kid sailed into the harbor—older or younger, male or female—our boys and their friends swam over to invite the new kid to outdoor games ashore. New friends were few and far between so kids got to know each other before they sailed away.

We continued in conversation with Nick and Earnest, feeling a sense of kindred spirit. As we got up to go, we promised to keep abreast of each other's departure plans in attempts to stay together. It was hit or miss since they berthed in a marina far from the Alfred Victoria Waterfront.

At the last second, I queried Nick about the bulky cast on his hand.

"I lost half of my thumb during a robbery in front of my five-star hotel in Durban. I exited the front doors, turned the corner, then bam! Two youths accosted me and tried to grab my backpack. I fought back. Everything I owned was in that backpack: boat papers, passport, credit cards, and cash! One of the guys pulled a knife," Nick said.

He held up his cast.

"This was all I have left—half a finger. I'm a musician and right handed. Never found my finger. Passports, cash and credit cards—all were gone," Nick said with a look of dismay.

My fears about violence in South Africa were confirmed. I didn't have the heart to bring up the issue of AIDS and tainted blood. Later, we shopped for jerry jugs to fill with diesel fuel and extra water. The boys ran off to peruse V & A Waterfront Mall shelves to fetch specialty items.

One morning Peter called the boys up on deck to review the proper procedure for reefing the mainsail. Each of the boys had a go and grasped the method quite easily. When it came to my turn to practice, I remained supine, lounging on the deck. I suddenly found myself swaying. I felt dizzy and weak. In the cool air of early winter, I felt hot beneath a wool sweater. I tore it off.

"I'll just watch you guys tackle it," I said with far less confidence than I felt. What the heck was going on with me? *Just the stress*, I told myself.

The pounding of fists on deck bolted Peter awake and out of bed in the darkness of night. He dashed into the dark cockpit as a cacophony of what sounded like stampeding bulls resounded. I stumbled behind him, grabbing a rolling pin, my weapon of choice, along the way, for what, I hadn't a clue. Clambering into the cockpit, I expected to see a gaggle of men, but my mouth went slack-jawed when I saw golf ball-sized hail hammering the bridge-deck at the back of the boat.

The giant balls rebounded off the decks and into inky waters. Around us floated a bumpy white carpet. Illuminated by ambient light, the large hail resembled bobbing eyeballs. I ducked back inside to avoid being hit. Sounds of crashing hail echoed from the sides of the boat. I felt as if I was inside a steel drum plunging over the Hoover Dam. The roar was tremendous. Curious, I ducked my head outside. In the fading moonlight, the sky was heavy with bruised clouds; lightening streaked across the sky. The pyrotechnic display was mesmerizing.

Alerted by the raucous noise, the boys stumbled from out of their cabins. We peered together through the ominous darkness, dumbfounded. The docks misted in layers of large hail as high winds buffeted, sending floating hail careening against pilings in small waves. Strong gusts bucked the boat, straining mooring lines. A winter gale was upon us.

Peter hollered, "Grab more warps. Let's get this baby nestled back in her crib!"

The boys sprang into action. Leaping out of the cockpit, they threw open deck lockers, thrusting entire bodies into depths of giant bins to claw out ropes. As the boys darted about with lines, our boat began to resemble a spaghetti factory. Wet piles of rope were strewn wide across decks, folded into fat loops like fettuccini. Nimble fingers hastily tied rope ends into bowline knots. Together the four lads leapt onto slick docks to secure lines around dock pilings while checking for damage and inspecting cleats. Any minute, a cleat could tear out of the dock, sending *Scud* into concrete pilings.

"Be careful! I shouted. "Don't slip!"

One trip to the hospital and it'd be all over.

The low pressure that had descended upon us was a red light to stay in port, but it was a green light for the kids. The next morning after the storm, they hit the beach, eager to ride the big waves. I stood in the foggy haze and stared at Table Mountain. It was every shade of orange in the morning light.

All of the boys appeared in the cockpit doorway early the next morning, donned in the ubiquitous uniform of the surfer: board shorts, rash-guard, wet suit, truckers cap, dark shades and flip-flops. I quickly grabbed my camera gear and followed along behind them. Together we began the long trek to Greens Point, the first surf site on the boys' bucket list.

We passed through a park, void of visitors because of the cold temperatures and gusty winds. I sent the boys on while I stopped for take-out at a coffee bar. As I fumbled for empty change in a knapsack, my eyes darted at the large headlines splayed across the Cape Times newspaper.

"Boy, 14, Is Second Victim in Less than a Week." I grabbed the Times and tossed down a few coins. Slowly, I ambled out of the shop with a pit in the base of my stomach.

At the park, I lowered myself onto a bench to read the story as coffee swirled in the cup.

"Tim Stewart, 18, from Capetown, was attacked while surfing off the popular King's Beach in Port Elizabeth and needed surgery to repair his leg. At least eight surfers and body boarders have been bitten by sharks on the same coastline since May. One of the most horrific attacks was on champion body boarder Neil Stephenson in May—his badly mauled right leg needed amputating."

I lowered the newsprint, drank coffee, and laid my head back onto the back of the cold, wooden bench. This voyage had turned into an adventure fraught with way more danger than I had ever anticipated.

I knew sharks. Sharks inhabited the Florida coasts; surfers were accustomed to a few sightings a year. But in South Africa, the cold waters of Antarctica attracted an abundance of seals, which lured in predator sharks like the mako and great white. I breathed a great sigh.

My dire warnings to the kids elicited a mute response and roll of the eyes. I decided I would plant myself on the beach and analyze each wave with my long lens. At least I could alert the boys to any lingering sharks. If they wouldn't heed my earlier warnings, maybe at least now they might.

I met up with the boys at the park, and together we stood in silence. All around us lay in ruin. The sidewalk lay smashed into broken slabs of concrete, and a stainless steel fence had folded upon itself from the raging sea during the previous night storm. Where once there had been a lawn was now a salty pond due to storm surge. The sea was still angry. Long barrels with foamy heads curled onto the beach, crashing with violent force. The weather had restrained a fleet of merchant ships offshore, their half-mile long vessels flagging from China, Panama, and Japan.

The boys momentarily forgot about the storm ruin and focused on the sea. In the foreground, elongated ribbons of kelp undulated in the current, its blades wide and green and resembling mermaid hair. The kelp bed extended from the low waterline to the edge of the surf. Behind it rose barreling waves. As they collided with the beach, water raced up the embankment before receding into the sea, pulling rocks and storm debris along with it. I made sure to stand back to avoid being dragged into the rip. High winds tore at my jacket and clawed at my pants. I felt tiny next to this display of pure, violent power. The sight was formidable.

Adam and Warren moved to don gear: black wetsuit, board, and leash to the ankle. Off they went into the sea. Sam and Gary stayed behind to regard the scene. Sam looked sanguine, but Gary less so. He appeared more daunted by the thunder of the sea. Eventually, Sam pulled on surf gear, grabbed a boogie board and jogged into the sea. Gary stayed back. In time, he pulled away to walk the beach, alone with his thoughts.

I set up a tripod, mounted a photographic zoom lens, and pretended to scout for good shots while acting as a lifeguard. All three boys had donned black wetsuits, so it was hit or miss seeing who was up and who was down. They were so close to the ships anchored behind them that it was a short swim to reach them. My belly cramped as I watched the scene unfold. It seemed as though the whole ocean was rearing up ahead of them, gathering itself to hurl down upon the surfers like a raging sea serpent. In time, my fingers became numb from the cold, and my eyes sore from peering intently into the view finder.

I sat and studied the three black forms, ready for any sign of trouble. I didn't have a chance to save them if anything went sour. But keeping vigil was the best I could do.

All of a sudden, Warren shot off his board and harpooned straight into the sky, flying, flying, and flying. I let out an audible moan and jumped up to press my face into the viewfinder. The lens zoomed into the scene. Warren's surfboard was still careening backwards like a slingshot, a rooster tail of spray scudding from the board tip. He landed in the water, far from the board. I darted the lens back and forth, left and right, scouting for sharks. Nothing. My heart thudded in my ears. Any second now, I half expected to see a fin cut through waters. I was ready to tear off my coat and charge into the surf. When Warren surfaced, he looked around to all degrees of the compass, and then turned to chase the drifting board.

My body trembled, imagination running away with me.

Hours later, when the surf team eventually rode a wave into shore, they dragged weary bodies up the beach.

"Hoorah! Man! What a ride! Awesome!" Warren hollered as he lumbered towards me.

"Ah man, that was SO sweet!" exclaimed Adam.

"Best, Dude!" yelled Sam. He slapped Gary on the back. "Dude, why didn't you come in?"

"Maybe tomorrow, Sam. I'll see," Gary said with a sigh.

"What was with the sky diving act?" I asked Warren, trying to sound nonchalant.

"Oh, that? Yeah. Weird. I was going like a train on a big one when something grabbed my fin. I thought I was a goner. Shark, probably. But no, when I caught up with my board, fat blades of kelp were entangled around the fin. Funny, huh?" Warren's face glowed with animation.

For the next two weeks, the boys surfed every beach around Capetown, putting miles under their flip flops. At each site, I stood sentinel on the beach with my weapon of choice: a new set of binoculars, tripod, and zoom lens. If I had to grab a shark by the tail and reel him into the beach to save the boys, I would. I'd done it before when shark fishing in the Bahamas.

Was it shark fishing with the boys that had fueled a carefree attitude towards sharks, neutralizing their fear?

I only had myself to blame.

12.

Jaws

Bull Shark Snared at Twilight.

If you are lucky enough to find a way of life you love, you have to find the courage to live it.

—John Irving

I taught our sons how to fish for sharks when they were young.

"There's the shark! I see it!" Adam, age six, hollered.

Warren's eyes went wide, their little faces bright with anticipation. We were living, at the time, aboard a steel boat in the Bahamas.

"Where? I want to see!" Warren shouted, leaning over the side of our inflatable dinghy.

Toes treaded air as the boys bent far over dinghy pontoons until their noses touched the water. A shimmering shape lay motionless on the sea floor—a shark. It wasn't going anywhere. Two concrete blocks anchored its jaw to the bottom. Because of the blunt snout and wide head, it looked to be an eight foot long bull shark. The bull shark was one of the most aggressive sharks known to man.

Last night at twilight, I had wired the remains of Peter's catch— one grouper and two snappers— to giant hooks. The head, entrails, and tails were intact. Attached to ½" chain links, the fish undulated in the current as if alive. After placing the rig in a cut at the far end of the harbor, I dumped chum from a bucket. We were sure to snare a shark by morning.

My imagination ran wild during the night, with eager anticipation. I was relieved when the first bit of light streamed through the hatch, weary from having stared at moving constellations all night. Sleep deprivation felt like a morning hangover.

After gathering ax, cutlass, plastic bags, bucket, and handheld VHF radio, I jumped into the dinghy where the boys were already waiting with the family dog.

"Hurry up, Dad!" Warren shouted.

Warren was donned—like his brother—in a white robe. I'd sewn them for sun protection and air ventilation. A sunhat with flaps completed the uniform.

"You go ahead. I'll stay back to gather weather," Peter said. "Radio me when you have your shark. I'll bring in the troops."

It was summer—hurricane season. A storm could develop out of a tropical low at any time. Consequently, Peter spent long periods listening to broadcasts from the US National Weather Service via single-sideband radio every morning and many evenings when conditions were ripe. Internet weather wasn't yet an option. Snail mail and radios like the VHF and SSB were our only sources of communication.

With the young boys settled in the dinghy, I roared off to the ocean cut where I had set the shark rig at dusk the previous day. The boys were excited; the dog barked incessantly, knowing what was to come. When we came upon the site, I motored to a set of buoys. Attached to one buoy were two concrete blocks, serving as a crude anchor on the seafloor. The 2nd buoy served as a trip-line, keeping me from having to get near the shark.

"Help me pull this monster in," I said. The boys' little bodies raced to the bow of the dinghy.

"Mom, it's hard!" Warren shouted.

"Here, let me," Adam said.

"Just go slow and steady," I said.

Together we worked as a team to reel in our catch, struggling with the concrete blocks until we finally pulled the set into the boat. We began shortening the 2nd line. Suddenly, the dinghy began to swing sideways, jerking left and right.

"Mom!" the boys shouted in unison.

"It's okay. Don't worry. Just stay seated in the middle of the boat," I said

Quickly, I tied the line off to an eyebolt at the back of the boat. With twenty feet of rope still attached to the shark, I throttled forward … ever so slowly. After a tug, the dinghy made way with the big bull in tow.

Nothing and everything can go wrong.

At the beach, the dog launched out of the dinghy, the boys after her.

"Run and get some rocks," I said. "We'll need it to anchor the shark."

I wanted to keep them busy while I calculated my next move. The boys disappeared into the scrub in their robes, looking like trick-or-treating ghosts in a tropical bush. They gathered up mini-anchors of limestone while I tossed the rig onto the beach. I kept the bull twenty feet from the beach so that no one could get hurt. While I gathered my tools, my musings went to the dire warnings of Gloria Patience, who had first taught me how to shark fish.

"I had two sharks bite the end of my fiberglass Boston Whaler. Trashed my outboard too. What makes you think you're so invincible in that silly ride you have? That inflatable boat!" Gloria Patience had yelled at me.

Known as 'Shark Lady,' Gloria once lived on the island of Great Exuma and was featured in National Geographic Magazine. She hunted sharks for the large colony of cats in her backyard and sold shark teeth to jewelry craftsmen in Nassau.

Outside the Laundromat one day, she shook a gnarly finger at me and pulled out a photo. True to her word, a large gash crossed the right side of her Boston Whaler. Torn fiberglass and serrated edges streaked down the hull; jagged teeth marks dotted the outboard engine.

"One bite to your bubble of a dinghy and you're a goner!" Gloria harangued.

In remembrance of Gloria, I had left the dinghy at the far end of the beach and away from the killing site.

"Boys, grab this rope. Now tie it off around a palm tree, near the bush," I said.

Even at their young ages, they knew how to fashion a bowline, the most ubiquitous knot known to sailors.

"When I heave in the shark, stay away from the jaws. OK? Do you want to help filet it?" I asked.

"Yeah!" Adam shouted.

"Uh huh!" Warren added.

"Ok then. Here we go. Ready? First, I want you to stand next to that palm tree over there until the shark is high and dry on the beach. Got that?" I asked.

They nodded their heads in agreement and trotted up to the tree located two meters away. They stood with rapt attention on round faces. I began to pull the shark, ever so slowly.

As I pulled the rope in, I backed up to the high water line, just in case ....

When the shark's snout broke the surface at the water's edge, blood gushed from giant jaws. Attached to them was a grey head that was wide and full. The body was about eight-feet long. I tugged hard, backing up, digging the soles of my feet into the sand. Progress was slow. Suddenly my feet slipped in the sands, and I fell onto my derrière. I quickly wound the rope around my waist, using my hundred and twenty pounds to act as a belaying pin. The shark felt like it weighed just less than half a ton—there was no way I could get it high and dry. I lay back on the beach to take in my breath and think.

I gathered myself up and walked over to the concrete blocks to better secure the line. I looked at the struggling shark: droplets of water ran across the snout; a fluke of tail writhed; gills lumbered with a belabored breath. It was painful to watch. The shark struggled against sure death.

I entered the water behind the shark. Yellow eyes followed my moves. I grasped the tail, pivoted the shark on its belly, and dropped the caudal fin above the waterline. The shark was midway up the beach now.

"Quick! The line!" I shouted to the boys.

They ran down the beach from their hideout in the bush. On their approach, the great shark suddenly gave a leaping roll of its stout body, writhing violently. Rig chains rattled. The boys fled back to the tree.

We watched in horror as a giant head twisted round, touched the caudal fin, and then writhed back the other side. In a matter of seconds, the beast was back in the water.

"Oh no," I muttered in agony.

I raced forward, grasped the rope again, and pulled hard.

"Oh, no you don't, you bully! Get back here!" I yelled.

I ran up to the fluked tail with a rope this time and, as fast as lightning, tied a bowline around the fluke. I quickly retreated, keeping the line taut. I kicked over a nearby concrete block and secured it fast.

"Quick! The tail rope! Secure it!" I shouted to the boys.

Sure as any great hunters of the sea, the boys charged for the rope. Adam grabbed the lead end and headed back up the beach to the palm tree, Warren in quick pursuit. Together they wound the rope around the skinny trunk until they came to the rope's end—nearly a dozen wraps. I laughed uproariously. The hunt was getting fun.

"Where's your limestone anchors? Let's anchor the rope even better by loading it with the rocks," I said.

"Yippee," the boys shouted.

They gathered up the little rocks into the lap of their robes and dumped them next to the tail rope. One by one, the rocks were placed on top of the rope, acting as additional anchors.

With the head and tail secured tightly with rope, concrete block, tree anchor, and rock anchors, the shark wasn't going anywhere. We stood back to study our captive.

The eyes were big and menacing. The pupil was black as midnight, marquise-shaped, set against a backdrop of yellow iris. It resembled the eye of a cat. A set of formidable triangular, saw-edged upper teeth was erect and narrowly pointed. The lower teeth were finely serrated. We moved about gathering tools to filet the beast.

"Mom, look. Its eyeball is following us," Warren said.

Adam walked up to the shark and moved left and then right, testing its eyesight. Sure enough, the shark followed his every move. An eerie feeling overcame me. Best to gut this beast fast. It was creeping me out.

The bull shark boasts of a ferocious reputation. Many experts consider the bull to be the most dangerous shark in the world. Joined by the great white and tiger sharks, they are believed to be the species most likely to attack humans. They have a pugnacious disposition and a tendency to head-butt their prey before attacking.

I picked up my trusty cutlass and moved to the anus. With precision, I cut from the anus to the gills.

Whoosh!

A large gush of urine emptied onto the sands, liquid and transparent. It felt warm in my hands. With deft fingers, I removed the organs as the shark began to bleed out. In time, shark eyes grew vacant of life.

"Thank you Mother Earth for blessing us with this catch," I said aloud and placed my palm on its flank.

"Yeah, thanks, Mother Earth," Adam and Warren mumbled together.

It was a traditional Native American Indian custom after a hunt to be appreciative of food. Every part of the shark was utilized. A German friend would craft lederhosen from the skin. Dad would hang the jaws in his office. The flesh would be roasted over a beach bonfire, and shared by our friends tonight.

A roar of outboard engines announced the arrival of a fleet of dinghies. Families had come to photograph and learn the biology of the shark. It was the science lesson of the day. I handed the offal around for each child to handle. Their eyes went wide with wonder.

Three hours had passed before I was able to hack through the tough skin to divide the flesh into steaks. The sun climbed; it grew hot. As I knelt over the body, sweat dripped from my face onto the knife handle, creating a slippery mess. I carved, pulled, and hacked. At last, a small ax split the cartilaginous skeleton of the back, and I was done.

Later that night, six families gathered around a beach bonfire to grill the flesh. The stars were out, and a full moon hung low and bright, shining through a canopy of palm fronds. It was bright enough to cause the palms to blow fuzzy shadows around them. A light breeze tickled the needles of casuarinas pines, sending a soft melody of the *swoosh, swoosh* across the night breeze. We could see far out across waters that were still and flat. Someone brought out a guitar. Singing began.

Over the next few years, shark fishing with the boys fizzled out when the local politics began.

One day, a sailor cornered me in town. His tanned face came in close, brows furrowed. A twisted snarl across his tanned face sent a malevolent air. I drew back from him, but he came at me, close and aggressive.

"You have no right killing sharks in the harbor!" he yelled.

"I don't kill sharks in the harbor. I catch them in the ocean cut," I countered. Hands on my hips, I stood tall in my 5'3" small frame.

"You're drawing sharks around the boats!" he continued.

"Guana Cut is three miles south of the boat anchorage. You have nothing to worry about," I said firmly. With that, I walked off.

Once back on the boat, I relayed my personal attack by the stranger in town to Peter. I felt violated and angry over the incident.

"We'll play a trick on him," Peter said. His eyes twinkled with mischief, and his face creased into a wily grin. He picked up the microphone of the VHF radio.

"Hailing Morning Glory, Morning Glory. Scud, Scud, over."

Yacht *Morning Glory* hauled from Florida, owned by Tim and Debbie. They had been cruising the Bahamas with us for a year.

"*Scud, Scud. Morning Glory* here," said Tim. "How are you doing, Peter?"

"Great. Say, Tim. Tina just shot a goat, and we're cleaning it on the back of the boat. It's a good time to fish with all the chum floating around. Come on over for some mutton dinner later on. We'll get the kids together," said Peter.

Over dinner that night, we all had a real laugh. But my joviality in shark fishing took a dive.

"You know, Tina. The gestation period of a shark is two whole years. That's a long time for a mother to be carrying her young," Debbie commented.

Carry her young. Baby. Gestation period. Eve.

With that, I felt chastened. It was time to stop.

Together over a period of three years, the boys and I had landed half a dozen sharks: black-tipped, white-tipped, reef, tiger, and lemon. But the ocean needed sharks. They were critical in the ocean ecosystem. As a top predator, they fed on the sick and weak, keeping schools of fish healthy. The sentiment echoed throughout the cruising community.

Our days of shark fishing were over.

13.
Near Mutiny

Martial Arts at Sundown

Teenagers. Everything is so apocalyptic.

—*Kami Garcia*

Peter continued to labor over conflicting weather reports, trying to determine a weather window for departure to Namibia. Any day now, surely. When favorable weather announced a good sail from Capetown, we walked the docks to chat up the local fishermen, querying them for advice. More than once they shook their heads in disbelief, and we stayed. Their warnings were dire.

Sam grew restless. Although Gary and our sons continued with homeschooling lessons most of the day, Sam became agitated in the confines of the boat. Many times he vanished during the day. I have no idea where he went. I worried about his safety. Severe racial tensions often manifested into violence in Capetown. We were frequently warned about walking alone without a companion.

"Don't go out at night here. Never walk. Always take a taxi," warned the Victoria and Alfred Basin Marina gatekeeper.

It was only a matter of time before the inevitable occurred with Sam. While working in the galley one late afternoon, I overheard Sam holding court with the boys. "Dude, we bust out, tonight. Girls! Clubs! Some booze?" Sam said.

My hands clenched, and I ducked into a dark cabin, ears alert. Later that night, I heard the patter of feet in the cockpit. It was late. Sure enough, all four boys were gathering up to climb onto the dock.

"Where are you all going?" I asked politely, with a strain in my voice.

"Just out, Mom," Adam said. Gary was mute, his usual quiet manner. Warren too, but he let his brother do all the talking. Sam pulled himself up short to me.

"We're just heading into town for a little walkabout," Sam said. "No worries!" "Yes, worries. No way," I said.

"We'll take a taxi then! You're way hyped out on the fear factor." Sam countered.

I shot him a sideways glance. In the glow of the cockpit lights, he looked like a petulant boy. I ignored his comment for a moment.

"No, no town carousing tonight. You have the entire marina compound to explore at night where it is safe. Cafes. Shopping," I said.

"We don't want to shop," Sam said, raising his voice.

"It's not safe. The country is still recovering from Apartheid. All the locals have warned us," I insisted.

"Oh Mom, you're exaggerating. Nothing will happen!" Adam argued.

"You don't know that!" I said flatly. Our quarrel brought Peter out of bed.

"What's going on?" he asked.

"The boys want to go to a nightclub," I said.

"No way. Cruise the shopping boardwalk of the marina, but no going outside the gate. It's just too dangerous," Peter added.

Gary pulled down his baseball cap so that it covered most of his youthful face and hid the brilliance of his big eyes. His calm demeanor was a soothing distraction next to Sam's building tirade.

Peace prevailed, but Sam was fraught with frustration and anger. As the boys lumbered down the dock, Sam yelled an expletive and gesticulated wildly, pin-wheeling his arms. Capetown was our first port since our guests had first boarded. We hadn't even begun the ocean crossing. I quaked at the prospect of being at sea with a testosterone-fueled Sam. I tried to focus on his good humor and other good traits. As I gazed up into the heavens for inspiration, bruised skies stared back at me as if an omen of bad things to come.

Sam's temperament continued to grate against mine. His thunderous tirades created stress in our otherwise peaceful family. His brother, Gary, didn't have any control over him either. Easygoing and polite, Gary was a lot like his mother. Gary's quiet, sweet presence lent a peace about the room. When faced with his older brother's tirades during a manic crash, small-framed Gary stood mute and afraid. More than once as younger brothers, I had seen Gary sprint into island bush as his stocky brother rumbled after him, lost in fury. Hot on his trail, Sam screamed threats and abuse.

Discipline with my boys was laughable. How could I handle a raging Sam at sea? I was afraid that my parenting skills were weak, at best. I spent many hours ruminating over the issue with Peter. He wanted to send Sam home, but I insisted we finish strong. I didn't want to disappoint our sons. They were fond of Sam.

"I'll be too occupied with handling the boat under sail, managing the systems, and gathering weather to help you with Sam," Peter warned me.

"I know. I want to give him more time. You know the adage: Sailors rot in port. Maybe he'll straighten out at sea," I said.

"You'll have to take him on. It's up to you. I can't invest time in a radical crew member," Peter said.

"I know. I understand. Leave him up to me. I'll make it work," I said.

Peter left the stateroom to tweak the sailing instruments as I pondered my situation. My lack of power over our sons troubled me. I thought back to when our sons entered their teen years, back to the day when Adam slipped off a salty swimsuit and left it in the middle of the salon floor. It was a game changer for me.

"Hang up your wet swimsuit, please," I asked.

Nothing. No answer. He shrugged his shoulders as if deaf.

"Hang your wet swimsuit up," I repeated, a bit louder.

Nothing. No words. No snappy comeback. No action.

"Hang up your frigging swimsuit!" I yelled.

The dripping suit remained on the floor.

What could I do? I fled to the stateroom I shared with Peter, collapsing into tears. I stared up at the ceiling and allowed myself to vent. In time, I calmed down and reflected. Suddenly, I felt stupid. I had allowed my ego to manipulate me, seeking power instead of peace. It was just a silly swimsuit. After much talking with my inner spiritual self, I decided I would simply collect the wet suit next time, and hang the darn thing up myself. Why ruin a beautiful day and an otherwise healthy son/mother relationship over a piece of clothing? I would choose differently next time. I would call in my Zen influences to seek peace over power.

Our extended families who lived stateside considered us permissive parents. True, if one's type of parenting included spanking, but Peter and I decided long ago that we would never, ever strike our children. Although I have felt the inner rage at times during explosive teenage outbursts, I chose instead to breathe deeply and remove myself from the room to avoid further negative engagement. Once, I kicked a favorite pair of tennis shoes of one of the boys over the stern of the boat when standing next to them during an outburst. It lead to him jumping overboard to retrieve the shoes, and surfacing with a cooler self, emotionally.

Peter and I decided never to spank because it breaks trust and destroys the spirit. My parents used spanking as a discipline. It failed to curb my behavior. Enduring spanking with a belt as a child only made me angry, afraid, and sad. I could never share my inner soul with my parents because of the mental anguish. I didn't want such a negative environment for our sons—ever.

Church events, formal schooling, and arguing over who had to clean dirty rooms were non-events in our family. Rather, we spent decades teaching our sons differently: follow my example. Peter and I wanted to teach our children well through natural living. If we treated each other with love and respect, our sons would follow suit. We engaged them in homeschooling and family sports. We free-dived with our sons, spearing lobsters and fish for dinner. At night, we lounged around beach bonfires listening to their inner thoughts, cares, and concerns. Peter competed with them in beach volleyball. I taught them how to windsurf and cook. Their friends' parents became our friends. We hung out together— considered un-cool in most teen social networks. Why send our kids to a school where the trend of violence was escalating, and where bullies were an issue? Our sons had never heard of ADHD, Ritalin, OCD, CBT, Ecstasy, Vicodin or OxyContin. I intended to keep it that way. I wanted our children to grow up protected, admired, stimulated, and knowing they were loved.

And yet, once again, Sam corralled the three boys in the main salon into scheming. I was fishing out a snack for Peter in the galley, hidden from view.

"This time, our plan has to work! Capetown nightclub, here we come!" Sam enthused to his group of admirers. A thunderous clap announced a smack on his lap. "Lap dance, baby!"

The snickering of laugher resounded around the table of minors. I stood in disbelief. *Sam just won't give up!* I thought.

"Adam, Warren, your parents are far too strict. They treat you like babies. They're crazy. You have a right to explore places on your own. No way would I treat my kids like they do you! It's disrespectful!" Sam hissed.

The boys' conniving continued in the main salon about sneaking into Capetown for wild fun.

"How are we going to even get into a nightclub? I'm only sixteen," Adam said.

"Yeah, and I'm only fourteen. How's that going to work?" Warren asked.

"I'll sneak you in! I'm a master of disguise. You're tall. Piece of cake. We'll craft some fake IDs, tip the bouncer," Sam urged.

"I don't know, Sam," Gary said.

"Oh, come on! Think strippers! Hotties!" Sam said.

"But it's dangerous out there," Gary said.

"Nah, that's just a rumor, something Tina made up. Maybe your mother should buy a green beret with her name stenciled on the front. Listen, we'll just get a taxi!" Sam insisted.

This same rant had been uttered up to a dozen times before. Due to the stress of imminent departure and my fatigue (whatever the source), I'd had it. No more mouthing from an unappreciative crewmember, who, up to this point, had ushered in nothing but trouble.

I marched up the stairs and went straight to Sam. Pressing palms tight together, I bent over double and leaned into Sam's face, up close and personal.

"I don't appreciate you creating discord with our sons. You either become part of the solution of all of us having a great crossing, or you become part of the problem. You decide," I said, loud and firm. My palms punched the air in front of Sam's face, fingers just inches from his nose.

Sam sat and studied my face for a very long time. My words hung in the air.

"Uh, do I have something stuck in my teeth?" I asked with lips pressed tightly.

Sam managed a weak smile. With that, I marched to my stateroom where Peter reclined in repose over a book. I was shaking all over. A headache formed above my brow, tight and mean. I collapsed into tears, the only way I could vent my anger. It was no longer any fun. All my fears about dealing with four testosterone fueled lads had come to fruition.

"It's going to be a long two months at this rate," Peter said with a moan. He put his arm around me in comfort. I tried to smile to hide my feelings, but I didn't know whether my face cooperated or not.

"Maybe once we get back out to sea, Sam will do better," I said, with far less confidence that I felt.

The next day, Sam was on the phone with his parents at a phone booth inside the marina mall. Later I learned that he had asked to mutiny and take Gary home with him. In sage counsel, his parents talked him out of it, encouraging him to try harder and stick it out.

14.

MADNESS

Foredeck Work

Madness is somewhere between chaos and having a dream.
—RM Drake

We planned to depart for Namibia at the tail end of the approaching near gale, and got busy making last preparations for the impending voyage. We had been at the marina for nearly three weeks now. Storms had come and gone. High winds howled at night, announcing winter. The fishermen were cautious and remained in port.

Nervous energy fizzed in my blood so, on impulse, I jumped off the boat and stepped onto the dock and into the near gale. Peter jumped down to join me. The shock of air, redolent with a foul fish odor, stole my breath away. I gasped as the stiff spray hit a piling beside me and struck my face like steel darts. Together we strode down the dock and came upon a fisherman mending nets.

"Haai, goeie dag," (Hi, good day.) I said with a smile, knowing he was busy and may not want to chat. "Hoe gaan dit met jou?" (How are you?)

My introduction was the depth of my Afrikaans terminology. I worked at knowing at least a dozen phrases before we visited any country, but I was hopeless with gaining the lilt of the Afrikaans language of the South African.

The fisherman wore neon-yellow foul-weather gear with rubber boots up to his calves. His hair was windblown, his face etched with hardship and creased from the sun. He was a hard man of middle height, with a beard so blond and heavy that the lower part of his face looked as though molded of iron. Heavy shoulders were like beams and he had the chiseled arms of someone who could a crush concrete block like a Styrofoam cup. He could judge this weather almost as accurately as any expert meteorologist.

Peter spoke up. "You think we should leave a full day after the nor'easter has passed or wait longer? I'm concerned about reaching Namibia in time before a new gale blows in."

"It's a real crapshoot, I tell ya.' But study the mouth of Table Bay from the bridge before you sail. And keep an eye on those nor'easters. Those storms can crunch your pretty little boat like matchsticks." Large calloused hands cut through the air as he gesticulated.

Although the fisherman spoke English, we needed a translator. The diphthong in "mouth" was nearly homophonous with *"moth"* and he sounded like his mouth was full of marshmallows. As recommended by the fisherman, Peter and I made it our morning habit to walk the marina bridge to study the conditions of Table Bay and gain insight into weather patterns.

A couple days after Sam's near mutiny phone call home to his parents, he seemed to have adopted a strategy of containment that worked. He settled into a comfortable pattern of taking the kids out to dinner at night within the confines of the large marina complex. The boys' nightly escapades served as terrific entertainment for them. South Africa boasted of some of the best beef in the world. For a few dollars, a massive steak—the size of a dinner plate—was served with a forest of curly fries. The prettiest girls waitressed at the Spur Restaurant, where low cut blouses and short skirts were the uniforms. The Spur Restaurant was the HOOTERS of South Africa. On the way back to the boat, they often stopped to play with gaming machines, returning full and cheery. I knew they didn't pass through the marina gate because I had visited the guard and asked him not to let the boys pass at night. Cash ensured his loyalty. True to his word, the gatekeeper kept his promise, which I determined from my daily visits to the gate.

Sam seemed to have gained a better insight into the forthcoming voyage as well. An energetic, even euphoric mood supplanted an agitated temperament. I began to relish his liveliness and wit, laughing uproariously at his antics. He delighted in holding court with the boys as if on stage, his electric personality belying his previously, irritable self.

I continued to look after the kids during our ocean passage like a mother hawk. At any time, something could go horribly wrong. I was determined to prevent disaster by confirming, talking to, and teaching the boys. I knew how precious life is; no one under my care would fall into disaster. This was the underlying problem between Sam and me. He could not understand.

Sam finally began to grasp the ground rules. The manic low of last week seemed to have passed or eased a bit. I prayed for no rockier periods. He needed to keep busy. I hoped that getting him to tutor the other boys in High School trigonometry and calculus would help. His keen intelligence was a delight to observe. Hopefully, his inner storm would remain in the genie bottle.

"Don't be dazzled by my mathematical prowess," Sam said, eyes rolling back into his head. He flipped his hand offhandedly into the air. "Math is one of my hidden talents. I try not to brag." Guffaws resounded. From the galley below, where I worked unseen, I eased a sigh of relief, hoping his good humor would last.

15.
INSIDE THE SKELETON COAST

500' Dune Jumping, Namibia

Maybe some women aren't meant to be tamed. Maybe they just need to run free until they find someone just as wild to run with them.

—*Candace Bushnell*

"Ah, but a fine night it is for sailing, my lassie!" Peter cooed. South Africa lay in our wake after an early morning departure. The dogwatch was mine. Time to face nature and the blackness of night.

Was Peter kidding? I looked astern where my eyes were drawn up and up as a large wave uncurled, and then pushed *Scud* forward like a speed train. Rooster-tails of spray shot off the sugar-scoops. My knees felt weak. I leaned against the closed doors of the main salon entryway for support, taking it all in ... very slowly, breathing in and out, in and out.

Wits gathered, I strolled over to seize the helm with earnest—still shaky and trying to appear more confident than I felt. Peter gave me a rundown of prevailing conditions and potential hazards while I adjusted the helm-strap for security. After his last warning of "keep a sharp look-out for unlit things," he kissed me goodnight and disappeared into the warmth of the salon, bolting the double doors to block out wandering spray. I wanted to ask him to leave behind an imaginary red emergency button for nerves, but I prided myself on handling passages well. It's just that it had been awhile since we'd seen gale conditions.

I took in my surroundings: The main sail was triple reefed, along with the jib—now no bigger than a diaper. Bright moonlight illuminated crests of waves with shimmering silver as high winds chorused through the rigging. The winds sucked the liquid caffeine out of my mug faster than I could drink it. I tossed the last few ounces of black coffee into the depths of the cockpit, giving up trying to guzzle it before becoming airborne. Leviathan spouts of spray rushed to claw at our stern. *Scud* raced before it like a majestic swan, gathering feet beneath her for take-off. She steeple-chased up the wall of a wave for lift-off, and then slid down its slope into a yawing abyss with a gut-swooping drop, only to rise again to repeat the cycle.

"You go, girl!" I yelled into the raging winds. Suddenly, I felt transformed, empowered with this strong vessel beneath me.

My mind raced along with the boat, and suddenly something clicked: Peter always did an odd thing before each passage by throwing out heavy items to maintain a good payload for the boat. In order for the boat to move fast, it needed to remain light. After witnessing his tirade of discarded items, I began hiding favorite books and items dear to my heart in my panty drawer. *He'll never find them*, I thought.

Wrong.

One day I discovered my stack of beloved nautical magazines missing. I cornered Peter in the galley.

"I threw them out to keep the boat light," he said.

"Those were mine!"

Our debate grew heated and was repeated many times. Going light meant more speed, and no one likes getting to port sooner than me. So after several rounds, I threw in the towel—albeit grudgingly. I am a peacemaker at heart and detest conflict. Years later, we passed more than a few cruising cats in our company as word spread about our light payload. (Men gossip like old ladies at the well.) In time, wives told of how their mates did an odd thing before going on the passage: shoes, deck boots, books, and clothes went missing. Eyes wide, I nodded in bogus disbelief and horror.

All was not dire straits on *Scud*, however. My reverie snapped back to attention when a whistling snort sounded in the near gale. I peered to see porpoise cutting the dark surface through the swells, a ghostly glow of phosphorescing plumes spinning off their underwater tracks, forming an ephemeral luminescence that turned the surface to radiating ginger-beer bubbles. The dolphins darted beneath our twin hulls and back again, teasing me with their mischievous grins of pure pleasure that shimmered in the moonlight. Their beauty moved me to tears. *Maybe they are an augury of better things to come*, I hoped.

We were finally en-route to Namibia from South Africa. Rounding the Cape of Good Hope had been uneventful—like child's play. This passage was altogether different.

A grey, soupy fog blanketed us against the Namibian desert, reducing visibility to 0.5 nautical miles because of the Benguela Current. The vast current swept frigid waters up from the Antarctic, merging with the warm Atlantic waters and running all the way to Angola, Namibia's northern neighbor. The resulting thick, impenetrable fog tormented our souls. Also, ever-changing sea-beds and unpredictable currents with their sudden arrival, and then sudden disappearance made charting with accuracy difficult. Sandbanks drifted and reformed. Charts were useless. Peter glued eyes to the depth sounder to keep abreast of any sudden change in depth. All night long I heard shouts between Peter and the crew.

"Depth?"

"Twenty-one feet!"

"Fall off!" A bit later: "Depth?"

"Forty-two feet!"

Labeled the infamous Skeleton Coast, the intrepid desert coastline was notorious amongst raconteurs of the South African Yacht Club as being a sailor's graveyard.

"The Gates of Hell," sailors penned it.

"God's land made in anger," echoed the Bushmen of Namibia, the hunters and gatherers of the desert.

The coastline lay in ruin from bleached whalebones, the crumbling hulks of shipwrecks, dead plants, and the footprints of infrequent desert creatures—all on a desperate search for sustenance.

Rumor has it, thousands of rusty hulks from shipwrecks and the lives of many more sailors have littered this desolate coast for centuries. We saw more than a few rusting hulks abandoned on the coast. Once shipwrecked, sailors wandered the desert in search of refuge, food, and water. Their bones joined those of desert animals, dead from thirst.

As if to support this ghostly theory, the *Moeb*, a 120 foot fishing boat crewed by 19 townspeople from Luderitz, sank the day after we arrived in Namibia. Unmarked, unlit mooring lines criss-crossed the deep waters off the Namibian coast for the diamond mining vessels that mined the seafloor. The *Moeb* had fouled one of such mooring lines in her prop. The fishing vessel yanked abeam of steep seas and rapidly sank at night. All men on board perished in inky waters.

"Worst in Maritime History" was splayed in bold letters across the local paper the morning after we arrived.

The nutrient rich Benguela Current had brought the good and the bad, but not altogether the ugly. An extra knot of speed raced *Scud* north, and once the gale abated, abundant sea life began to appear. Jackass penguins, right whales en route to breed in warmer waters, and fur seals with liquid brown eyes entertained us with their hilarious antics.

Purple hues faded into orange with the arrival of dawn, and sunlight supplanted the ghostly grey fog. In its place rode a sea breeze, heavy with a fish odor that jetted from shore. As we entered Luderitz Bay in Namibia, crimson flamingos danced on spindly legs, and spectacular rock formations rose before us. Like plums fallen beneath a tree, Hansel and Gretel's fairy-tale architecture peeked out from the quaint German village of Luderitz.

Over tea and biscuits, we met our neighbor, Ian, a former sailor and Canadian merchant-mariner. I stopped by their boat when headed back from town and invited them over. Ian had jumped ship years ago and married Sophie, the lighthouse keeper's daughter. She possessed the grace and charm of royalty, with her stately ways. Her light brown skin was shiny and stretched over a fit frame of small stature. Warm eyes stared back into mine as she told of her childhood. Reared in a remote area, she had grown up in the desert where her pals were fur seals and flamingos. Lizards often wandered into the tiny kitchen to steal food.

"Vipers were the worst," Sophie said, eyes wide. "They often hid under my bed for warmth at night. Every afternoon after homeschooling lessons, I climbed the 500 spiral-steps to the lighthouse summit to give my father tea, often with my two or three sisters in tow."

Ian and Sophie drove us to the lighthouse on Dias Point. It was named after the Portuguese navigator, Bartolomeu Dias, who landed here after opening a new sea-trading route around Africa to the Orient. Today, the lighthouse is automated, a sign of modern times when Luderitz exploded into the 20th century on a single day when a boy walked on a remote railway track back in 1907.

While shoveling sand from tracks, the boy discovered a mere sparkling pebble of 21 carats. Word spread, and the diamond rush was on. Fortune seekers arrived in ox-carts with brooms, shovels, and enamel basins. During nights beneath a full moon, the townspeople crawled with tin cans tied around their necks, scouring desert sands as high winds abated. They found the exposed, glittering diamonds sitting atop sand dunes, winking in reflected light. Coinage temporarily disappeared, and diamonds were used to barter for flour and sugar.

When the big guys arrived—the De Beers conglomerate—the valuable industry became organized and the hunting of diamonds outlawed. Theft became rampant. Employed native miners hid diamonds in suitcase handles, hems of skirts, inside cut-away heels, and holed books. Homing pigeons carted off heavy bundles of un-cut diamonds. For every $3 million worth of hand-mined diamonds, 90% went missing.

We became fast friends with Ian and Sophie. They adopted us as if we were visiting family members. Tomorrow, they promised a drive into the desert for dune-surfing. After days at sea, the boys were eager for serious sport.

At daybreak the next morning, we clambered into Ian's roomy van. We embraced the empty desert sooner than I could finish my takeaway coffee. Only a single, narrow road led into white oblivion. A dull sky and sand merged into one mysterious flat haze. We drove until shouts from the guys in back trumpeted the appearance of colossal sand dunes in the far distance. When all six of us spilled out of the van, I glanced at the stout shovel that protruded beneath Ian's seat.

"In case we get stranded," he said. "High winds spring up without warning. They move giant sand dunes across roads like creeping caterpillars. If you're not home before nightfall, the road can be buried and you with it. Coastal desert dunes were also one of the only places in the world where the phenomena of roaring dunes occur, creating a perfect storm of sand grit and air that rumbled as loud as a low-flying plane."

Crikey! I thought and hustled the rambunctious guys into the desert void to hurry things along.

We trampled over hot sands to the 500-foot (154 m) dunes. The guys mustered atrophied leg muscles up to the summit while we hung at the bottom listening to Sophie's childhood tales of the last big diamond rush. The sun caught its zenith and then arched. Warren suddenly landed at my feet in a dusty heap inside a tornado of whirling sands that collapsed over him. We looked up to see Sam close behind, barreling down with his entire linebacker frame, galloping on a fast descent with imaginary ski poles. Gary followed, leaping into a spectacular cartwheel. Adam brought up the rear.

The scenario was repeated many times before it was time to go.

After shoveling the guys back into Ian's van, we clattered off to Kolmanskop, a diamond ghost town. Miles of fenced land passed by dotted with yellow signs affixed every 100 meters that announced: "Fine of N$200,000 and imprisonment of two years if illegal entry without a valid permit."

We were in the Sperrgebiet, *the forbidden territory*. These were vast tracks of land, closed off after the discovery of diamonds. Conscious of the reckless tendencies of youth, Ian abruptly turned around in his seat to stare intently at the guys in the back.

"Never go in there!" Ian trumpeted.

Kolmanskop resembled an abandoned stage set: dilapidated buildings flooded with sands, discarded furniture adorned old boardwalks, and remnants of rusty railways lay scattered. The boys scaled walls, climbed ladders onto loading platforms, and swung from ropes onto mattresses of sand as we nosed about the ruins. Ian and Sophie led us into an empty theater and dance hall, perfectly left intact as if the last dance had just ended. An eerie draft wafted between walls that whispered ghostly notes of reverie.

As the sun arched lower, Ian hurried us off further into the desert to complete the tour. We arrived at an abandoned whaling station where American whaling ships once harvested their trade. A corroded ship hull lay partially submerged in water, and a sun-bleached whale carcass protruded from sands, bones stretching into the sky. Tools of the whaling trade littered the site: an enormous black cauldron and boiling utensils.

Ancient railways led from the whale bones towards the bay where they disappeared into shallow waters alongside the ship as if the last whale had been cranked, boiled, and sold to the highest bidder.

Back in the van, the floor was beginning to look like a shallow beach. Sand stuck to our shoes, clothes, and body. High winds shoved it in, quicker than we could hand-sweep it out. Heading back into town, Ian abruptly skidded to a stop.

"Look!" Sophie shouted.

We mashed our faces against the windows to peer into the void, jostling for position but saw nothing. What looked to be a cross between a horse and an antelope suddenly materialized out of the grey curtain and loped towards us.

A gemsbok! Long, sharp horns stretched above its magnificent head, striped with narrow black and white ribbons of fur. We sat mute in utter silence and reverence. The stately gemsbok sensed our intrusion and bolted off into a beige infinity where swirling desert sands had turned the sky into a beige vault, merging the sky and terrain as one.

On the drive back to the harbor, shifting sands floated across the road as fine as baby powder. It swirled in eddies, resembling drifting snow. The sun was beginning to set, casting a pale shadow across the roadside dunes. We were a solitary van on the road in the middle of nowhere. I gave a sigh of relief when we came upon *Scud* tugging at anchor. The lagoon was still as a milk pond, sheltered from the open sea.

Early the next morning, I awakened to the disappearance of Warren and Gary. A cursory glance revealed surfboards stowed in the bow lockers, but we were missing a dinghy. With the binoculars, I scanned a vacant landing dock at the town quay.

Casually—appearing calm and collected—I queried Adam and Sam as my hands shook. The boys were seated at the salon table, crafting the world's largest model catamaran out of cereal boxes, sushi mats, mounds of duck tape, and AAA batteries. I knew they'd lie for their brothers as bros do, but I gave it a shot.

"Have you seen Warren and Gary?"

"Nope," Adam and Sam chorused.

Peter, pre-occupied with charts, hadn't a clue either. I was baffled. Could they have gone to the diamond fields? The forbidden territory? Surely not!

I remained in mental disarray the rest of the day, distraught and desperate. No one else seemed to share my concern. Without a dinghy, I was stranded on the boat. No one could go in search of the missing boys. Ian's dire warning raced through my mind as I threw myself into provisioning lists, knowing it was hopeless. With five men onboard—one a football linebacker—we went through so much food that lists were useless.

At dusk, Warren and Gary roared up in the dinghy just as skies turned a deep purple. My heart hammered in my mouth, and epithets were ready to explode from my once sweet, motherly lips. Clambering aboard, they collapsed into mischievous giggles on the salon settee like naughty school boys and began to empty their pockets. Semi-precious gemstones spilled out onto the table, glistening in a rainbow of shiny colors: leopard skin jasper, green aventurine, and black obsidian. I was astounded! Alarm seized me, however: they had sneaked into the forbidden territory and smuggled out rocks!

Warren's Stone-polishing Invention

Filled with mirth, they told of their escapade like regular raconteurs. In the early morning mist, they had rowed away without engaging the outboard until out of earshot. Once sighting the Sperrgebiet beach, they had ventured ashore to explore. In the unfolding of their escapade,

Peter's eyes danced with amusement, but Warren caught my livid scowl. Knowing how my heart swelled for him, he teased me.

"No one saw us, Mom! I swear!" Warren shouted.

Words caught in my throat, and I answered faster than I was ready.

"The stones are … well, gorgeous, of course. But you … you left me behind!" I wailed.

As soon as the words erupted from my quivering lips, I clamped my hand over my mouth in stunned disbelief. What had I just said? I cringed. Our son had inherited my adventurous streak. Audacious adventure stuck to us like peanut butter and jelly—the poor devil.

16.

NEAR COLLISION

Diamond Mining Ship, Namibia

Even the darkest night will end and the sun will rise.
—Les Miserables

It was the beginning of winter. We departed from Namibia early one morning in the cruelest of weather and most murderous of seas. We were forced to sail in less favorable conditions lest we become stranded in port due to the onslaught of worsening winter storms.

Dusk brought dense fog that held the captain and crew in jitters. It was as if a white tide had swallowed the sea. The horizon disappeared. In the sky, the sun was reduced to a minuscule gray disk as it slowly set. As night came, tendrils of fog drifted into the cockpit and a chilly, desert breeze blew out of the southwest. *Scud* was making way in a little over 400 feet of water, roughly 65 nm offshore of Luderitz.

Because of the fog, the crew would be jumping from bunks all night long, so they manned the night watches while I indulged in much needed sleep, but sleep betrayed me.

A crackle came over the VHF radio. The voice sounded as if in a panic. I bolted upright.

"Sailing vessel heading northeast, this is the *Discoverer*. Come in! Come in!"

Peter jumped up from the main salon settee where he had been cat-napping during Sam and Gary's watch. Gary felt unsettled about assuming a watch alone in the cockpit, so Peter set them up as watch-mates. In time, Gary would need to pull his weight.

Peter had insisted on being close to the cockpit action to maintain a tight ship and to keep an eye on the fog. It was mandatory for the boys to hand steer instead of engaging the auto-pilot, lest they doze off to sleep or become distracted. Peter kept a standing compass and a flashlight on the shelf next to him for a regular check of *Scud's* heading. He needed the assurance that the watchman was keeping a sharp course.

"*Discoverer*, this is the sailing ship, *Scud, Scud*. Do you read me? Come in," Peter shouted into the radio.

He jumped into position at the navigation system to study the radar screen. Normally when immersed in fog, the radar unit is left on standby instead of fully shut down for rapid booting in an emergency. A full power-up required an agonizing sixty seconds to load.

"Sailing vessel, you are on a collision course. Change course immediately!" called the mariner a second time.

"All hands on deck!" Peter bellowed. Bodies clambered up from dark staterooms.

Peter vaulted out of the navigation station and seized the helm from Sam. "Adam, stand by the radar!"

Warren, Sam, and Gary sprinted towards the foredeck at the bow like a gaggle of Olympian runners, leaving Adam at the navigation station. I joined them, and together we stood staring intently into the foggy gloom of a black sky and a black sea.

"Where is the ship?" Warren yelled.

"I don't see anything!" shouted Sam.

"Quiet! Listen for the sound of engines!" I pleaded.

Adam stood ready to engage the radar dials. "Come on, you bugger.

Come on!" The radar unit had not remained on standby but fully shut down. Precious seconds passed in waiting for the green glow to illuminate.

"I'm releasing the port jib sheet! Douse the sail!" Peter commanded the foredeck crew.

The halyard was released as the boys pulled the jib down, securing it fast to the port lifeline. Twins engines roared to life. Peter steered *Scud* along at a hare's pace, sensing trouble and anticipating doom.

From my viewpoint on deck, a vast blanket of white hung over the sea, illuminated by the steaming lights of the boat. The mist swirled in eddies, opening up small holes and then closing in just as suddenly. An eerie silence wafted as we waited. The night air was cold and wet. We stared into the blackness but saw nothing. Visibility was a mere ten feet ahead of us. Time passed in slow motion. The air was tense. Hairs rose on my neck.

"There! I see something!" Warren shouted.

"Dad, quick!" Adam shouted from below. "It's a ship. She's right in front of us!"

I ran down to stand beside Adam and gaped in terror at the radar screen. Two blinking blips were rapidly emerging as one. I stood mute with dread for a moment and then vaulted back into the cockpit. Peter handed me a spotlight to shine alongside the port hull and into the sea. Scanning the horizon revealed nothing but when I illuminated the hull I was shocked to discover a long warp passing close. *Scud* inched along ever so slowly while the warp remained in view. Seconds passed as it ran free of the stern, just missing the prop. The last thing we needed was the prop to become fouled, leaving us stranded at sea—like the *Moeb* disaster.

The beam of the light followed the warp as the end came into view, finally disappearing into the depths of the sea. I turned the beam far ahead this time to follow the leading end. It led across surface waters at an angle in the distance. But to where? Attached to what? Suddenly I was mute with terror when the realization struck. It was the anchor rode of a ship. A diamond mining vessel! The vessel had anchored into the southerly wind, and we were approaching fast down upon it on its port side.

Peter's eyes landed on the deadly target and then he knew. Quickly, he thrashed the helm hard to starboard. *Scud* flew away from the ship's side that looked to be a half mile away. Another two warps eased by in the gloomy mist. By now, Peter was in communication with the ship, a disastrous collision avoided.

"Diamond ship *Discoverer*, this is the sailing ship *Scud*. We are making way on a heading of 300 at 2 knots. Over," he said.

"Roger. Hold your course," the captain of the diamond ship answered.

Once clear of the diamond mining vessel, we sighed in relief. Sam stretched his fat palm in front of Adam for a high five. They smacked in unison and patted each other on the back.

"Great job, guys. Well done," Peter said.

We languished in the cockpit, fully aware of how quickly events can turn sour. The jib sail filled and engines were cut as we maintained an average speed of 7 knots under sail. *Scud* ghosted along in the gloom. All eyes were sharp, staring at the foggy expanse of blackness.

"I want some ice cream," Sam said with a moan.

"I want pizza, Sam," Gary crooned.

"I'll take a fat steak and fries," Warren shouted and slapped his knee. "Just like those babies we had at the Spur Restaurant in Capetown."

"Yeah!" Adam intoned.

"Just beans and rice, beans and rice for me," Peter chanted.

And I need a stiff drink.

17.

ROGUE WAVE

Warren and Adam Searching for Whales with Peter.

Life is a shipwreck, but we must not forget to sing in the lifeboats.

—Voltaire

I awakened to someone caressing my foot. It was Peter, announcing my 2 A.M. dogwatch. When he turned around to head back on deck, I luxuriated beneath the covers. A low, eerie sound of *ooooohm-hummmmm* reverberated through the hull, like that of a pipe organ. The eerie call was the wind in the rigging as the air filled the hollow boom. Rushing waves echoed through the hulls, sounding like volumes of cascading water. I stumbled into the main salon, peeled open one sliding glass door a short way, and stuck my head through the opening.

"What's it like out there?" I asked Peter, who was struggling with the helm. "It sounds wild!"

"We're in a Force 8, a fresh gale. Waves are three meters. Gear up tight." Peter shouted back in a muffled tone.

We exchanged a single glance of knowing that left me tense and nervous.

I timed my entry into the cockpit by waiting for a lull in the wind so that I could pull apart the heavy set of doors. After shutting them behind me, I stood mute as I took in the scene before me: Peter had attached himself to the helm-seat by a thick rope, and was clad in neon-yellow gear. Around me, huge black seas thundered, hitting us broadside, battering our new ship. Each time a wave struck from astern, the hulls shuddered and lifted up, moving away from the swell. Now and then, a gnarly one broke over the rails, sending a river of sea water down the leeward side, ending in a swirling froth at the stern. I took a deep breath for inner calm and gagged as misty seawater assaulted my throat. I grabbed my neck.

Peter raised the binoculars and slowly swept the jagged horizon. Only a sliver of moon infrequently peeked through bruised skies, bathing crests of waves.

"Anything I need to know?" The cacophony of raging surf ate my words, but Peter got the gist. It was customary to give a brief report when handing over the watch to the fresh crew.

"Maintain tight control of the helm. Make certain the waves hit on the aft quarter. Don't let her rear up and turn into the wind, or else you'll be broadside of the waves," he shouted. "Holler at any time if you need me. I'll be right in the main salon on the settee."

After Peter untied himself from the helm seat, I flung myself into it before the winds could rip me away. Peter quickly fastened the rope around me.

"Keep the main salon doors closed. They're locked from inside to avoid flying open when the boat cants." His lips moved, but I could only hear a few words and guessed at the rest. Doors. Locked.

We balanced against the violent pitch and roll of the cockpit as he gripped the helm chair. He smiled, edges of exhaustion smoothing away at his cheeks and corners of his mouth. Ever the vigilant Captain, sleep for him on passage was slow and hard in coming. Camped out in the main salon, he was always on call. Before turning around, he kissed me, and then was gone.

Once setting the auto-pilot to self-steer, I took up the binoculars to scan the horizon. Where light blinked in the peaks of waves, my pulse leaped. With a lightening in my stomach, I realized it was the shimmery glow of bioluminescence. Reaching for the flashlight, I shone it forward. On the foredeck was a mere diaper of a jib sail set and the main was triple reefed. I scanned to the right: flying fish darted out of waves, gliding off into the raging void. One landed on deck and flopped. It joined the group of others that studded the trampolines. Breakfast—if the winds didn't get them first.

I released the auto-pilot to enable self-steering and settled in for a long night. The wind tore at my rubber jacket and pushed waves even higher, but *Scud's* wide-flared bows were cleverly designed to cleave them apart. She ran like a bull, sleek and fast, taking the swells on her starboard quarter most of the time. When the swells hit from astern, she flew down each crest in an explosion of white foam with rooster-tails shooting off twin sterns. Landing in the trough, blue-water pushed through the trampolines on the foredeck, but *Scud* twisted and broke free, jerking side-to-side to steady herself, rising, ready for the next hit. Each time it seemed that she may not rise to meet the cliff of water that bored down on her, but *Scud* proved her integrity by rising each time.

The water was an inky black under the thick cloud cover. Together as a family we had lived through Caribbean hurricanes, but I had never seen water like this: so menacing and cruel. It glittered in iridescent blackness, moaned and growled in an ugly display of anger.

In the deep valleys between the crests, the wind was blanketed, so we fell into an unnatural stillness. An eerie silence enhanced the menace of this towering slope of water that would soon tumble upon us. In the trough, *Scud* heeled and threw her head up, climbing the slope in a gut-swooping lift that buckled my knees. As she went up, the cockpit tilted back, and a sliver of the moon filled the view from the cockpit with a vista of the low scudding cloud.

The wind tore at the crest of a wave ahead of her, ripping it away like downy feathers from a burst pillow, splattering custard-thick spume against the armored glass of the windows. *Scud* drove her wide bows and nosed into it, carving fat wedges of racing blue over her head and twisting violently at jarring impact. At the crest, she dropped over, surfing down and breaking out to fall free and repeat the cycle again.

I remained wedged into the helm-seat, swaying like a camel-driver to the thrust of the sea, turning aft every few minutes to check the swell astern. Having come to grasp the movement of the boat, I reached for the coffee thermos, but it lay just out of grasp. I watched in dismay as the thermos whirled about the cockpit floor, bobbing in seawater. Man, I needed a caffeine fix so bad: it would be a long and lonely two hours at the helm without its moral support. I judged the next towering swell, set the helm to auto-pilot, and with half a dozen quick moves untied the rope that imprisoned me. I crossed the span of the cockpit in those fleeting moments while *Scud* steadied in a trough.

A roar resounded so deafeningly loud that I stopped dead in my tracks and peered up. A colossal wave was climbing towards the heavens. It began to barrel down upon us as it clawed at the stern with frenetic energy. We were in its path while stuck in the bottom of an enormous abyss into which we had helplessly fallen. I felt like a doe, rigid in place from the oncoming headlights of a racing train.

The wave looked to be fifteen-feet high. If the hole closed too soon, the force of the breaking wave would bury us completely. My stomach turned to ice and struck me into silence. An uncomfortable premonition of terror invaded my senses.

Rogue wave. It was as lethal as a predator in ambush. Hidden by the dark and turbulent waters, it was a dead sailor's anecdote of lore.

There was no time to get back into the helm-seat. I wedged myself in behind the cockpit table, splayed tightened limbs against surfaces, and steeled for impact. In slow motion, the rogue wave curled over the boat. My mouth opened with an anguished scream that grew mute against the cacophonous roar and impending doom. The giant wave crashed on top of me, crushing my ribcage and squeezing breath from my lungs. I lay buried in its death-like grip as seawater pounded my lithe frame. Seawater flooded around me, pooling and swirling in the cockpit. The demon had knocked me off my feet, leaving me in a tangle of spiraling limbs in swirling waters. As the wave began its rapid descent, water eddied like mini tornadoes, creating a fierce momentum all of its own. The devil was receding fast, and taking me with it.

I clawed at space as motor neurons collided in my brain. I felt fear as never before. It segued into terror as I fought against the pull of the wave. When at last I found my feet, I lurched for the doors in churning waters and hurled my body against them.

Locked from inside. *No!* A blood curdling scream flew from my throat. I pounded the doors with clinched fists like a battering ram, begging for life.

"Help! Let me in! Let me in!" I shouted.

They all came to me like flying angels in the night: Peter first, then Adam and Warren. Sam and Gary ran up from below as well, eyes wide with concern.

They hurled open the doors. Seawater pooled into the main salon. I tumbled into Peter's arms. He slammed the doors behind me.

"Dear God! I was nearly swept overboard," I wailed, shaking violently. I was cold and had come undone; beaten and broken and tired to the very depths of my soul. I wanted to go into my cabin, crawl under a blanket, and sleep—for a very long time. I choked up, feeling defeated. I wanted to give up.

"How did it happen?" they chorused in unison. Their words of alarm for my safety tumbled out.

"Rogue wave!" I muttered breathlessly.

"It's okay, Babe," Peter said. "I'll take your dogwatch."

Adam turned to face Peter. "No, Dad. You just got off watch. It's my go. I'll take Mom's watch. It's too rough out there for her."

Peter looked haggard. Beneath his eyes were deep ridges, the color of slate and large enough to hold a small pearl. I felt my knees buckle under the weight of my despair and had the urge to vomit as nausea rose in my throat. I swayed, and Peter drew me in closer. I wanted to cry but held back, not wanting to expose my frailty amongst these big men-boys. *Too rough for me?* Had I had lost my inner battle with the sea … with myself? I had never whined for sympathy in my life. Fighting back waves of queasiness, I rapidly summed up my options.

I had come on this outlandish adventure in search of a new experience. No, I had not been mentally prepared for the dangers, but I still felt a stir of pride and a sense of accomplishment in having gone this far. In a slow heartbeat, the rumination diminished and slowly—in time—my despair lessened. Panic eased. Abruptly, an outrageous feeling overcame me. I felt the rush that extreme adventure brought, even in the midst of adversity. I began to laugh hysterically, releasing all the pent-up energy and fear stored over the last several weeks.

The laughter came in liquid fire bursts like that of an assault rifle. It sounded strange in my voice. Who was this woman of wild adventure, laughing uproariously after facing the threat of probable death?

Confused by my strange outburst, the guys stared at me with incredulity, their mouths like black holes against the green-glow of electronic screens nearby. The glow gave them a bilious cast, teeth blackened as if Halloween party-goers. They watched me in tense, electric silence.

"I'm going back out there," I said with a determined voice. Suddenly my mind felt clearer, and I was thinking sharply. "I won't be beaten."

Turning around, I collected the wayward thermos of coffee and climbed back on my camel, closing the double doors behind me. When I heard the click of the lock, it sounded like the marching bell to freedom. I had risen to a new, higher place where I intended to stay. I may stumble along the way again in the future, but I was happy in knowing I would arise again and start over.

And finish.

Just as my watch finished, Gary took his turn at the helm. Before securing the rope around him, Peter asked him to go forward and bring down the reefed jib.

"It's your go, Gary. We need to bring down the jib on the foredeck. The wind is building," Peter said.

The color drained out of Gary's face in the green glow of the electronics. He wringed his hands.

"I'll get S-S-Sam. He'll do it for me." Stammering, Gary stood still as stone

"No, Gary. Sam needs his rest too. Secure the deck lifeline around your inflatable lifejacket," Peter urged him in a soothing, but firm voice.

I could feel his heart hammering in my own ears. While the storm raged around us, Gary leaned against the helm, uncertain. I carried his uncertainty. I had been in his shoes.

"You can do this, Gary," I said with warmth and placed my hand on his shoulder. "Your Dad would be proud."

In time, wits garnered and safety gear attached, Gary made his way onto the leaping deck and into the girth of the storm. I watched with huge admiration from the helm. My heart swelled. With one swift yank as he had seen a dozen times before, Gary collapsed the diaper-sized jib as spray buried him. After properly securing the sail, he strode back towards the cockpit with deliberate, but careful steps. When he landed next to Peter, he was smiling like the Cheshire Cat.

"Way to go, Gary. You did great," Peter said as he thumped him on the back. "Now climb in the helm seat. Your next watch-mate takes over in two hours."

It was Gary's first watch alone.

18.
DEATH OF A MASCOT

Adam Prepping Spinnaker.

Coming together is a beginning; keeping together is progress;
working together is success.

—*Henry Ford*

The next day at noon, conditions had eased, but seas were still lumpy. I sauntered out of the main salon and into the cockpit to see the guys fussing over a seabird that had alighted on *Scud* during the tempest of the storm. Perched on the starboard lifeline, it fluttered to the deck and gazed intently at us. Nearby, a tiny tray of bread crumbs and a bowl of water lay within reach. The poor thing looked like it was starving and exhausted. It had long wings, a tubular nostril, and a hooked bill. I'd seen it soar low over the waves, gliding along the troughs with ease as its wingtips touched the surface. It was a shearwater, having earned its name by the way it "sheared the water" in flight.

"My God, it's beautiful," I said. "Is it eating or drinking anything?"

"We can't get it to take anything. It mostly rests," Warren said with concern.

The bird squatted down, tucked legs beneath a full breast, and blinked. A stiff breeze ruffled feathers that were as white as snow and just as exquisite. I tilted my head at a particular angle as brilliant hues winked across plumes. Sunlight refracted oil into a magnificent iridescence of silver, gold and a very light blue, creating tiny dancing rainbows.

I gazed at Warren.

"No wonder she's resting. Shearwaters migrate from breeding islands in the South Atlantic before flying to the Northern Atlantic to feed. That's 6,000 miles each way, every year for sixty years. Amazing stuff, huh?" Homeschooling, as usual, happened with accidental science and biology lessons.

Grunts from the crew affirmed the day's brief lesson. They gazed at the bird, worried it refused to eat.

"Maybe we should put out canned fish instead of bread crumbs," Warren said with a sad lilt in his voice.

"I never bought any. You guys hate canned fish," I said. "Next time we catch a fish, let's dry strips into jerky. We'll have sustenance for weary birds next time. How 'bout getting back into lessons for today? I'd like to see an essay on the migration of sea birds."

Gary tapped his brother on the shoulder. "Sam, help me with my chemistry?"

Sam's face lit up with a wide grin. As an assistant resident school teacher, he worked daily with all the boys whenever they needed help. Peter and I were delighted. Sam was a natural teacher. He possessed the intelligence and wisdom to open his students' eyes, to think harder. Sometimes I caught them all horsing around, air wrestling with arms. But overall, brotherly teasing kept the lessons fun and interesting.

Now that Sam had adopted a new attitude at sea, I felt more relaxed around him. Our battles ceased. Maybe sailors do rot in port. Sam had come to be a leader after having been at sea for more than a couple of days. Having graduated from high school with honors, Sam assumed the homeschooling lessons with our sons, relieving Peter and me from the duty. It was a great relief. I realized that we were indeed lucky to have him aboard. We had come a long way since rounding the Cape of Good Hope. I felt proud of our teamwork. We all sacrificed for a genuinely happy outcome day after day.

"Yeah, and after you finish teaching Gary, I need help with algebra," Adam called out to Sam.

Later in the afternoon I was kneading bread dough in the galley when I heard a shout.

"Fish!" Adam hollered from the cockpit.

I scampered up the main salon stairs and sprang out of the main salon to see Adam pulling in yards of monofilament line attached to a large yoyo. The yoyo had replaced previous fishing rods due to the constant explosion of rods from oversized fish, sending the entire rig into the sea along with the prized fish. Instead, we adopted the practice of using the plastic yoyo, a method we learned from the Venezuelan fishermen when cruising the country a few years ago.

Adam stood sentinel on the sugar-scoop on the stern of the boat, slowly reeling in his catch by hand. Warren stood behind him with a net. Sam stood near both of them on the sugar-scoops with a gaff. That left three big guys all bunched up between two steps. At the helm, Peter steered the boat further off the wind to slow the progress of the boat. Water pooled at the boys' feet as they struggled with the fishing line. The sight made me reel with anxiety. *Scud* was making way at six knots, down from ten knots, but still... anything could happen.

"Come back into the cockpit, boys. It's too dangerous for you to stand out there like that," I shouted.

It was to deaf ears.

"Mom, we're fine. Really," Warren shouted back without turning his head, refusing eye contact. Rooster tails of spray leaped off the stern from the speed of the boat.

"Sam, come on. You guys get back in here!" I implored.

"We got this," Sam yelled back.

Damn it! I thought. We were on a far reach, out in the middle of nowhere. I thought of Sam's mother and imagined how horrifying it would be to make *the call*. It's the call no mother wants to either receive or make. I imagined a scene much like when a military chaplain and officer arrive at a home of the deceased, clad in dress uniform to bear the worst news possible to the bereaved. Here, it wouldn't be death from war, but death due to a fish yanking its victim into the depths of the sea. No, that would not do. With that image, I seized a rope and sprinted over to Warren and Sam and Adam, and began the makings of a square knot for each.

"You're crazy, Mom! The rope will trip us up. Get away!" Warren countered, moving away from me.

Keeping them safe was an arduous challenge—like herding cats into a bathtub. Frenetic action blurred before me as the boys fought the fish. Relenting, I stood by with a life ring … just in case.

Adam and Warren and Sam struggled with the fish. A mountain of monofilament began to pool around their feet.

Not long ago a tragic boating incident was relayed to me from a captain aboard a sport fishing boat. We had been attending the festivities of a sport fishing tournament in Green Turtle Cay, in the Bahamas. Late in the afternoon, a dozen sport fishing boats rolled in with their catch. As a family, we walked the docks and stood mute as entire dock carts, larger than wheelbarrows, were loaded with giant fish: mahi-mahi, tuna, wahoo, blue and striped marlin. While the yacht crew cleaned the fish, we hung by the cleaning tables, mesmerized by the rapid swish of the blades against the shiny skin. Two crewmembers passed back anecdotes as fast as any raconteurs of the bar while downing Kalik beer, the Bahamian brew of choice.

"Dude, you know that kid, Kyle, from North Carolina?" the tanned fisherman asked. With deft fingers, he peeled the skin back from a shark filet. Clad in the uniform of a fisherman—board shorts and designer t-shirt, his sun-bleached hair pushed out from under a battered cap. He wore a pair of white rubber boots. Blood oozed down from boot sides, and large scales shimmered across the toes like tiny mirrors.

"Nah, don't reckon I do," answered his buddy while quaffing beer.

"I was on the *Miss Betsy* at the Hatteras Offshore Fishing Tournament," continued Bootman. "Kyle was 1ˢᵗ mate aboard *Byte Me* fighting a yellow-fin tuna the size of a refrigerator. When he tried to land the fish, it suddenly came to life and decided to make one last run. The fish dove deep. Suddenly, that kid was in big trouble. He had reeled in that monster and let the line land at his feet. When the fishing line zinged back out to sea, the fish dragged Kyle overboard. There wasn't a thing anybody could do. Awful, man." Bootman screwed up his face and spat.

"Freak thing, dude," Buddy replied.

"Kid had been fishing on the back of the boat since a little tot."

"Sick."

"Yeah."

— •◦• —

Armed with that dreadful memory, I dashed close to the sugar-scoop, grabbed the fishing line, and began looping it back around the yoyo. Together, we crowded the small space, and things got out of hand.

The fish thrashed wildly about in the water. As the distance between the fish and the boat lessened, it fought more violently. Ever so slowly, Adam and Warren hauled in the monofilament as Sam stood by ready for action with the gaff. Together they looked like three stooges on the steps, acting crazily and yelling at once, caught up in the frenzy. At one point, the fish leapt to throw the hook, and we gasped in unison. It was huge! A two-foot long tuna! Twenty pounds, at least.

"Get a knife! Gloves! A bucket!" Adam and Sam and Warren shouted together. The energy was frenetic and the air tense. Gary dashed about the cockpit in search of a bucket. Peter cautiously steered the boat to lose the wind and slow the boat down. I continued threading the yoyo and praying for calmer heads to prevail.

And then it all went wrong.

I jumped backwards into the cockpit with the yoyo to give the boys more space while keeping a sharp eye on them. Safety concerns? Shot to hell. The boys moved feverishly all over the place. Not sure of what to do, I played lifeguard with a horse collar of a lifejacket.

Adam got the fish up close and jumped back to ease it into the bucket. Warren took a big swing of the gaff, but missed the target, and ended up thumping the fish on the tail. Sam stabbed at the air with the net. Suddenly, the line slackened, and the tuna garnered the energy to take one last leap into the air. It thrashed its tail, gained altitude …

Plop.

The shimmering fish disappeared into the depths, leaving ripples in its wake. The boys stared mutely at the spot where it had dived. The air singed with incredulity and then fury.

"Damn you!" Adam shouted.

"I didn't do anything wrong! It was your fault!" Warren yelled back.

"Idiot!" Adam hollered.

"What's your problem?" Warren bellowed.

"I had the knife ready, dude!" Sam shouted.

"I got the bucket," Gary said gently.

The three stooges gesticulated wildly, pin-wheeling arms, laying accusations. Three yelling testosterone-fueled man-boys sprinted into separate staterooms, slamming drawers, hitting fists against walls.

There goes a new boat, now aged. I thought. I didn't bother with motherly scolding. Discipline out here wouldn't work. There was nowhere for them to exercise their anxieties at sea out in the middle of an ocean. No place to jump ship. No way to calm down.

Gary stood mute in the middle of the cockpit as long arms dangled at his side. When my eyes rested on him, his eyes twinkled with mirth. He shrugged his shoulders and, in calm repose, strolled over to the lifeline to study the sky. After a moment, he turned to gaze at the horizon behind the boat, looking intently for signs with the binoculars. A seabird rode the trough of a wave nearby. After fingering the destroyed pink skirt on the fishing lure, he supplanted it with a new yellow skirt that glinted with sparkling dots from sunlight. He tossed the line back into the sea and sat down on the sugar-scoop step to wait. Time passed.

Zing!

"I gotta' fish! I gotta' fish!" Gary roared with delight.

Footsteps resounded all at once like a buffalo drive. Pouting boys bounded up the stairs and through the main salon doors all at once, colliding into a messy heap in the cockpit. Mayhem ensued with each assuming their role of who was on the bucket, knife and gaff. Out of respect, they all stood in reverential repose behind Gary, giving him ample room to fight the fish. Shouts of encouragement resounded through the balmy air.

"Steady as she goes," cooed Sam.

"Feed that baby in slow and tight," cautioned Adam.

"Nice, Gary," Warren enthused.

I held my breath. There wasn't any cautious gathering in of line. No lifejacket. No guard duty. *Just land the thing!* I thought. We needed this rush like an addict needed his fix. A successful landing would give us the high we needed. We were all weary of the same ole food: canned chicken, beans, and rice, wilted carrots and cabbage. Fresh fish was a prized delicacy. *The brothers' mother will never know,* I told myself.

Gary reeled in the fish ever so slowly. This time, when the fish jumped out of the sea, it looked to weigh a good thirty pounds, bigger than the last one. Gary pulled the line in and yanked at it tightly to avoid slack. When he had the fish under control and close to the boat, he hesitated. At his feet by the water's edge, the fish fought wildly for freedom.

"Sam, you take it," Gary sighed. As a lover of the living, he hated to kill.

Sam moved in, took hold of the line and with one mighty yank, landed the fish on the sugar-scoop. He kept the line taut into the air as it flipped violently. Suddenly from behind, Adam and Warren sprinted like double linebackers. They plunged on top of the fish and wrestled it down as scales and fish slime sprayed surfaces.

"Wow! Another tuna! It's bigger than the last one!" Sam thundered.

I tossed the boys a small rum bottle. They poured a long slug into the gill of the fish and thanked Mother Nature. The great fish succumbed to the pleasure of spirits and then to its death shudder. All were quiet until the great fish finally lay still.

Gary smiled, glad to have escaped the killing. Congratulations came from all around—bear hugs, whoops, and hollers and the clapping of backs as if we'd just won the World Cup.

Night brought a splendid feast of fresh fish with recalls of landing the big one. The event had presented a medley of exuberant activity. Morale soared. The boys united as a team and in good time. Winds receded even more after the great gale and peace fell onto *Scud* ... or at least I believed it to be true.

When I heard a moan and an anguished sigh early the next morning—I knew. The wretched sigh was a familiar sound. Adam discovered the dead shearwater on the side deck. Lying on its side, the feathered body wallowed back and forth to the cant of the boat, one pretty wing extended into the midair. Gorgeous white feathers fluttered in the light breeze.

We had just caught fish for the poor thing. All of us had become attached to the stunning bird. She was our mascot.

The day had been fraught with the good, the bad, and the ugly: the juxtaposition of experiencing utter joy along with bitter despair. It gripped me with unease. Landing the fish felt remarkable and our languishing spirits soared, but the death of our pretty mascot, the shearwater, sent the crew reeling into a feeling of despondency. Also, striving for continual safety at sea while allowing risky behavior had led me into a state of exhaustion. If I watched the boys too carefully, they grew angry. If I watched them too little, an accident could erupt at any time.

I needed steady emotions onboard, ones that ran true and consistent. It seemed a fleeting task. Emotions like anger, sadness and despair were regular happenings on shore, but the same emotions segued into extreme ones at sea, ending in drama and sending a crewmember into an emotional downward spiral for days.

On the other hand, benefits arose with intense scrutiny of emotions at sea. One felt more alive. Awake. Attuned. I juggled the heightened state of awareness and drama with resulting insomnia. It was 4 AM. I watched the mast light draw figures across the sky, begging for sleep while planning the next day's menu.

19.

St. Helena

184-Year Old Tortoise, Jonathon

*History, despite its wrenching pain, cannot be unlived, but
if faced with courage, need not be lived again.*
                                        —*Maya Angelou*

In early morning light, the island of St. Helena lay enshrouded in
fog. Wisps of fog swirled and thinned as *Scud* rode the current in
light winds. Though the big island lay a mere ten miles ahead, it was
as if we were approaching the underworld. The mist created a mystical
energy that seemed to pulse. It lured us forward, beckoning our wayward
souls as if willing to possess. The view captivated us. For no reason, we
whispered amongst ourselves, wanting to hold the spell.

St. Helena lay in the middle of the South Atlantic as if dropped like a giant boulder by the gods haphazardly during a brawl. It was the most remote country in the entire world. There were no airports on the island. The only way to reach the island was by The Royal Mail Ship *St Helena* from Capetown, nearly 1200 miles away. The nearest land was Ascension Island, which was 700 miles to the northwest, and South America, 1,800 miles to the west. These distances overwhelmed me. Despite the exhaustion that fogged my brain and cramped my muscles, I felt a stir of pride, the old sense of value achieved. Half of the Atlantic Ocean now lay stretched out behind us. We were already halfway across. I felt elated. I reached out, grasped Peter from behind, and threw my arms around him. He squeezed my arms in reply.

"Nearly there, Babe!" he shouted.

I watched the boys in front of me as they passed around the binoculars. The four lads looked like young schoolboys under their shaggy bushes of sun-bleached hair. Their soft murmurs penetrated the breeze. Bronze hues of morning light gilded their tanned bodies. I smiled. They had come so far.

Sam held court.

"First thing I'm doing is dragging my scooter ashore for some serious off-road biking," Sam announced, turning back to look at me.

His teeth flashed white in the low light. His wide grin split his face in two. A look of respect supplanted his once frozen, impudent look. The fleeting moment took me aback. Together we had fought long and hard to reach an understanding. I decided to ride the fortuitous change of tide.

We still had another two weeks at sea before land-falling in Brazil. We had not allowed any electronics onboard—no movies or video games. Instead, the boys played Monopoly and cards, devising entertainment while enjoying the natural beauty around them. Hopefully, the crew would be adequately stimulated and challenged enough to remain in high morale

For two months, Peter and I had tried to turn the boys into the bold men that lay just beneath their skin, I trusted Sam's new respect wasn't simply based on the euphoria of a landfall, but on renewed integrity for himself, and us.

I was especially proud of Gary. He had stared down fear by grappling with a small sail in a storm by himself on the foredeck at night. His watches were assumed single-handed now.

When I saw the jagged peak of St Helena poke through the mist, I was elated. The boys exchanged high-fives. The sky was still gray, but you could see the sun fighting to take control.

Suddenly the water exploded in front of us. Two dolphins charged at our twin bows riding the waves. We ran up to the bows and threw our bodies down to peek over the rail. The dolphins passed near enough that we could see their skin patterns and wide grinning mouths. Three more appeared to port and then more to starboard. Then suddenly they were all around us. The great mammals circled the boat, ducked beneath the twin hulls and surged up on the other side. Their huge grey triangular fins sheared the surface as they blew through the vents in the top of their heads. Tears came to my eyes. The dolphins' surprise visit was one reason we cruised: to experience life raw and hard, and then high and bright.

Peter saw my tears streaming down my face. He drew me in so close that I felt I couldn't breathe.

"Isn't this magical?" Peter hummed into my ear. His whiskers tickled my face.

"Oh yes!"

Entering Jamestown Bay, we dropped the hook in the sapphire-blue water beneath the shadows of looming volcanic peaks. The magnificent peaks stretched through the clouds. A deep valley divided the island, surrounded by jutting cliffs. Two impenetrable peaks fringed a barren and forlorn looking inner valley. The only sign of life was red roofed houses that studded the gorge against a backdrop of orange volcanic earth. Morning sun refracted stunning hues of pink and red against volcanic sands.

Getting ashore was quite a feat. Since the anchorage was an open roadstead, protection from the large swell was nonexistent. Because it was the austral winter, swells were mild: 3-4 feet at most. But in a matter of weeks, the weather would drive us out.

With the six of us crammed into the dinghy, we faced a challenging effort in remaining dry while getting ashore. Landing anywhere on the island except at the public landing was impossible. One would be not only shipwrecked upon landing, but the victim could be swept back out to sea. The public landing consisted of a stone wall beneath a canopy constructed of a set of twin bars. Attached to these bars were three fat ropes. One needed to grab hold of the landing rope as the swirling sea swung the dinghy against the wall. Rumor had it that Prince Edward ended up in the drink there many moons ago.

Peter held the engine in slow reverse to counteract the sweep of the sea. Once he felt the dinghy being propelled against the sea wall, he steadied the boat.

"Go!" Peter shouted to Warren.

Warren grasped the fat rope, kicked off from the side of the dinghy, swung away from the wall, then made a perfect landing.

We all followed in turn with Peter taking up the rear to tie off the dinghy to a rig and pulley. An hour passed before we found ourselves neatly packaged to trump into town. My legs felt wobbly, and vertigo assailed me, creating a swaying march. Land sickness was the curse of every sailor after a long passage at sea. A few hours passed before we all felt stable again.

This island was like none other. A long dirt path lead us along the waterfront where fishing boats the size a Mom and Pop could manage lay dry docked, some awaiting fresh paint. At the end of the wharf, we came upon a whitewashed castle entrance flanked by ancient cannons. The castle was a museum and overlooked the harbor where the East India Company once plied their trade.

In the heyday of sailing ships, the crew rested at anchor after many months at sea on the return voyage from India and provisioned ashore in St. Helena before heading back out to sea. When the Suez Canal opened with the advent of steamships, the tall ships no longer called at St Helena. The local population plummeted.

A lovely archway at the castle gate framed Jamestown in the distance. I looked overhead to the coat of arms that depicted the English East India Company. Horse carts, bales of hay, and rugged seamen once stepped through this ancient gateway. As we made our way to Jamestown, the island's main settlement and only harbor, we came upon a single lane road and were astonished to see a village virtually unchanged from a hundred years ago.

The old Georgian town hugged a rugged coastline. The village lay in a deep canyon between two highlands that emptied into the sea. Three roads led out of the village: one ran up either side of the steep canyon and the third track lead to a plateau perched 500 meters above Jamestown.

I was eager to venture down the trail and made a mental note of its location.

Brightly colored shops and houses were painted in blue, green and yellow, lending an atmosphere like that of a small English country village. The houses nestled close together in rows on both sides of Grand Parade and Main Street. An occasional late-vintage car passed. I wondered why one even needed a vehicle in these parts. People with dark European features entered shops and strolled sidewalks. They descended from mostly planters, government civil service workers, and former soldiers. I noticed Chinese features later in the afternoon when parents collected their school children. They were descendants of itinerant workers hired to work the once productive flax plantations. African features were prominent as well. It was one big melting pot of humanity and everyone getting along. *Our American politicians need to study their community ways,* I thought.

A friendly wave across the street drew my attention. I touched Peter's elbow. We were holding hands, my petite fingers hidden in his great palm.

"Morning," said a stout man. "You just sailed in, right?" Biceps pushed at his short sleeves. His tanned face and thick fingers announced his trade as a fisherman. His smile did not touch his mouth but crinkled his blue eyes slightly. A battered cap covered most of his graying hair.

"Yes," I replied with a smile. "We sailed in from Africa."

I felt a swell of pride in saying this. I had overcome my fears . The new personal growth felt like liquid gold in my veins. I vowed not to let fear ever defeat me again. Fear made me feel trapped, small and insignificant. Next time, I vowed, when I see my old fear surface, I will consider it, let it pass over me, through me.

"You must have tea with me and the wife," the fisherman said warmly.

"Thank you," Peter said, after introducing himself.

"I'll see you around town then. Everybody knows you're here. I own the red and blue fishing trawler on the wharf."

"She's got nice lines," Peter answered. "We walked by her this morning."

Wherever we ventured, the Saints waved and greeted us warmly.

After clearing customs and paying a small fee, we stopped at Anne's Tea Shop for coconut fingers and pumpkin fritters, foods influenced by the Malay, British and Chinese cultures. Toward lunchtime, the smell of sweet cakes was replaced by the rich aroma of curry, Pilau (a Southeast Asian dish) and roasted fish. The waters surrounding St. Helena were nutrient rich for tuna and were the island's main export. No wonder a large dolphin population resided in the waters around the island.

We raided the sole grocery store in town and were stunned to see many shelves bare. Although the freezer was stocked with fish and chicken, scant produce or eggs were to be found.

"The RMS *St. Helena* isn't due for another week, maybe two or three weeks," the ancient proprietor said. "Stop in again whenever it arrives and unloads. Maybe we'll have something for you." A gnarly finger, bent by rheumatoid arthritis, drew circles in the air as the short, stocky woman spoke with a thick twang. We were the only shoppers in the store.

Peter and I headed back to the boat for some much-needed rest while the boys ventured further into town. There was little crime on the island, so they couldn't get into too much trouble other than physical injury from an outlandish feat. I needed a stress-free stay on St. Helena like all the sailors before me. So far, the patron saint of the island, Saint Helena, had upheld her namesake by keeping watch over us during our passage. As a guardian of archeologists, I prayed she'd keep watch over these rambunctious teenagers as they tumbled down rocky ledges, jumped off cliffs, and who knew what else?

The next day, an open vintage truck the color of dull rust collected us for an island tour around the forty-seven-square-mile bit of land. An aging but agile man greeted us warmly. His large callused hands were the color of onion skins, darkened with liver spots. He was short and fit. His firm frame gave evidence to years spent in the field or perhaps at sea.

"Morning, folks," he said. "My name's Joe."

Joe put two hands the size of canned hams on the hood of the truck.

"This here is Bessie. She might be very old, but she'll get us where we need to go," Joe said.

Prehistoric it was, but Bessie's charm was piercing. On the island, late model vehicles were simply repaired. The younger generation learned from their elders in how to keep a car running. Where I grew up in the Carolinas, vehicles were discarded like old toys. We grew tired of the color or model and replaced it with a shinier, more impressive ride. Purchasing a new ride was not so practical on St Helena. To obtain a newer vehicle, one would have to be shipped in from Africa on the

RMS *St. Helena*—assuming the ship made it. I admired the low carbon footprint the Saints followed.

We piled in like giddy school kids on a field trip. I stole the front seat, along with Peter. I wanted to spy the island beauty up front and personal. I prided our family in observing a low carbon footprint as well. We hadn't owned a car since we first started cruising thirty-five years ago. We walked everywhere instead of driving.

Driving through Jamestown at a camel's pace of 20 mph (the legal limit), a single lane led up a precipitous volcanic ridge that rose 1,600 to 2,300 feet. Etiquette required the driver coming down to make way for upcoming traffic. Driving on the left hand side of the road complicated matters further. Once two vehicles stopped in front of us, hugging the inner slope, while the female drivers gesticulated wildly, engaged in town gossip. With a wave of Joe's hand, they parted and moved on.

Inside the volcanic range, the coast was barren and dotted with cactus. We passed through hillsides of flax that grew so close to the road, its tall blades brushed the hood and sides of the truck. Across the flaxen void, silver undersides of leaves refracted morning light. The field of blades undulated in the breeze like a massive breathing machine, ebbing and flowing, left and right. The view was breathtaking. I wanted to jump out and run through the field of flax naked, allowing my fingers to touch their velvet surfaces. Peter's hand took mine as our eyes met. I knew he too wanted to do the same.

The flax field took me back to when I once ran topless as a prepubescent tomboy with my Kentucky female cousin. We ran down extended rows of corn taller than my short frame. I giggled and screamed with delight as we raced against each other, grabbing at cornstalks as we ran. In back, the boys wrestled while taking in the views. Laughter reverberated forward. Their joy was a welcome treat.

We passed willows, poplars, and Scotch pines. After three miles, we came across fields of redwood and black cabbage trees, big oaks, cedars and bamboo, banana trees, eucalyptus. In an ebony forest, we stopped to see Napoléon's gravesite. A small mound fringed in a decorative, wrought-iron gate lay situated in a remarkable glade of lavender morning glories. Although the body of Napoléon had been returned to Les Invalides in Paris long ago, the gravesite announced a critical passage of history. We paused as Peter gave a spontaneous history lesson.

"Napoléon Bonaparte was one of the most brutal military

commanders in history, leading France to the Napoléonic Wars and dominating European history for nearly two decades. Before his final defeat, he had seized much of continental Europe and slaughtered nearly 6 million people, both military and civilian."

"Ugh," moaned the kids in unison.

Peter eyed the boys, holding their attention.

I was taken back to when, in Paris, long ago, Peter and I studied masterpieces of Napoléon in the Louvre by Paul Delaroche. We were early in our marriage, awaiting final finishing touches on a new boat in Sweden. To pass the time, we toured Europe in a battered VW camper van during winter, camping alongside rivers and in the middle of fields. Though very cold, it was terribly romantic. We spent long hours strolling down the Rue de Seine alongside the River Seine, arms around each other's waists. I counted him in my life as being one of the best blessings bestowed upon me. I never took him for granted. Around us in Paris at that time was the highest concentration of art galleries and antique dealers in the world. History engulfed me.

Peter made history exciting for me. Where, before, I narrowly passed history courses in college, especially European history, I now reveled in historical research because of our foreign travel.

My mind returned to the present moment when Peter launched into a moving account of how the French Revolution had come to pass. His knowledge of European history captivated me and made him a marvelous traveling companion. Peter's voice drew me in.

I looked around at the boys. Their heads were cast down upon the gravesite of Napoléon. Surrounding it was a simple setting, a lovely knoll: tall oaks, willows, and eucalyptus, a lawn of luscious grass.

"Joe, why is there not an inscription on the tomb? No one would know this was Napoléon's gravesite if they just happened to it. There's no entry sign on the road either," I asked. "For a man as powerful as Napoléon was, the site is rather insignificant."

"That's intentional. The Governor at the time, Sir Hudson Lowe, insisted the inscription read 'Napoléon Bonaparte'. But the French wanted the Imperial title of 'Napoléon' since royalty were signed by their first names back then," Joe said. "As a result, the tomb here in the Valley of Willows was left nameless." He held both arms out, palms to the sky and shrugged.

Peter jumped in.

"You must consider what brought about the revolution to fully grasp it. The French Revolution was a time of social and political upheaval in France, much like our own American Revolution when we fought against the British for freedom." Hands in his jean pockets, he stood stately and calm as he sought to draw the boys out.

"You see, the French government was deeply in debt after the American Revolutionary War, which they helped bankroll until they were nearly bankrupt. After failed crops, the French needed cash and placed tough taxation schemes upon the peasants which became inflamed. The peasants resented the privileges enjoyed by the clergy and aristocracy—like castles and mansions. The peasants demanded change and got them. The period of Enlightenment arose: Human rights were restored, women marched on Versailles."

Peter pointed at me, and I lifted my hand to my brow in mock salute to the women of Versailles.

"In time feudalism was abolished," Peter continued. "This resulted in the National Republic replacing the previously established monarchy. The people executed King Louis XVI soon after."

We all had eyes on Peter, breathing in history, feeling the impact of Napoléon's gravesite.

Peter's eyes twinkled when he spoke. I marveled at what a fine educator he was. His passion for history was evident. He remembered historical details and facts about political figures that had escaped me long ago in the halls of educational institutions. For me, history was something I memorized and then forgot. Not for Peter. He lived and breathed history. "Here's where Napoléon came in," Peter said again. He was on a roll, holding the boys with rapt attention. "After the execution of the King, the French government collapsed in a coup d état led by Napoléon. It was the last year of the French Revolution because Napoléon established an empire and French society underwent a transformation as feudal, aristo-cratic and religious privileges disappeared. Old ideas about hierarchy disappeared under the mantra of liberalism, nationalism, socialism and the practice of total war. Thus began the deadly Napoléonic Wars."

"Did he get to keep any of the booty?" Warren asked. "I mean, where's your stash, dude?" A round of smirks and giggles echoed in the dark forest. Sam kicked the back of Gary's knee where he had been supporting most of his light frame. Gary tumbled into a heap on the grass.

"Hey, what about those wenches? Aye?" Sam added. "I'm thinking luscious European babes for Napoléon, mind you!"

Booty. My mind took me back. Where did we leave our lost bag of gold, the Krugerrands valued at $10,000? A hotel? A rental car? There was one happy cleaning maid somewhere, cashing in the lost bag of gold somewhere—the little wench.

"Well, yes, Sam. You're quite right. Although Napoléon was married, he sired many non-marital children."

Joe added to the fray. "On his deathbed here in St Helena, Napoléon called out for Josephine, his one true love, who had horrible teeth. That's why you never see her smiling in portraits. Napoléon divorced her because she was unable to bear him a child. She had a way with men, I understand. Although she was a widow with two children when Napoléon met her, she was no saint—she was the mistress of several men, including Napoléon's boss. During the French Revolution, Josephine and her husband were imprisoned. He died under the jaws of the guillotine. Napoléon was obsessed by her, though she was six years older than him."

"My kind of woman!" Sam shouted, and punched the air.

As we made our way along the grassy trail back to the truck, Sam tossed down his mobile scooter, jumped aboard and pushed ahead of his buddies. The boys charged after him like the Pied Piper in hot pursuit down a long trail. At the truck, Sam folded his scooter, and we piled in like army ants.

Heading down a steep incline towards the harbor, Sam leapt out of the back of the truck with his scooter just as the truck wheels began to pick up speed. The loud cheers from the boys announced Sam's revelries. I glanced back. Perfectly balanced on the scooter, Sam weaved left and right along the single lane road, rapidly gaining speed on the descent until he nearly reached the truck's fender. I gasped. *Not here. Not now. No injuries. Please.* In a matter of days, we needed to depart from St Helena to beat impending bad winter storms. The last thing we needed was a patient in the local clinic on an island without an airport. The RMS *St. Helena* could take weeks before reaching Capetown from here if we needed to get anyone off the island for surgery. We couldn't leave anyone behind either. My fingers dug into my pant leg, willing inner calm.

Om Mani padme Hum, Om Mani padme Hum, I chanted like a Buddhist.

On a distant hill, Joe pointed out Napoléon's place of internment, the Longwood House. It lay nestled amongst rolling hills of low and lush greenery, far away from any other home. Barely 4,000 people reside on St Helena and over a quarter of them lived in Jamestown, the capital . As we exited the truck, Sam came roaring in like Napoléon himself, except on a scooter instead of a rearing white horse. I had to hand it to him: Sam possessed pizazz.

A smell of verdant earth rode in on the afternoon breeze as our guide, Joe, opined about Napoléon.

"The French emperor was confined at Longwood House for six years where he penned his memoirs and wrote love letters to Joséphine de Beauharnais. He emperor hated it here. Though the estate was a twenty-three room house, he bitterly complained about the damp, windy conditions. As you can see, there are few trees surrounding the house for protection. Rumors flew of his poisoning by arsenic upon his death, but his doctor ruled the death as stomach cancer," Joe said.

Inside the Longwood House, antiques, doilies, and heavy red carpets lent a depressing air. Peter wanted none of it. He disdained warfare, believing in the sanctity of human life. With a whisk of his hand through the air, Peter marched out of the dismal house.

I lingered behind to feel the presence of Napoléon. I relished museums. Where Peter dashed through hallways of interest, I read every plaque, eyed every exhibit.

Clambering back into the ramshackle truck, Joe chugged down the hill as Gary ran after Sam on the scooter. A former field runner, Gary was on Sam's tail until we reached the Plantation House, the residence of the Governor. It was a stately home built by the East India Company, and the Governor still resided in the mansion, often holding garden parties for privileged guests. Gazing at the mansion, I felt it still held its charm. A beautiful forest of oak and mahogany surrounded the mansion, fringed in a magnificent lawn inhabited by otherworldly looking reptiles.

We traversed the great lawn to study the giant land tortoise that stood sentinel, regarding us warily. Joe came to stand in front of us, and we all spread out on the luscious lawn.

"That's Jonathan, the oldest living tortoise to date in the world and perhaps the oldest living reptile. Jonathan came to the island from the Seychelles in the late 1800's," Joe said with a wide grin.

The graceful turtle moved slowly across the carpet of green as we watched with rapt attention. Adam leaned down to stretch on the grass for a close up-eye view of Jonathan's face from a foot away as the tortoise slowly grazed, unbothered by our presence. Quite the contrary—he seemed to be posing for photos as I snapped away.

"The land tortoise has been known to travel three or four miles in a day on rugged terrains like that of the Seychelles and Galapagos," Joe added.

He was moving along at a pretty impressive clip for his age and size, inch by inch.

"Despite Jonathon's old age, he still has the energy to mate regularly with Myrtle and Emma, the younger females too," Joe said with a chuckle. He pointed to the far corner of the garden where a wooden structure housed two females. They were content grazing without the attention of the paparazzi.

"The local school kids believe the slave burial ground not far from the mansion is haunted. They should know—they play soccer at the site. They say a cold air invades the great mound now and then."

Warren nudged Gary with his elbow with a mischievous look in his eyes. Gary's cobalt-blue eyes danced with mirth. Vivid memories crowded back of when they disappeared together to scour for stones in the diamond fields in Africa. I watched those two devils intently.

"Shh," Warren hissed at Gary, throwing a pointed chin in my direction. I felt like the schoolmarm on a field trip.

Joe went on.

"Over 5,000 bodies were unearthed at the haunted soccer field by archaeologists recently when preparations were being made for the new airport. Long ago, slave ships were rescued by the British Royal Navy when they suppressed the slave trade in the Caribbean," Joe said.

Peter joined in with Joe.

"The slave ships traveled what was called the Middle Passage, or the 2nd leg of a triangular route sailed by European ships. Ships departed Europe for African markets with manufactured goods that they traded for purchased or kidnapped Africans. The Africans were transported across the Atlantic as slaves and then sold or traded for raw materials. The raw materials would be transported back to Europe to complete the voyage. It was, no doubt, one of the greatest crimes against humanity. They suffered appalling conditions," Peter said. He looked down, his once cheerful countenance eroded by tragic history.

"Even when rescued by the Royal Navy, the victims still suffered horrific conditions in the refugee camps here on St Helena. There were so many of them: over 150,000 were brought here during the years of slavery. Babies, young men, and mothers made up a lot of the group, and were in the prime of life. When they died, they were placed in a massive grave," Joe said.

Joe stopped talking and hung his head in the sad reference. After a bit of time, he recovered himself and continued with the sad reality of St Helena's history.

"The English East India Company brought in so many slaves that nearly half the population of the island was 'black gold.' It was two centuries before slaves became freed. On this island, there's not one bit of racism. Every black person, Malay, British, and Dutch are God's children. We've all intermarried. There's not a lot of options for mates around these parts, as you can tell. Color never matters here. Respect does," Joe finished with a flair.

St. Helena was a remarkable little island indeed. The more I learned about it, the more I longed to come back and reside on a pretty knoll in a little house with a white gate.

20.

JAIL TIME

Jamestown, St Helena

An ignorant person with a bad character is like an unarmed robber, but a learned person with a blog is a robber fully armed.

—Mickey Kaus

The following morning our breakfast was interrupted by the sudden arrival of *Running Wind* with Nick and his autistic son, Earnest, onboard. As they motored up to *Scud*, the newly hired Captain and the female 1st mate appeared in the cockpit. Earnest lingered on the bow, grinning wildly and gesticulating like a pinwheel. The journey seemed to have made an impression on him. He looked happy.

A couple days later, we met up with Nick and Earnest in town and stopped to have curry at Anna's Tea Shoppe. Nick appeared highly stressed in contrast to his son, who sat calmly in quiet repose.

"I don't know what to do," Nick said, wringing his hands. "I had to bail my Captain out of jail this morning. He got drunk at the White Horse Pub last night and punched a man who hit on his fat girlfriend, Nora. The landlord of the pub called the police." He threw his head back and let out a sigh.

Peter was deeply concerned. "You're kidding! Where did you find this captain—what's his name?" Peter said.

"Patrick," Nick said with exhaustion. He wiped his brow with a napkin.

"What are you going to do?" Peter asked.

"Dump all the booze overboard and not allow any aboard once we sail. That's what!" Nick was beside himself—and with good reason. "It's life or death out there on the high seas, especially with winter coming. I don't need the problem of an alcoholic onboard too!"

"What made you hire him?" Peter asked.

"He came recommended! For years, he's been the professional captain for the South African manufacturer of my boat, delivering new catamarans for clients all over the world. I figured he was okay," Nick added.

"Can you handle the boat yourself?" Peter asked.

"No. I've never sailed before in my life on an ocean passage—just small lake stuff. I'm from the Midwest. This ocean passage was going to be my beginner's instruction lesson into sailing on bluewater," Nick said with a shake of his head.

"Well, you can't exactly ship him home and hire a new captain. There's no way off this island," Peter said.

"Yep. I know. Tell me about it," Nick added.

"Look, I think we can help you out. Why don't you depart the same day as we do? We can maintain communication via single-side band radio every morning and evening. Do you have an SSB?"

"No. I couldn't afford the radio. I'm on a budget and newly divorced. My ex wife took nearly everything except the boat."

Peter tried hard not to reveal his shock. Earnest was a delightful person and had accomplished great things in just being out here. But he couldn't crew: couldn't stand watch alone, handle sails and lines, or manage jam-cleats. Earnest was gaining the experience of a lifetime, and I hoped it wouldn't end badly.

I thought back to when our sons asked to bring Sam and Gary on this trip. Peter and I had been concerned: the brothers had never endured an ocean passage, taken long watches, or handled emergencies at sea. This ocean crossing was not a walk in the park. It was a very serious endeavor, and doing it without the right preparation would be like trekking up the Mt Everest trail and forgetting your oxygen mask.

This was why Peter insisted Sam and Gary assume watch-taking alone from the get-go. If they couldn't pull their weight, both would be shipped home. Crewing is serious business. If you don't do it right, you or someone else could die or become injured in some accident.

Nick agreed to rush provisioning to be able to depart with us.

"We're planning on departing in one week; we're already gathering GRIB files for weather info," Peter said.

Nick massaged the mutilated forefinger that he injured during the robbery in front of the Durban high-end hotel. The final stitches were removed at the St Helena clinic. Swollen red patches were still visible. It seemed like Nick was on a bad luck streak. When we parted ways with them at Anne's Tea Shoppe, a sickening feeling pervaded my gut. My intuitive inclinations usually rang true. I prayed this one didn't.

Our final days in port found us busy with boat chores. Water jugs needed filling, food purchased, systems analyzed, and weather data gathered. Peter and I took on the provisioning, lest the boys return with less nutritious items. After their morning school work and chores, they disappeared to surf on the other side of the island or venture into town.

The mail boat still had not arrived, and I was getting desperate. Few vegetables were available other than cabbages, carrots and potatoes. These would have to do. I missed green leafy salad makings, ripe tomatoes, and broccoli. I struggled with finding eggs. They were not available, anywhere. *Surely someone raises chickens here*, I thought.

Peter and I decided to investigate the outback for the mysterious missing eggs. Rumor had it that Half-Tree Hollow had eggs. We prepared to set off at first light since we knew it would be a long hike. No one bothered to mention we had to climb a ladder to reach Half-Tree Hollow.

Sure enough, as we headed toward town, we paused to take in our surroundings on the wharf and plan the attack to acquire eggs. I felt desperate. The four boys devoured eggs for breakfast, and I needed eggs for quick bread and snacks like pastries and cake. Two weeks on the high seas with four growing teenagers would be unpleasant without them.

Jamestown lay on an igneous rock inside a small enclave in James Valley, sandwiched between two steep cliffs—referred to as *the Highlands*—that are carved from volcanic rock and unsuitable for building. The terrain resembled the surface of the moon, barren and void of trees. Half-Tree Hollow lay on a plateau 500 meters above Jamestown. Taking the road to get there was out of the question, as it would mean sharing narrow switchbacks on a dusty, very narrow track, and would take most of the day.

Jacobs Ladder

Facing the town, we turned our heads to all points of the compass to determine the shortest route. "Why not take the short-cut?" I asked. "It's right there! That little ladder. It'll save us mountains of time."

Peter agreed, and off we set.

Once we reached the bottom of the ladder, we stood in astonishment as our necks strained up and up to take in its size against glaring sun. A vertiginous row of 699 steps ran straight up at an angle of 45 degrees. Each step was set a foot apart from the other and the same as wide, giving it a hefty climb at 600-feet (183m) from sea level.

"Yikes! I need a cable car for this thing!" I said.

"Aw, come on Babe. You can do it!" Peter said. "Whew, would you look at that!" He pinched my biceps and blew out a breath of air.

He could make me laugh in the worst of times and he seemed always to get his way.

"Ok then. Let's get on with it," I said with a chuckle.

We started off. I led to gauge the pace. My short legs struggled with the steep incline, but I grasped the rails when needed and moved at a decent clip. If alone, I would have preferred to limp along at a turtle's pace and take all day. I didn't want Peter passing me up lest he considered me frail and frumpy. But after one hundred steps, my breath caught and I felt dizzy. These were not normal steps, but more like a ladder to a rooftop. Determination pulled me forward until I counted past 300 steps. That was barely halfway. Sweat poured down my shirt and pooled in my flip flops.

Peter paused beside me, barely breathing. As an avid runner, this was an easy challenge for him.

"Wow, would you look at that view!" Peter implored and whistled softly, shaking his head.

How sweet. He was permitting the pause for me to catch my breath. What a gentleman! I took in my moon-like, crater surroundings.

A cobalt-blue sea stretched far beyond. Stillness hung over it all. Not a breath of wind moved. The sky was a milky blue, filled with the haze of St Helena's volcanic sand. The Harmattan haze began to shut out the sun and extended in every direction out to the endless ocean. A patina of dust carpeted the rails, stuck to our clothes and filled our nostrils. We were both silent as we leaned against the rail lest we lose our balance from distraction and barrel back down the steep steps. I fought back vertigo and breathed deeply.

Time stood still. Neither of us moved, lost in thought.

"How long do you think we'll sail, Babe?" I asked quietly.

Peter shrugged. He kept his eyes out on the ocean. The masts of *Scud* and *Running Wind* were still as steeples.

"Maybe always. I love it out there on the ocean. I feel alive," he said. I couldn't read his eyes because of his dark sunglasses, but I knew t he crow's feet at the corner of his eyes were dancing.

"Sometimes I wonder if we're hiding. You know, as if the real world is somewhere else. But the real world is what we create for ourselves. Right?" I said.

Peter threw me a winning smile and drew me into his arms on the cramped stairs. I felt close to this man, happy in our simple life. I liked the way we enjoyed nature together and sought out adventures. His good parenting skills juxtaposed my less admirable ones. I felt supremely insouciant in our union. I felt it more strongly now, right here, at this moment.

Fluffy clouds drifted in with a light breeze, wrinkling blue water with sparkles, dispersing some of the haze. I watched in wonder as an old man entered the ladder at the base and began climbing at the clip of a young man. He carried a basket in each hand, never grasping the rails. The space between us closed at a rapid rate. My Zen was quickly supplanted by my ego.

"Let's get a move on," I said.

"Roger that!" Peter knew what I meant. He pulled out in front of me, instead of me leading the way. He began whistling. The only time Peter whistled was when he felt nervous or bored. Bored, he was not. I smiled and picked up my pace. Now and then, I glanced between my moving feet to gauge the progress of Mr. Olympus. He climbed in my shadow a couple hundred feet down the precipitous steps.

Where previous sweat had dried in an instant from the lack of wind, sweat now stained my t-shirt. My hands started slipping on the rails. In a matter of minutes, my toes slid around in my flip flops like wheels on ice. Why had I not worn sneakers?

"Oops. Oh, ha!" I guffawed. Slippery sandals always took me back to a time with my two sisters.

"What's so funny?" Peter asked, surprised at my outburst.

"Oh, I was thinking about Lilly and Carol. We once sang a trio in church. Carol hit a wrong note, got the giggles, and sat on the floor, hidden behind the podium. Lilly and I tried to finish the song, but Carol yanked at my dress to get me to join her on the floor. Lilly and I were doing a pretty good job of holding our own, until Lilly hit an off note too.

"Mother stared us down, willing us to behave. Her face was scarlet with fury. Lilly succumbed to Carol's shenanigans, but I grasped Lilly around the waist, unwilling to let her abandon me. I was overwhelmed by the absurdity of it all. But I belted it out anyway.

"We were singing 'Onward, Christian Soldiers. And then it was all over. I wet myself. Rivulets of yellow liquid trickled down the insides of my legs. I blushed and felt hot in the un-air-conditioned sanctuary. My feet slipped while I was fighting to keep Lilly upright. Carol was stronger than me and won out by pulling her down I sang alone. Then it fell apart."

"I couldn't hold it any longer: urine, sweat, and tears—knowing that I'd get a whipping—flooded my sandals. Holding my head up high, I stopped singing. Together we marched off to find our way to the front pew. My kegel muscles were as tight as a drum skin.."

My chatter brought us nearly to the end of the ladder, just as Mr. Olympus excused himself to pass us. We gave way respectfully, admiring his gait. He waited for us at the top. Whereas we were panting, he wasn't even breathing hard.

"Greetings. Welcome to St. Helena. You're new here," the Saint said.

"Yes. Thank-you. Do you walk up this ladder often?" I asked

"Every day. My granddaughter lives in the village. The wife and I prefer it up here. Jacobs Ladder is 699 steps. It keeps me young, but the wife—her knees, you know," he said.

"Why is it here?"

"Jacobs Ladder used to be the Ladder Hill Railway, used to bring up the manure from stables and stockyards in Jamestown to the inland farmers here in the highlands. When the supply ship sailed in, the mechanical railway was used to ferry supplies to Ladder Hill Fort here in what is now Half-Tree Hollow. When it fell into disrepair, old timers like me used it as a shortcut to town. You should see the kids. They ride the rails down on their feet and backside!" said the kind Saint.

We found the sole grocery shop a few ways down the road. It was tiny, more like a roadside stand. "Any eggs?" I begged the proprietor.

"No, my dear. Not till the ship comes in," she said.

When we sailed out of port three days later, the ship *RMS St. Helena* still had not reached. A gnarly weather system was due. *Scud* sailed out of Jamestown Bay with *Running Wind* in our wake at first light.

21.

QUEEN OF OCEANS

Wild Horses on a Morning Walk

All things are artificial for nature is the art of God.
—*Thomas Browne*

We departed early morning on a favorable forecast with *Running Wind*. In our wake, St. Helena shrank until her twin peaks dropped into the ocean amidst a lacy curtain of light fog. The island grew grayer and more spectral with each advance of *Scud* toward the west, until at last the fog closed around the island and it was no more. By mid-morning, *Scud* sailed out from beneath the wind shadow of the big island, allowing the trades to fill in. Peter and the boys launched the spinnaker. A great curtain of green and yellow cast against a backdrop of the deep blue ocean, looking majestic.

Expectations of landing tuna were high since fish was St. Helena's main export. Fishing lines were set. When the boys pulled out the board game of RISK after school lessons, I prepared a feast for the much anticipated tuna. In the background, I heard the boys invading countries, conquering and defending. It sounded like Napoléon's strategy of war all over again.

"Hey, you're out of troops, Dude, so send your French attack packing!" exclaimed Warren.

"Ah, but next time I'll conquer England because I'll roll a bigger number. Just you wait!" Gary quipped.

Invading troops in defenseless countries competed; dice and soldiers moved in and retreated. Their banter inspired joy and reminded me of a snowy day before a roaring fire, playing Monopoly with my siblings.

The RISK gamed dragged on. Hours of play became a day.

"Say, how about putting away this game? It's all over the place," I said.

"Yeah, soon, Mom," Warren said.

Day two arrived and still the game was on.

"Today. It's got to go," I said. "I implore you!"

"Yeah, right, Mom. We will. Promise," said Adam.

Day three arrived, and still the game was on.

The board and pieces blanketed the main salon table, taking up valuable space needed for studying charts, serving food, and working on school books. I couldn't take the clutter anymore. That evening when cleaning up, I accidentally knocked the board and pieces went flying: red, yellow, green and blue soldiers. I gathered the gaggle of weaponry and men, tossed them back on the board, straightened them in a totally disregarded fashion, and went on my merry way. The next day was near mutiny.

"Someone is cheating! My country is gone!" Adam wailed.

Oops, I thought. In time, games of poker supplanted RISK, and hard gambling commenced.

"I call and raise you five beans," Adam announced to Sam.

"Ha! I'm all in, but I'm playing real money now, not beans," Sam said.

"You're on!" Adam quipped.

"Fold," said Gary.

"I call and raise you $5," said Warren.

"Show what you got, Sam!" Adam said.

"HA! My three of a kind beats your two pairs!" Sam said to Adam, smacking him on the back. "And I don't want your beans either. Cash in, dude."

"I don't have $10," Adam said.

"Then you can do my turn of the dishes," Sam countered.

I never knew who had clean-up duty since their betting messed up the flow chart. In the beginning, the boys compiled a group chart of boat duties. If I cooked, someone else did the dishes.

The boys were obviously enjoying themselves with poker. I left them to it. Sam was a master at betting. His mathematical genius could count cards, leaving him winning most of the games.

Fish dominated our diet for the next ten days as we sailed ever closer to Brazil, the final landfall of our Atlantic Crossing. I couldn't believe how relaxing and enjoyable this leg had been in contrast to our passages around and out of Africa. Gone were the gales, fog, and diamond mining ships. All that remained were empty sea lanes.

"Have you seen *Running Wind*?" I asked Peter one morning.

"No, I haven't seen them since the first evening after our initial departure from St Helena. I'm sure they're alright," Peter said.

I felt uncertain.

"What did you make of the mishap with the Captain and the fouled spinnaker?" I asked.

"Yeah, too bad."

We'd been enjoying curry with Nick and Earnest in St. Helena one day when Nick shared the incident.

"We were on passage from Capetown to St. Helena when winds escalated from a steady breeze to gusty conditions, threatening to blow out the seams of the spinnaker. Patrick ran forward to douse the spinnaker, but was distracted and hadn't given enough attention to the control line. The line had pooled around his feet. As he began to collapse the sail by pulling on the halyard, the control line shortened. The spinnaker sock started to come down, and then the control line tightened around his ankle. He lost control of the sail. The control line whipped him up to the head of the sail at the top of the mast. He dangled upside down, trapped and entangled in the line, whipping back and forth with each canting of the boat," Nick said, his face mapped with terror.

"Oh my god! What did you do?" I asked.

"Unless I did something, someone was going to get killed. Natasha was screaming. She abandoned the helm and ran forward to bring him down, but she neglected to engage the auto pilot. So, of course, the boat veered off course and ended up wrapping the spinnaker around the shrouds and spreaders. It was terrible, I can tell you that!" Nick said.

If it weren't for the fearful look on his face and the lack of booze in his tea, I would've imagined this whole scenario had been invented. But bad things can happen at sea quickly if you don't have your act together.

"So I took the helm so that she could free Patrick. But one mistake led to another until raging chaos ensued. Eventually, I was able to run forward and help, but the spinnaker halyard had twisted during the partial collapse and the shackle had snagged. In the end, we had to pull out a deck knife to shred the sail so it would collapse. Once the rig was free, we were able to bring in Patrick." Nick collapsed his head into his hands.

"It was horrifying," wailed Nick. "He was cut up, bruised, and had contusions and a busted ankle. He was in the sky whirling about and kept hitting the mast every time the boat hit a wave. Natasha threatened to bring up a pistol to shred the sail. I refused! Later, I ran across an empty Vodka bottle in the galley. How didn't I see that they were both intoxicated?"

Suddenly, my musings with Peter over *Running Wind's* woes were caught short by a shout from the bow.

"Ahead! Something there!" hollered Adam. "Noon target! Dead ahead!"

I left Peter at the helm and ran forward to join Adam as the rest of the crew clambered up on deck. Sure enough, a large shape floated on the water. It resembled a bizarre fish of some kind. As we sailed down upon it, a giant eyeball the size of a dinner plate gazed back at us. It looked as if the giant fish would ride the current between our twin hulls. On a spinnaker run, there was little time to change course.

"It'll fit between the hulls! Don't worry," Peter shouted from astern.

The giant fish remained motionless on our approach, and I feared it dead, but no. Just as the fish rode between our twin hulls, a curved dorsal fin moved. It was alive! It was the most peculiar fish I'd ever seen. It looked like a giant fish head with wings. It was about three meters long and seemed to be basking on the water's surface for warmth. It was gone as quickly as we had encountered it.

I dashed back inside to scour our field guides. After a bit of research,

I learned that it was an ocean sunfish, the largest bony fish of the sea. It can weigh up to 5,000 lbs. and reach up to 14 feet long and 10 feet wide. They feed on jellyfish. I vowed to collect all trash at sea, especially plastic bags that resemble jellyfish. A bag to an ocean sunfish would be instant death.

After ten days at sea, *Scud* drifted quietly into the Baia de Santo Antonio as a full moon rose from a tall peak, silhouetted against the brilliant moonlight. All crewmembers were needed on deck to safely anchor the boat. The entrance to the bay was straightforward in deep water without the added dangers of negotiating a narrow channel or entrance. Few yachts were in the harbor, except for some fishing vessels moored close to shore.

On our slow and cautious approach, the neon-orange orb of the moon hung low and bright, shining through a spray of light clouds. Once inside the harbor, I picked up the binoculars and sighted a glowing white beach that shimmered in the moonlight as palm fronds danced a lacy shadow across the sands. The full moon dappled a slight surf that rolled into the harbor, sending boats jostling. A vast peak extended out from shore, standing sentinel atop a peninsula. It was a jagged, rocky pinnacle that resembled a phalanx—an appropriate setting for passionate Brazil. The full moon was the only source of illumination, other than navigational screens. It was all we needed. Flashlights were left stowed. A full moon entry into a harbor was a sailor's constant prayer.

We ghosted in, and the hook released with a clatter into a patch of sand, easily sighted by moonlight. The village near the bay lay in quiet, and the noise of the boat anchoring echoed across the bay.

I stood motionless, listening to the beckoning of nature without really seeing. An owl hooted, and yet other birds were quiet in their nocturnal state. The truth lies in nature. The sound of nature at night soothed my soul. I listened to nature like a blind woman. When I focused on the palm fronds fluttering in the dappled light on shore, I heard the vibrations as they shimmered into one rhythm, a million atoms joining as one. God was their director, and I was in attendance.

The magic was everywhere, all around me, hidden in rhyme, song and images. The ocean, the whales, the dolphins and the fish were the same as me: particles. They were just in a different form than me. I loved hearing particles speak. All you had to do was open up and listen, but you couldn't hear unless you loved.

Peter joined me at the bow on the trampolines where I lay, listening with my heart. He knelt down along with me. I could feel his exhaustion. His keen awareness and captaining skills had brought us all across this vast ocean. .

We were a true team now. We had begun rather roughly, but we had endured after never giving up, always trying and always seeking. Six vibrant personalities inside a small space of forty-four feet by twenty-four feet felt like a holding cell. Now it was a palace gilded by spiritual growth. No one could have anticipated such rewards. Sam and Gary had become like sons.

Peter held me so close that his heart beat rapidly against my own. In a short time, his breathing became labored, and I knew he was asleep. I was equally exhausted for the same weariness. The physical fatigue was bewildering. I pushed away the concern and rode the high of our landfall, ever following a positive outlook.

Next morning, we were up early to clear customs.

"All right!" Warren yelled. "My ride to McDonald's has arrived!"

"I'm right there with you, bro," hollered Adam.

"Take me!" Sam said as he tumbled in to join his comrades.

"Don't forget me!" countered Gary.

I dashed up on deck to see a mega yacht that had arrived sometime during the night. On its back deck was a small helicopter, large enough for two people. The boys were fighting over who was to be invited first—as if they knew the owner on board. I giggled to myself.

"Oh, and you know Rachel Welch?" I asked Sam.

"That's a small point unworthy to consider against my gifted prowess. We might have a date for this evening, in fact!" Sam quipped.

Oh, he was good. I was surely going to miss out on Sam's humor. His laughter refreshed me every morning. I never knew what he was going to say.

"Only three days in port, then you must be gone," said the gendarme on shore after we cleared customs.

We understood. In fact, we had known the requirements to visit Rio de Noronha. A visa was required to visit the mainland of Brazil, but we had neglected to obtain it in South Africa. We didn't want to make landfall on the mainland: only the outlying islands. Hurricane season was upon us, and we needed to reach shelter in the Caribbean in time.

We jumped into high gear. Time was of essence as we prepared for the final route to Grenada where Sam and Gary were due to fly home. We drew up a verbal chart of duties for each crew member and sent the four boys off.

They left together to jerry-jug water and diesel fuel. Peter stayed aboard to maintain systems (engines, pumps, gears) and plan a navigation route for our impending passage. I provisioned in town, using freelancing villagers as taxis. My ride ended up being a red convertible beach buggy that I loved. My driver sped down the quiet country road that led from the wharf. We passed a man on a horse in tow of four other horses on a joint tether, an ox and cart, and modern wind turbines—a juxtaposition against the toil of a farmer's field.

Provisioning complete, we prepared to attend the village dance on our last night in the harbor. The boys were eager to show their dancing abilities, and I was eager to join them. I hadn't attended a public event for nearly six months. My Portuguese was basic, but would have to do. Peter opted to stay on the boat for some much needed rest and to maintain a sharp lookout since gusty conditions prevailed. It was difficult for him to enjoy himself if he was worried about the boat.

"Stick your thumb out on the wharf. Plenty of folks are headed your way," a kind fisherman told me earlier in the day. His eyes twinkled with genuine pleasure, proud to show off his country. "Don't worry. These are country people. There hasn't been any crime on this island since the pirate days!"

I took him at his word.

By eight o'clock in the evening, we found ourselves riding in the back of a dilapidated pick-up truck up a narrow, grassy trail in the forest.

In the waning moonlight, we drove along a bumpy track. A thick canopy of limbs created dancing patterns of light across the road behind us as we sped forward. I felt the boys move apart beside me. Suddenly, Warren stood up and grabbed hold of the truck cab in front. We hit a big bump in the track, and I looked forward in time to see a massive branch headed our way. Gary followed my gaze.

"Watch out!" Gary shouted to Warren, and yanked him back down.

"Dude!" Sam yelled. "Don't knock yourself out before your Portuguese Sheila gets to dance with you!"

All day long, the boys had been talking about the gifts of Latin girls. They meant the way they danced, surely?

We heard the music before we saw it. A loud bass resounded around the bend, and we drove up to join the myriad of vehicles already parked in the field. We thanked the driver profusely, and I offered to buy him a beer as thanks for the ride.

"I pode comprar uma cerveja?"

"*Obrigado,*" he said. After handing him a cerveza, I joined the villagers who lounged upon a patchwork scene of colorful handcrafted quilts and sat on makeshift chairs of coolers and tree stumps. Surrounding them were various family members.

Here there were no low-riding jeans, tattoos, body piercings or punk hairdos. I wished Peter was here to enjoy the jovial, family festival. He was shy on the dance floor, never planting his feet firmly in one place. His inability to dance well was always overcome by the moves I made around him, using his body much like a Maypole. All I wanted were his eyes on me, and to be in his arms as he caught me when I went flying.

The boys made their way around the back where beer and wine were set up atop a folding table, served by a couple of elderly fishermen. I watched them from where I stood. Tall for their ages, the boys rose a good foot or two above the Brazilians, which made it easy for me as their chaperone. I knew the fishermen were not questioning their ages. Here in the remote countryside of an off lying island of Brazil, I doubted carding was an issue. Three generations of family members had their eyes on the young foreigners in town. Though I didn't mind if the kids sneaked a beer or two, intoxication would not be permitted, especially since we were setting off on passage at first light to Grenada tomorrow.

I stood off the dance floor admiring the young girls and their male companions. Bodies intertwined, moving like liquid gold in energetic samba and salsa moves. The Brazilian beat held me transfixed, as did the women around me, whether old grannies or young mothers. Their wide hips gyrated back and forth as they chatted amiably. I smiled at their transparent display of physical pleasure. Their young toddlers and babies slept peacefully across soft blankets that carpeted the field of grass, despite the beat of the loud bass. Now and then, someone pulled out a bottle of milk for a baby or a snack for grandma.

Overhead, a tangle of yellow lights illuminated the dance floor. As partners twirled, a patina of dust rose from spinning heels. The school-aged girls wore dark skirts, flowing black hair following their petite bodies like party streamers as they whirled, stamped, and flexed. Their rhythmic pelvic movements were intoxicating. When the dancers moved into a feverish trance, the musicians played louder, holding the end of the song until couples were spent.

Their passionate intent resembled the ritualistic love dance Peter and I had boogied on a particularly lively Friday night, accompanied by Dire Straits' "Love Over Gold" when onboard the boat alone. As it blared across our decks, we disappeared into each other, and I fell into the song: "You're a dancer..."

Even now, watching the couples move with languid form, I closed my eyes and began to tilt my body, left and right to feel the rhythm run through my veins like a liquid rush. I relaxed, and a marvelous feeling of well-being draped over my battered self. Stress and worry in anticipation of the next passage melted away. I began to feel transformed by the energetic atmosphere. There was no other place that I'd rather be.

My natural dependency upon dance as a way to erase anxiety paralleled with the beginning of Brazilian dance. When European settlers arrived in Brazil, they brought African slaves with them to work the sugarcane fields. The slaves introduced their customs, songs, and music. The predominantly Catholic elite upper class of Brazil frowned upon the African dance, considering the samba and other dances to be lewd and obscene. The Brazilian slave dances grew into a subversive culture and disappeared underground, where slaves continued their unique African dance. The slaves used it to ease away their frustrations at having to deal with their conditions. The word "samba" is derived from a Bantu word, meaning 'to pray' or 'to invoke the spirits of ancestors.'

Once slavery was outlawed, the African dances exploded onto the Brazilian scene, gaining more acceptance with time. Today, the Brazilian carnival is an explosive release of energy as dancers and music invade the streets to perform the exuberant dance of the samba, salsa, and flamenco.

I first learned the more traditional Latin dances in the Dominican Republic when Peter and I sailed to Panama as newlyweds. Aboard the *Antilles*, we stopped on the eastern side of Hispaniola, taking long morning walks to explore seaside villages. More often than not, we ended up dancing in the middle of a dirt path with a myriad of locals when stopping at a vendor's stall for a cold drink. The handsome locals gave us pointers in dancing, laughing at our stumbles and missteps.

The Latin beat played in nearly every public establishment we encountered. Spontaneous dancing erupted on sidewalks, in bus stations, and beside waterfalls. If a patron wandered into an outdoor local watering hole alongside the street, he'd have a Coca-Cola and lead the cook or the waitress into a samba move. When we were present at such times, I looked on. When I couldn't stand still any longer, I'd jump to the infectious beat. Soon, we were a welcome addition to the quaint villages, no longer considered tourists, but more like dance enthusiasts. At such times, Peter simply stood still as he held me close. He never really moved, except moving his hips left and right, which was enough for me. The villagers smiled warmly and often invited us to join them for Café Santo Domingo and sweet Galletas Martín at their table.

It occurred to me that spontaneous dancing would be a welcome addition to the American culture. Imagine if we replaced the depressing daily news with romantic music for dancing? We'd have a fitter, happier American race. Calories would spin off, and endorphins would flood the brain. Our government should introduce a tax break for those who danced in public.

———•••———

When the flamenco beat arose across the dance floor in the tiny village of Antonio Bay in Brazil, the best dancers were led onto the floor to spin. Their fingers flicked into the night air with tremendous passion. The young girls excelled at the art of dance. Their male partners led them with magnificent grace and agility. From a young age, these children had grown up with dancing, following in the steps of family members who learned from former generations.

I looked over at the boys, who appeared stunned with the execution of exquisite dancing. I decided to wander over and encourage them. It was obvious I was their mother, as we were the only blonds in the gaggle of dancers. I approached Warren, normally the more confident on the dance floor. .

"Aren't you going to dance?" I asked the boys.

I couldn't figure out what was holding them back. They grew up dancing to the reggae/calypso beat in the Bahamas when as a young child. We took them to island dances much like this one, except along the wharf next to a soccer field. At such times, we made our way back to the boat in a sailing dinghy. Sometimes we stopped to douse our sail in the middle of the harbor and listen to the calypso beat just one more time before packing it in for the night.

"Yeah, sure. I'm just trying to pick out the hottest one," Warren said with a smirk.

"How 'bout that sweet lovely standing over there with her daddy?" asked Sam. "She's a winner."

I followed the direction of his finger to where a young girl stood. Her dark hair was full and long, and her calves thick as a working man's biceps. As I strained my eyes, I noticed a thin outline of a fuzzy harelip on the young girl's face.

"Oh, Sam!" I laughed. "That's not a nice thing to say. You're better than that."

"Oh, now there's a babe," Gary cooed.

Gary jerked his head towards a tall, lanky prepubescent with legs like a doe's, attired in black, the ubiquitous uniform of the night.

"Jail bait!" Adam hollered.

I made a mental note to keep a sharp lookout at all times. We didn't need the gendarme chasing us at sea. I pushed away the thought of a young man's fit of passion exercised in a hay barn. Scanning my eyes beyond the dance floor of dirt, I noticed some hay piles in the distance arranged in haphazard clutter. Party lights held them in deep shadows like coffins across the field.

Warren was the first to invite a Brazilian girl to dance. She accepted and, once in the middle of the circle of dancers, Warren moved into the typical American writhing motion of jerk and jump. His arms pin-wheeled awkwardly, legs launching out in various directions. His cap was on backwards and he wore dark sunglasses, completing the surfer's uniform, the cool attire of any young traveling American. The legs of his jeans trailed a ribbon of tattered string from constant dragging. He appeared under-dressed and out of place next to the young girl. She was well dressed for the evening's festivities. I sighed and shook my head.

The pretty girl disappeared into the crowd hurriedly after the first dance. Warren joined his comrades, who patted him on the back.

"Good show, Dude," Sam, Gary, and Adam said in unison.

Next up was Adam. The brothers were competing now. Adam jerked his long arms into the air, rocked his head back and forth, and marched. I covered my eyes. His moves were out of sync, and he refused to hold eye contact with his sexy, albeit young, partner. After a dithering show of a type of dance that I couldn't place, the girl abandoned Adam on the dance floor. Embarrassed, he walked off, bewildered.

When Adam returned to the safety of his peers, they tore him apart.

"What the heck was that? She blew you off, Bro!" Warren shouted.

Sam slapped him on the back.

"No worries, Mate. She's not a looker," Sam said. Guffaws resounded; bellies shook with hilarity.

Gary and Sam never had a go at the feat, although I was dying for a good laugh at witnessing their blunders too. The Brazilian girls wanted to be held, cooed, led and twirled. Gyrations, chants, and wild gesticulations did not cut it for these lovely Sheilas. My heart went out to the boys. At least they had tried. How brave!

I soon found myself swaying my hips to the beat, trying to follow the movements of the women around me. Occasionally, I missed a beat and had to pause to catch up with my invisible instructors.

Suddenly, a man approached me and asked to dance. I turned my head to inspect the women behind and beside me to assure me of his invitation … *me*? Surely he meant someone else. I couldn't believe my lucky stars. I was so ready to tear up this dance floor.

The stately man wore a fine attire of silk slacks and a Chambray shirt, announcing him as a traveling business man. The Brazilian took my hand and led me to the very front of the dance floor, directly in front of the band.

Ooh, this is nice, I thought. I glanced over at the boys. Their jaws dragged, mouths open in black O's.

The beat segued into a rapid crescendo of samba beat. My partner held me tight with both hands, so I could transfer my weight to him. Taller than me, he fairly carried me with him like a human doll, and I was so grateful. His expert direction allowed me to follow his lead by relaxing into his moves. When his hips thrust to the right, I followed suit. When he stepped forward, my foot shot backward in time with the rhythm. I kept my knees slightly bent and liquid. Once I manifested confident foot moves, I put the swing into my step. I allowed him to twirl me into oblivion, engaging my abdominal muscles as I moved my hips. When he let go of me, I swung my arms in a dramatic display. When he pushed me away from him, completing a full twirl himself, I responded in the same, and he caught me on the return swing. Lights spun around me as my partner led me around the dance floor.

Who *was* this man?

Soon a spotlight centered on us. So intoxicated with his own moves, my partner led me to the source of the spotlight—a TV video camera! Three men stood behind it, handling a variety of cords, microphones, and lights. Mr. Dancing with the Stars increased his feverish pitch, twirling me faster, harder, and more elaborately. The crowd thinned, leaving us more space on the floor. They circled around us.

I suddenly lost one of my shoes and quickly kicked off the other one to keep pace. Colorful lights, faces, dancers merged and blurred as I grew weary. The spotlight grew hot on my skin. Sweat began to pour off my body. As my partner continued to bend me, twirl me, toss me, and wind me around his torso, beads of water spun from my body. When the spotlight and music finally dimmed, we paused, and I took the opportunity to thank him. It seemed as if I'd danced for more than an hour.

I found my shoes trampled, broken and scattered in bits around the earthen dance floor—a small sacrifice for a splendid evening. Back in the bed of the pick-up truck, we wound back through a forested track. Peter met us on the wharf.

"How was it?" Peter asked.

"Mom got discovered," Adam said. He raised two fingers in each hand, miming quotations.

"Yeah, she outdid us all," Warren added.

"I'm taking dancing lessons when I get home," Sam said.

"I'll never attempt a dance floor in my life if faced with that again!" said Gary.

"Really?" Peter said.

"Yeah! Dance with me, Babes!" I said, but by the time the dinghy arrived back at the boat, I was already nodding off. Fatigue had overwhelmed me once again, except, this time, I had a smile on my face.

22.
CLIFF DIVE

Seven Sister Falls, Grenada

Cowards die many times before their deaths; the valiant never taste of death but once.

—*W. Shakespeare*

Sam and Gary flew out of Grenada shortly after our arrival at Prickly Bay. Although Adam and Warren were sad to see them go, Peter was ready to have the boat back to ourselves as a family. It'd been nearly three months since the brothers had first arrived to join us as crew in South Africa. Although we hadn't needed them as crew, they had provided wonderful friendship and entertainment for our sons, for which I was very grateful.

The first morning after our arrival in Grenada, Peter and I were up early to relish the quiet morning alone on the bow. *Scud* lay anchored amidst a fleet of sailboats, hailing from ports all over the world. Their colorful signature flags adorned the riggings. The harbor lay fringed in hilltops and studded with brightly painted houses in hues of blue, yellow, and orange. Waters were green in shallow parts, turquoise and azure in deeper parts. The lagoon lay in shadow as the morning sun gilded hilltops. As an orange orb rose, the tropical mist gave way to morning humidity. Fishermen began to drift in from their nightly excursions in dugout canoes, heavy on the waterlines with cargos of fish. We studied them while I tried to summon a lightning bolt of energy from a mug of caffeine.

Today we were trekking to the Seven Sisters Waterfalls with other teens in the harbor. Once the word was out that we were taking our sons in a *jitney* (local bus), other teens in the harbor jumped on the bandwagon. Last night during our discussions over dinner, it was decided that we'd all jump from the top of the falls—a tall order for this old cruising broad. Could I do it? Of course. Should I do it? Of course not. But ... would I do it? That was the question that nagged me now. Was it a sage option at my age? I decided that if Peter did it, then I would too, as he's the most sagacious one of either of us.

The day before our morning departure to the falls, we had headed into St. Georges to the Farmers Market together while the boys completed their schoolwork. The market was a patchwork of vibrant squares of fruits and vegetables piled into vast triangular mountains of all shapes and sizes. Some looked otherworldly, like the achiote from South America. The seeds of achiote were ground and made into a bright red dye that the Tainos Indians of the Caribbean called bija. Bija delineated their male virility and repeled mosquitoes. Culinary chefs today used achiote paste to flavor spicy cuisines.

A large Grenadian woman towered over her mountains of field vegetables. Her arms were strong looking, pushing at the sleeves of her floral blouse. Muscled hands with large fingers gently passed over the vegetables as she placed them in my basket. A man's navy hat shaded her dark face.

"Fresh tuna for you today?" the Grenadian woman asked as she whirled a machete in the air. Beside her lay a gorgeous tuna that was so large that the tail extended past the end of the wooden table. The bright eyes of the tuna announced that it had been landed before first light in a dugout, but not long after. The price was shockingly low, and I grabbed two kilos.

After filling my basket with an array of brightly colored produce, most of which I'd never seen until now, I asked the woman how to find the Seven Sisters Falls.

"Catch the first morning jitney that heads into the Grand Etang Forest Reserve from the main road," she said.

In the morning, a gaggle of teens waited for us on the beach. They learned of our tour into the rain forest from Adam and Warren and joined in with our group. We guided them down a hilly road until we came to Grand Anse Road, a narrow two-lane stretch of pavement bordered by canopies of overhanging foliage. We had heard the jitney before we saw it. Thunderous reggae music blasted from around the bend. When the battered van rounded the corner at breakneck speed, children donned in blue and white school uniforms fled into ditches in quick retreat lest they be turned into road kill.

I jumped back to merge with the stately palm behind me for protection. Peter lifted his hand in a request for a ride, and the van skidded to a stop. Dust devils and stones burst from beneath the rear tires in rooster tails of spray. I half expected the contraption to break into a wheelie. The six-person van boasted proud hues in the Rasta colors of red, yellow and green. "Rastaman" was written in scarlet letters down both sides. Arms and torsos protruded from tiny windows, caked with a patina of dried mud.

"Crikey! Are we boarding this death trap on wheels?" I hissed to Peter.

"What choice do we have with all these kids?" he asked.

"Who are they all? What boats do they belong to? More important, where are their parents?" I asked.

With less confidence than we felt, we boarded the overcrowded bus, passing coins to the conductor who was a young boy wearing a bulging bobble-hat of multi-colored wool in the colors of the Ethiopian flag. Mothers of ample girth squeezed closer, collecting young children onto their laps to make room for our group. Half-seats were pried open and yanked down. Numerous limbs hung suspended from open windows.

In the hot air, I fought to catch my breath while gazing around at the death-trap. Peter looked apprehensive—a bad sign, as he's definitely the more composed of us two. But the teens were in high euphoria over the thrill of the ride and, more likely, the joy of the raucous tunes detonating from the oversized speakers in front and back.

Our driver drove like a madman bent on speed. Bodies slid to the right, then left and faces mashed against windows as the van rounded corners. I knew what my seat-neighbor had eaten for dinner by the aroma wafting from his breath. Body odor rose from the mass of humanity, gathering into a thick cloud overhead. More bodies boarded. I counted twenty-two persons inside a van that was intended for eleven. I shut my eyes and pulled down my sunglasses, willing myself to ease into the rhythm of the adventure. *Part of the experience is getting there*—I said to myself over and over.

An hour later, we entered the dark Grand Etang Forest Reserve and were the last to get off. I thanked the blessed Universe for our safe arrival as we spilled out onto the pavement, rubbing sore limbs and crunched elbows. In a flash, we lifted into uproarious laughter at the impossibility of it all.

At the trailhead, we were delighted to find a mona monkey perched on a wooden gate. He donned a sweet look as if waiting for chocolate peanuts. His white rump and the brown agouti fur on his back was full and shiny. His legs and tail were black, and his face was a blue-grey color with a dark stripe that made him look like a bandit. He looked to weigh about ten pounds and was the size of a medium-framed dog. All at once the monkey jumped from the gate post to a nearby tree and jumped onto Warren's backpack.

"It's after my bananas!" Warren shouted. He yanked off his pack and drew out the bananas from the side pocket to pass one to the monkey.

"Look! Another one!" Adam shouted.

Sure enough, the enticing aroma of the bananas drew in other comrades. Shy and hesitant at first, the monkeys inched over. Soon, Warren had them feeding from his hand. The cute apes took the bananas gently and peeled away the skin with nimble fingers, stuffing cheek pouches with succulent fruit. When breakfast was over, the monkeys quickly left.

The teens charged up the road and disappeared into the dark void of the tropical rain forest while we bantered about our ride from hell. Though nearly late morning, it was cool beneath the tree canopy of vines along the dirt trail that led to the Seven Sisters Waterfalls. Cocoa, nutmeg and banana trees bordered the skinny trail. Scarlet birds of paradise peeked from behind a curtain of elephant ears that grew alongside the riverbed. Hills formed a backdrop to the forest that now ran in a narrow belt along the river bank. Trunks were daubed with multi-colored lichens: sulphurous yellows, burnt oranges, blues and greens. We slipped and slopped along the muddy trail, following the rich sound of the teens' giggles.

We came upon a small forest of cacao trees. The pods were a kaleidoscope of colors: lavender, red, yellow and orange. A chocolate lover would have been in heaven, spellbound by the aroma. I picked a cacao pod up from the ground for a taste. The expected sweetness, but also the taste of banana was present, along with a slight tartness like a mango. I tore my eyes from studying my feet lest I tumble down the mountainside, and studied the lush vegetation more intently. Close by stood a band of banana and plantains trees.

"Foresters plant bananas and plantains next to cocoa trees to provide protection from high winds and offer shade," the fruit vendor said when I later returned for more tuna at the straw market after our rain forest adventure. "My husband, he does that too."

When the sides of my sandals began to tip, and I felt the crunch of something hard beneath my feet, I knelt down and picked up a brown kernel the size of a fat olive. I turned my head towards the top of the tree looming over me, and saw hundreds of pale yellow fruit that resembled yellow apricot. Several of the yellow fruits were split, revealing other-worldly-looking nuts inside. Hugging the brown nut was a rubbery blanket of red lace. Around the base of the tree were large numbers of the brown and red nuts. I collected a few and tucked them in my pocket.

I showed the tuna vendor my treasure when we returned to town later that day.

"Ah, you found the red gold of Grenada," she hissed excitedly, sucking breath through brown teeth.

"Wars have been fought over that treasure. It is the nutmeg. Before it came to our island, the East India Spice Company kept it all to themselves and hid it in the Bantu Islands of Indonesia."

She peeled off the rubbery red encasing of the brown nut.

"This red part here is the mace blade. Let it dry until it's yellow-orange in color, and then use it like a bay leaf in your cooking. Take it out of the dish before you feed your man. Grate the nut when it is dry. Follow dis' and your man will follow you to the ends of de earth, girl!"

Her island twang echoed, and as her smile broadened, a gold tooth flashed.

"You have problem with your man?" she asked, staring at me intently.

"Ah, no, not really. Well, he's distracted sometimes," I said.

"Oh then. You must see my sista'. She can make the diabless go away."

"The diabless?"

"Girl, don't you know? The diabless …"

And here she leaned into me and glanced around to ensure total privacy, "the diablesses are demonic women that come out to seduce your man! Ah, yes, you must call on my sista. She has special powers to help you."

"Ah, yeah, well…" and I grabbed my parcel and snuck out. Tuna Lady's raucous guffaws resounded as I dashed awkwardly across the crowded market, ricocheting off of natives, dropping half of my purchases. I left them as they rolled down the hill and into the gutter. Her laughter still haunts me to this day. I have never liked nutmeg since then.

Back in the rain forest reserve, out of the shade of giants, we wandered onto a brook where an abundance of flower petals caught the zenith of the sun. Scarlet birds of paradise peeked from behind a curtain of elephant ears, fuchsia ginger plants with waxy petals, and Chinese-red and neon yellow heliconias pushed up the verdant earth. We oohed and aahed, rounding a bend to discover hot pink anthuriums that held us in rapture against a backdrop of the lavender-colored Madagascar rubber vine. Giant ferns towered over my head, misted with beads of dew that twinkled like diamond studs in rainbows of morning light. Tree trunks were daubed with multi-colored lichens: yellows, burnt oranges, blues, and greens. I felt like Alice in her own magical Wonderland, lost in a supernatural forest. Was I hallucinating? The stunning beauty nearly brought me to my knees.

"My god, it's so beautiful here," I said in a weepy voice.

All at once, two Antillean crested hummingbirds darted by.

I followed their pace. The tiny birds performed a pattern of flight in figure eights and came to land on a pair of heliconias. Their minuscule heads were crested with emerald green feathers, tipped with iridescent blue-green ones. As they suckled nectar, I noticed what looked to be miniature peacock tails splayed across their foreheads like celebratory carnival caps.

We knew there were other unseen creatures of the dark forest. We could hear them: the croak of a giant bullfrog, the squawk of the St. Lucia Amazon parrot.

As we trekked higher into the rain forest, the dirt path gave way to a muddy track, evidence of a morning rainfall. We slipped along as we followed the laughter of the teens up ahead. Alongside the trail, tiny triangles of green kites moved in the dirt. I knelt down for a closer look.

"Peter! Look at this!" I said.

Together we knelt down side-by-side and snickered.

"Can it be? These little ants are carrying huge bundles!" I said, smiling.

We followed their rapid progression into the forest. The ants marched in unison and with the same beat. In time, the trail extended too far for us to follow, lest we lose our way back.

The rain forest drew me in along our trek. We passed an abandoned shed, remnants of a farmhouse. Had the house been destroyed by a hurricane? The roof was missing. It may have been lifted by a tornado, and dropped far out to sea. The shed of stone was partially hidden by a thick tangle of lianas. Their fat roots unnerved me. As a child I had nightmares of fast-growing roots overtaking and choking me. The jungle felt treacherous all of sudden. Evidence of entire civilizations had disappeared beneath encroaching vines with big teeth.

The gradient was not steep, but it still required careful going. The trail followed along the top of a ridge. One misstep off the trail and one would tumble down a slope carpeted in thick vegetation that ended in giant boulders strewn across the river. Shadows were growing long, so we picked up our pace to reach the teens. As the only guardians, I felt a responsibility for their safety, even though we didn't even know some of them. The trip had come together so rapidly. Our sons had made the invitations without our awareness. We had not consulted with the other parents. I pointed this out to Peter.

"That's the way of things these days with teenagers," Peter said.

After passing a white horse grazing on grass fit for a golf course and a pretty clapboard house painted a neon blue, we reached the teens. At the top of the grassy knoll, we paused to gaze down at the group. They lounged in various states of attire beside a deep blue lagoon that lay in shadow from the late morning sun. Waters steamed with wisps of mist.

Large boulders spotted with lichen bordered the far side of the lagoon against a backdrop of a rocky crevice, seemingly 200 feet high. Atop the crevice, lianas dangled from branches and kissed the falls. A torrent of water crashed into the lagoon at the bottom. Where the falls emptied, a great roar penetrated forest air. Shouts from the teens were barely audible against the rumble.

Warren swam to the bottom of the falls, fighting fierce current. He disappeared behind the cascade. Behind the wall of water, he appeared hazy while standing sentinel atop a great boulder.

"Come on!" I shouted to Peter. I couldn't wait to jump in.

Peter leapt down the slope easily while I negotiated my steps carefully. Barefoot, I grabbed at the fat roots of a gommier tree for balance but lost my grip in the end, landing on my fanny at the bottom. So much for grace.

At the bottom, a makeshift landing of dead limbs was adorned in colorful clothing: tennis shoes, tank tops, and shorts. Ahead of me, girls in bikinis stroked waters and lay supine like floating banana leaves.

"Come on, Babe! It's fantastic!" Peter shouted. Throwing my wrap to the side, I plunged in and swam over to him.

"Wow, it's cold!" I shouted. It felt marvelous.

"Let's swim behind the falls. Come on!" Peter said.

Together we headed out, but he soon broke ahead of me. Vast current from the plunge of the falls ripped at my swimsuit. I paddled against it, kicking hard. The roar of the falls was so great, I couldn't hear what Peter was shouting at me, but I knew his intention as his lips were moving rapidly.

Harder, harder, he mouthed.

I stroked and stroked. Breathing became difficult from the heavy mist of the falls. Fat water droplets clogged my throat. Every time I took a breath, water engulfed my lungs. I finned with my back to the falls to shelter my breathing from an incoming torrent, but as soon as I turned over, I was thrust back by two meters.

Dang! That just took me fifteen minutes to swim! I thought. I paddled harder. Just as I was about to reach the bottom of the falls, I choked on air and water and was pushed back. This scenario repeated itself. I could see Peter behind the falls now. The image of him rippled with haze and mist. When I saw him dive through the falls like an Olympian, my heart soared.

Peter reached me easily and took my hand to pull me forward as his strong body propelled us both through the heavy mist and current. When we reached the bottom of the falls, he plunged his mouth to my ear.

"Grab this rock and pull forward. I'll help you," Peter roared. He guided my hand to an indentation in the rock wall. There were several of them, expertly placed by sports enthusiasts. I slowly pulled, inching my way forward against the strong current. Soon, Peter's big hand reached down for me, and he pulled me into him atop a great boulder.

"Oh my god! Amazing," I shouted. I hugged him deeply. Tears welled in my eyes. He seemed to be forever pulling me out of the water with his large hands. My musings took me back to when he yanked me from Lake Geneva, and back into the Hobie. We had laughed then. We had laughed again when he later pulled me from Key Biscayne in Miami when I jumped overboard to save his favorite hat.

Water. In the Taoist tradition, water is considered an aspect of wisdom. It takes on the form and moves in the path of least resistance. It speaks of a higher wisdom. I felt that together we were aspiring to mimic it by following our family voyage around the world. We were learning a better life for ourselves.

Warren and Adam had already found their way inside the cave behind the falls, and we stood together as a family. It was an emotional moment. I felt our family love, solidarity, and intimacy. We were joined at the hip by our common thirst for adventure and the unknown. Giant grins erupted across our tanned faces. Beneath the vault of the cave, our voices were amplified. As our words echoed off rock walls, we watched through the tumbling cascade to see other kids fighting against the current. They tried to find their way to the falls and into the cave, but no one could make it. I was glad. This was our cave now: our secret family cave.

In time, one by one, we dove through the cascade. Under the water, it felt like a washing machine of rapid current. When I broke the surface, the torrent spat me through the current and across the lagoon as if a wad of paper. I climbed out when I reached the embankment and drew myself up into the sunlight. My skin riddled with gooseflesh from the cold, but my mind was sharp and my spirit high.

"Hey, there's a path over here!" Warren shouted. "I'm following it."

Behind him ran his entourage of new friends. Peter took up the rear in an attempt to watch over this gaggle of rambunctious teenagers. I elected to stay behind and soak up warm sun rays and take in the view.

After a bit of time, a young girl burst through the tangle of vegetation that, shortly before, she had entered. She was in tears, cut and bleeding. I ran to her.

"What happened? You're hurt!" I said.

"No, I'm fine. It's just that the gradient is steep and rugged and … scary. I thought I'd never get back down," the young girl said, between sniffles.

She gulped air. Fat tears welled from blue eyes. I handed her some water to drink. She walked over to the water's edge to wash off the bloody rivulets that ran down both sides of her legs.

"Some of those vines were mean," she said.

We sat together on the edge of the lagoon to wait for the rest of the kids to arrive. Time passed but, but no one exited back through the tangle of vegetation. I grew worried. I suddenly feared that no one was ever to come through the jungle hole.

"At the top, there is no return," the young girl uttered beside me, still shaking.

"At the top … of what?" I asked, afraid to hear her answer.

"The falls," she said.

"You can't come back down the way you went up? Up the trail?" I asked, surprised.

"It's nearly impossible because of all the recent rainfall. It's the rainy season. The gulch was raging with water. I stopped when I had to climb over giant boulders in the middle. I had to grasp roots to make my way forward. I was terrified!" she stammered.

"How do you get down when you reached the summit? Is there a way out to a road or something?" I asked.

"No. You have to jump or camp-out until someone pushes you to jump," she cried.

"But the falls are nearly 200 feet! There are boulders at the bottom!" I wailed.

"Yup, I know," she said.

My nerves grew taught when a tiny shape appeared at the summit. It was a young girl. The cascade released a roar so loud that her words were inaudible. I knew she was yelling because she faced sideways, gesticulating wildly at her comrades behind her, hidden from my vantage point far below. Her moves were aggressive. I watched in horror as she thrust her head into her hands and bent at the knees.

Oh, god, no. Don't fall.

She sat frozen in terror, obviously crying.

"Do you know her?" I asked the girl beside me as I pointed to the summit of the falls. *If there's going to be an accident, best to get the names early*, I thought.

"She's my friend on another boat," she said.

"And you are?" I asked.

"Amy," she said.

Color came back to my face when I saw Peter inch his way forward and take the girl's hand. He moved her body back towards safety.

"Whew," Amy sighed in relief.

I gulped, waiting to see who would replace the jumper.

A teen stepped up to the mount. He stood tall. From where I sat, I could see his fit frame. He wasn't donned in the surfer's uniform of board shorts and a t-shirt, but in Speedos. He balanced, slowly drew his arms up overheard, turned around, and leaned backwards.

"Oh no! Oh, my God. Please, no!" I wailed.

I threw my hands to both sides of my face as if to comfort impending grief. Boulders were strewn haphazardly across the bottom of the lagoon. *Boulders. Broken necks.* Tears welled in my eyes. All my faith dissolved into a sudden premonition of disaster and rushed down on me.

Why had we not insisted other parents join us?

The boy at the top of the falls suddenly poised on his toes. He fell into the air, touching his toes, straightening, and barely parted the waters with a splash when he entered the lagoon. I was stunned, mute with shock. It was indeed a very impressive dive. When he at last surfaced, I mentally placed a check by his boat name: *Toucana.* I congratulated myself on scribbling down boat names while overhearing the kids banter in the van and on the trail.

Now, who was next?

Next in the line-up was another young girl. Emblazoned with honor from the previous act, she barely paused when jumping. As she fell into the air, a scream worthy of Hollywood resounded through the forest, causing birds to rise from the trees. When she surfaced, I checked off her boat name too: *Papillion.*

All the girls had leapt but one. Two kids were left in the care of Peter.

But I couldn't see them. I knew Peter wouldn't jump, but I wasn't so sure with our sons. A dare to a teenager from peers is powerful stuff, and I wondered whether our sons would be brave enough to choose another way down. As of yet, there didn't seem to be another option other than jumping.

Warren stood tall and true next at the summit. My heart ached. His intent on diving the falls belied our familial solidarity in our secret cave behind the falls. At that moment, I hated him for this act of daring. I wanted to shout, but it was useless. From 200 feet up, I was a mere speck. I crisscrossed my arms over my head, pleading with my gestures. *No! Don't do this wild act!*

He fell into the sky, straightened his legs and landed. When his head popped to the surface and he easily swam to the side, I closed my eyes and said a heartfelt prayer of thanks. Amy released my hand, which was sore. I hadn't realized we had been holding each other up.

I ran to Warren, breathless.

"Where's Adam? Where's your Dad?" I shouted. My words hung limp in my throat as I grasped his arm. My heart hurt. I felt sick.

"They're coming back down the gulch. One girl crapped on herself and cried, so they're carrying her back down," he said.

Pals slapped Warren on the back in congratulations. I waited until I couldn't stand it any longer and began to collect our things.

When Peter and Adam emerged from the vegetation with the girl, she was a mess. Scratches ran with blood, welts from mosquito bites eroded her pearly white flesh, inflamed. Bruises dotted her legs and arms. She looked like she'd been run over by a boat.

"Are you okay?" I asked the young girl. She was nearly limp in Adam's and Peter's arms.

"She's fine. Just a little shaken," Peter said with a sigh. He gave me a look that said, *don't ask.*

"Yes, well. Wash off and get some dry clothes on. We have some sandwiches in our bag," I said, worried.

When I opened my pack, I pushed aside the mini medical kit and grabbed sandwiches, passing them out for our family and the injured girl. Back with her girlfriends, she quickly recovered.

"How did you get her back down?" I asked Peter.

"It wasn't easy. We had to carry her on our backs most of the way. The

Gulch was full of debris, raging water, and boulders. Good thing Adam was there. It was pretty terrifying for the girl," he said.

It had occurred to me that there were no public phones, no mobile phones, and no taxis. We were far from civilization. Only our Rasta jitney driver knew we were inside a remote rain forest, linked only by a two-mile trail to the main road.

Surely, he'll remember to come for us, I thought.

As we stood on the pavement waiting for our Rasta driver, I realized I had come undone. My thoughts went back to the secret cave where our family had pledged allegiance to all things good between us. I held that thought. The euphoria of our family unity and love unwound my taut violin strings, and I left the feelings flow. Once onboard Rastaman, I donned sunglasses, opened my eyes wide and sang along with the teens.

"No woman; no cry," I belted out. Bob Marley ran true for me. As we rounded the bend, a red orb plunged into the sea. It would be resurrected again with the coming dawn, along with a happier me.

Later, once we were back on the boat, I was eager to read up on the ants and the burden they carried that resembled kites. I sat with Peter in the main salon while he prepared navigation routes for our next passage. Field guides lay scattered around me.

"Those creatures on the forest floor were leaf cutting ants! It says here that they form the largest and most complex animal societies on Earth. They can build underground nests that can grow to more than 100 feet across by 260 feet wide to house eight million ants," I said, mesmerized.

Peter came over to join me, interested. I continued, pointing at references and images.

"You know those ants can carry pieces of leaf hundreds of meters in a procession like the one we saw? Each ant can carry a piece of leaf up to fifty times its body weight. That's like me hefting a wheelbarrow filled with fifteen gallons of water," I said. "Hey, kids! Check this out," I shouted.

The boys tumbled in from the cockpit where they had been chatting about the girls on our field trip.

"Oh yeah. We saw those too," Adam said. "They were pretty awesome."

"Yeah, it was if the ants were kite-boarding on the dirt!" Warren added.

"*Scud, Scud,*" someone shouted.

We ran outside to see *Running Wind*. Nick was standing on the bow, port side, holding a five-gallon jerry jug.

"We need water," he shouted. The captain maneuvered the catamaran close, so Nick could toss the jug. I dashed below to fill it from a shower hose. Peter lugged it back on deck to pass it back over the rails.

Later that night, Nick dropped the hired captain and his girlfriend off on the beach and dinghied over for a chat. He refused our invitation to come aboard and remained alongside *Scud*. He looked exhausted. Grey patches of skin lay beneath his eyes. He appeared thin and frail.

"Are you okay?" I asked.

"No. Not at all. We ran out of water in the middle of the beginning of our passage from Brazil," he said. His voice shook and his fists clinched, opening and closing. "The engine water hose overheated and melted, dumping all our fresh water into the bilge. It happened at night when we were motoring, so no one heard the bilge pump running and all the fresh water going overboard into the sea."

"No!" Peter said.

"Fortunately, I had packed away an emergency water supply in the cockpit bins. Each of us could only have 1 liter/day of water, based on the jerry jugs I had stowed. It was ample enough to keep us hydrated, but the extra water disappeared faster than I could calculate," said Nick. His face was masked in agony and he rubbed his forehead. "One afternoon when looking for a missing tool, I walked into the captain's stateroom and was shocked to see freshly laundered panties and bras dangling in the bathroom."

"Oh my god," I said. It was incredulous. "Who would do such a thing as use ration water for laundry?"

"A drunk. That's who," Nick said. "A nearly empty booze bottle was in the bathroom closet when I started investigating. We then had to lessen a liter/day to only one cup/day for each person. I had to sleep with the water supply to keep it safe. My son suffered terribly."

"What are you going to do?" Peter asked.

"I kicked them off soon as we landfalled. I'm looking for a new captain. Someone I know this time. No strangers!" Nick said. "I'm done with boats. This entire trip has been a nightmare...the robbery in Durban, the loss of my thumb, my captain in jail, the spinnaker mishap, and now this! *Running Wind* is up for sale. I'm never boarding this boat again once I reach the USA."

I felt heartsick for him. As he motored back to his boat, his back slumped forward in guarded repose.

"So sad," Peter said. "It goes to show you how one decision can ruin a lifetime dream. He wanted to sail the Great Lakes with his son. Such a big goal, gone into sudden ruin from just one bad choice of hiring a complete stranger as a captain."

"I know. I'm so glad you're an experienced and sage captain. Nothing went wrong on our entire voyage," I said.

"Knock on wood," Peter said, and tapped his knuckle against the deck.

23.
ARRIVING IN HELL

Australia

What the caterpillar calls the end of the world, the master calls the butterfly.

—Richard Bach

A well-endowed nurse with a round face got up close and personal in my face. I lay supine beneath a thin napkin while she stood sentinel over me in a medical clinic. Her eyes were wide. Her nostrils flared. Even though it was near freezing inside the room, her face was red as a cherry from either emotion or exertion. It was hard to tell. She weighed nearly three-hundred pounds, so I could imagine why she was out of breath as she scurried in and out of the room, yelling orders. She and I were not hitting it off. Her malevolent nature announced she protested on working over the Christmas holidays, especially with a disagreeable patient like me.

I was in the Myrtle Beach Breast Center in South Carolina, shivering on a cold table beneath an array of medical instruments while a team of doctors stared at my breast x-ray.

"Hmmm," a doctor uttered.

"Yes. There," another doctor confirmed.

"And there. Hum."

I found myself on the table after a routine mammogram. The doctors' words didn't sound good. Each one lingered for a few minutes and then disappeared until a different doctor entered the fray. The heavy door closed with a slight click, then re-opened with a new dizzying display of "Let's Play: Guess What?"

It was like watching a baseball game with Dr. White-Coat on 1st base, Dr. Black-Shoes on 2nd base, and Dr. White-Shoes on 3rd. Nurse Ratchet was up to bat. Her home run was guaranteed. *Place your bets, everybody,* I thought.

"What are you saying?" I pleaded with the nurse.

"It's palpable."

"What does palpable mean, exactly?"

Nurse Ratchet shook her head. Was it dismay or disgust?

After being poked, prodded, and analyzed, I was not a happy camper. It was December 22. In two days, I would be relaxing with Peter and our boys by a pool on deck #7 aboard the Carnival Cruise Ship with my Mom, sisters, and brother to celebrate the holidays. The Cayman Islands and Mexico reported warm temperatures during December. I was looking forward to it.

Peter and I had left *Scud* in St. Thomas and flown to South Carolina. My mother wanted to celebrate Dad's memories by gathering us together from all points of the compass for a cruise. Being delayed in this medical igloo was the last thing I had expected when I went in for my routine mammogram.

"What is it?" I begged.

"Inconclusive," Dr. White-Cloak muttered.

"Yes, possibly, but look here," Dr. Black-Shoes uttered, pointing at the x-ray.

"I see. And here, here, and there too," Dr. White Shoes said, scratching a chin.

Here, here and there?

What the Sam Hill was going on here, exactly? It was a phrase my Dad always used when he wanted to say fuck or shit, but Mom wouldn't allow it. I preferred he use fuck or shit. Life would've been way more fun, and honest, inside our mute family of six.

"I'm sure you're mistaken. You have the wrong x-rays. I'm a vegetarian, live a stress-free lifestyle in paradise—except for the last four months while I was crossing an ocean with four teenaged boys! I do not smoke, there's no history of breast cancer in my family, I'm only in my forties, I'm fit, and I swim two hours a day during lobster season! Otherwise, I jog. You're wrong. Wrong. Wrong," I whimpered, tears welling up in my eyes.

The doctors disappeared to consult in private. Only Nurse Ratchet stood over me. I would pry the truth out of her if I had to. I had a cruise to catch, shopping to do, and Christmas presents to buy. I only had two days to prepare for a week-long cruise with my large family aboard a cruise ship.

Nurse Ratchet was sweating now. Hands on her hips, she eyed me warily. Ratchet bent down to poke me some more. She jabbed my breast with her forefinger.

"See here? And here?" she said, and then moved over to the right breast to prod some more. "Feel that? Does it hurt?"

Ouch! It did indeed hurt, but I was not about to let Ms. Doomsday, Nurse Ratchet, get to me. But her next words did.

"You have breast cancer, probably Stage III by the size of those tumors. You aren't going anywhere on Christmas except for inside an operating room," she said.

With that, she marched out of the room.

No way. But, I thought. Maybe this is why I felt extremely fatigued over the last few months…exhausted most of the time.

I fell apart. Tears streamed down my face. Abruptly, I started shaking. I needed Peter here. Now. Badly. I wondered how I was going to make it back to Mom's house. The last time I drove home after having received the news that our baby was dead inside my womb, I cried all the way. I never saw the car that I pulled out in front of from a side street. It crashed into me, sending my car into an 180-degree spin that totaled the vehicle. Luckily, neither me nor the other driver were hurt very seriously. When the ambulance came, I refused entry. I refused to go anywhere near a hospital. My baby was already dead. What could a hospital do to save her now?

I'll never forget the kind woman who comforted me after pulling me out from the battered driver's seat of my car.

"My baby, my baby," I wailed.

"Where?" the woman shouted. She climbed into the back seat to search.

"No," I stammered.

"What?" she pleaded, worried.

I told her my story, stammering in tearful hysteria. The kind woman hugged me and stroked my head like a grandmother would with her grown child. I realized that I could have killed her with my negligent driving.

Surely God had held me in his grace at that time. This time when driving home, I needed to be centered before I got behind the wheel of the car.

Olivia Newton-John once said, "My cancer scare changed my life."

I would soon find out why.

Our family dream of sailing to the South Pacific would momentarily go on standby. But I was determined to pick up where we had left off aboard *Scud* in the Caribbean before this little hiccup happened. It was just a little side step. *We'll be back out there on the bluewater highway in no time,* I promised myself.

South Pacific Expedition—we would do this or die in trying.

ABOUT THE AUTHOR

Croc hunting, Great Barrier Reef, Australia

Tina Dreffin is an accomplished travel writer, world sailor and circumnavigator, and an advocate for women's issues. She moved aboard her first boat in 1979, and raised two sons, now grown, aboard various sailing vessels.

Tina Dreffin is author of *Bluewater Walkabout: Into the Caribbean,* available as an eBook, paperback, and in audio format. Her photography and articles appear in several magazines, including Cruising World, SAIL, International Living, Multihulls Magazine, Multihull Sailor, and the Caribbean Compass. She has also had work included in the anthology *The Best of the Caribbean Compass.*

You may view the route of her world circumnavigation: www.bahamascatcharters.com/family_circumnavigation.htm.

Tina currently lives aboard a catamaran in the Bahamas with her husband, and a Belgium barge dog named Bella–a Schipperke. Bella is known for her wild antics of swimming with Nikki, the wild dolphin. You can view the YouTube video of the *Dog and Dolphin Wrestle* here: https://youtu.be/k3Ixow3NfyE

Wild Dolphin Teasing Bella

Tina's sons now own their own sailing catamarans. Together they operate a licensed family yacht charter business in the Exumas, Bahamas where the famous swimming pigs reside on White Cay Bay nearby.

Book your next vacation with world renown chef, Tina Dreffin here: http://www.bahamascatcharters..com

Family Fleet

Tina's travels aren't limited to the sea. She and her family have traveled the world by train, donkey, horseback, bicycle, and plane. She hosts presentations of her photography and works as a motivational speaker, encouraging families to travel with their children, put down their devices, and get out and explore.

To learn of Tina's forthcoming books in the series of Bluewater Walkabout, drop your email address here for personal updates: www.bluewaterwalkabout.com

Email: tinadreffin@bluewaterwalkabout.com
Websites:
www.tinacarlsondreffin.com
www.bluewaterwalkabout.com
www.bahamascatcharters.com

Phone: WhatsApp: 1-242-524-0156
Tina Dreffin
6501 Redhook Plaza, Ste. #201
St Thomas, US Virgin Islands 00802-1306